ABRAHAM
LINCOLN
**IN THE
KITCHEN**

ABRAHAM LINCOLN
IN THE KITCHEN

·······

A CULINARY VIEW
of Lincoln's
Life and Times

**RAE KATHERINE
EIGHMEY**

Smithsonian Books
WASHINGTON, DC

This book may be purchased for educational, business, or sales promotional use. For information, please write: Special Markets Department, Smithsonian Books, P. O. Box 37012, MRC 513, Washington, DC 20013

Published by Smithsonian Books
Director: Carolyn Gleason
Production Editor: Christina Wiginton
Editorial Assistant: Ashley Montague

Edited by Lise Sajewski
Designed by Mary Parsons

Illustrations are from various 19th-century sources: those on pages 48, 49, 50, 113, 115, 137, 142, 143, 158, 159, and 219 are courtesy of The Florida Center for Instructional Technology; most others are courtesy of the Dover Pictorial Archive.

Library of Congress Cataloging-in-Publication Data

Eighmey, Rae Katherine.
Abraham Lincoln in the Kitchen : a culinary view of Lincoln's life and times / Rae Katherine Eighmey.
pages cm
Includes bibliographical references.
ISBN 978-1-58834-455-7 (hardback)
1. Cooking, American—History—19th century.
2. United States—Social life and customs—19th century.
3. Lincoln, Abraham, 1809-1865.
4. Presidents—United States—Biography. I. Title.
TX715.E3368 2013
641.5973—dc23
2013026631

Manufactured in the United States
21 20 19   5 4 3 2

In memory of F. C. E.

With thanks for his library of Lincoln books
where this work began

And to four remarkable young men—

Justin and Jack
Nicholas and Jonah

May you spend a lifetime of learning,
especially while reading under trees
with corn dodgers or gingerbread men at hand.

CONTENTS

INTRODUCTION

"**A**braham Lincoln cooked!"

The words leapt off the pages of my sixty-nine-year-old copy of Rufus Wilson's *Lincoln among His Friends*. I could hardly believe what I was reading.

Yet there it was. Phillip Wheelock Ayers, whose family lived three doors down from the Lincolns' Springfield home at the corner of Eighth and Jackson, described how Abraham Lincoln walked the few blocks home from his Springfield law office, put on a blue apron, and helped Mary Lincoln make dinner for their boys. Other neighbors' homey reminiscences told of Abraham shopping for groceries and milking the family cow stabled in the backyard barn with his horse, Old Bob. There must be more to this part of the Lincoln family story! The joyful prospect of research with books, pots, and pans immediately drew me in.

For me, food is the stuff of memory and of discovery. The cultural studies label is "foodways," but I think the best word is "cooking." And for the past two decades, cooking with century-old recipes, then eating meals made from them, has been my path for understanding and interpreting social trends and historical events.

Everyone has a favorite meal that brings forth a vivid memory or a dish that captures a moment in time: A taste of homemade peach ice cream immediately conjures up a summertime front porch. A holiday sweet-potato casserole Aunt Minnie always made brings memory of her to the table when she no longer comes. Sometimes the memory begins with food preparation. Just about every time I sit with a mixing bowl full of fresh green beans, I recall the blue-and-white bowl on my grandmother's lap as we sat in the screen porch snapping beans forty—no, fifty—years ago. I can almost see and hear the rowdy Tobias boys next door running around to the side yard, their Boston bulldog chasing them as fast as its stocky legs could carry it, and the porch swing squeaking as my grandfather sat, reading the paper and waiting for dinner.

I also remember vividly the first "antique" recipe I made, and the delight that drew me into this area of study. I had been struggling to understand everyday life for the Jemison family in 1860s Tuscaloosa, Alabama. I was doing public relations and fund-raising for the restoration of their antebellum town home. The elegant Italianate structure had many stories to tell—architecture, state-of-the-art engineering, political and Civil War history—all of it well documented. But I was searching to find a way to reach the lives of Robert Jemison, his wife, Priscilla, and their daughter, Cherokee. Then I found Mrs. Jemison's pencil-scrawled household notebook in the archives at the University of Alabama.

Mrs. Jemison had written down two recipes. The recipe for a "jumble" intrigued me. I've baked and cooked since I was ten. It was obvious this was some kind of cookie, biscuit, or muffin. The mostly familiar ingredients were listed. Measurements were sketchy in the style common to mid-nineteenth-century cookbooks. There were no directions. Several days of research among the century-old cookbooks in the library stacks and dozens of test versions baked in my kitchen later, I had the perfect reconstruction of Mrs. Jemison's jumbles. One friend, whose family had Alabama roots five generations deep, gave me the highest compliment: "They taste just like my great-grandmother's tea cookies."

My rediscovered jumbles were a crisp, not-too-sweet doughnut-shaped cookie. From them I was able to construct a life incident. I imagined Mrs. Jemison made a batch in the modern "range" she had in the basement kitchen and packed them in a tin for her husband to take with him as he rode off from Tuscaloosa to take his seat in the Congress of the Confederacy, meeting in Richmond.

Jumbles were just the beginning. Several other recipes had caught my attention as I carefully leafed through the fragile cookbook pages seeking jumble-like treats: cakes, breads, meats, vegetables. I began making some of them, too, just to see what they were like. They were wonderful! And I was hooked on this adventure of tasteful discovery. Now, thousands of recipes and five books later, I wondered: Could an expertise that began with the study of a family from the Confederacy ironically lead to an introspection of the man who dedicated his life to saving the Union? I began reading, thinking, and cooking.

The joy of studying history through cooking is that foods provide a complex sensory immersion into the past. This study, and the eating that follows it, is time travel at the dinner table and the only common experience that engages all the senses. An essay by food writer M. F. K. Fisher highlights the special power food memories have. In a 1969 book she recalled a dish of potato chips with lasting and real physical impact: "I can taste-smell-hear-see and then feel between my teeth the potato chips I ate slowly one November afternoon in 1936 in the bar of Lausanne Palace.... They were ineffable and I am still being nourished by them."

Food has the added benefit of being accessible. Everyone has to eat, and most of us cook to one degree or another. The most committed non-cook interacts and prepares food, even if simply pouring milk into a bowl of cereal. And, cooking is largely the same as it was in the nineteenth century.

On the face of it, that similarity seems an unlikely idea, but in my experience it is true. Of course there have been significant changes in the application of heat and cold for cooking and storing food, but to my mind, the *essentials* of cooking are unchanged from Lincoln's kitchen to mine or yours. Knives, forks, mixing spoons, and bowls; frying pans and stewpots—I still use the same tools as 1820s Hoosier pioneers or 1850s sophisticated Springfielders did. Butter, flour, eggs, milk, cheese; chicken, beef; carrots, turnips—we all still cook with the same ingredients. Mixing, stewing, braising, frying—the basic methods are the same as well. What's more, cooks across the country use those basic hand tools and those primary ingredients. In fact, cooking is the only task where doing things the old-fashioned way can be seen as practical, if not entirely modern.

Some other occupations continue to use traditional tools: carpenters still use hammers and nails, seamstresses use needle and thread. But if a carpenter used *just* a hammer and nails instead of a nail gun on a construction site, or if a seamstress made a dress entirely by hand sewing, each would be considered archaic, an artisan, or impractical. In the garden and kitchen, it is commonplace to grow and cook food by hand, using shovels, trowels, and rakes; pots, bowls, knives, wooden spoons. For a great many recipes it is, in fact, easier to chop the vegetables with a knife rather than get out the food processor, or to blend the butter, sugar, and flour with a fork rather than an electric mixer.

As to finding a recipe link to a specific time and place, luck has a lot to do with success. For my jump across time into Lincoln's kitchens, it would be wonderful to have a cookbook from Lincoln's mother with notes written among the recipes by his stepmother and another one from his wife, Mary, with menus describing what they ate and recipes for how they cooked it. But we don't. In fact, information about Lincoln's life is sketchy for the Springfield years and even sketchier for the log cabin days of his youth in Indiana.

The only body of sound evidence is Lincoln himself. During those growing years he must have eaten well. By the time the family left Indiana for Illinois, twenty-one-year-old Abraham was six feet four inches and weighed between 160 and 220 pounds depending upon who told the story. I've raised a teenage boy who grew to over six feet, and, as anyone who has fed teenage boys knows, the refrigerator and pantry seem to empty themselves just after they've been filled.

Known facts about Lincoln's diet and food habits are about as scanty as the provisions on those pantry shelves. I found some foods mentioned by name in some of the biographies. Anyone who reads broadly about Lincoln's early life and courtship runs into them, but these are, to use a food phrase, simply serving suggestions. I've run across some recipes and menus connected to Lincoln without reliable historical sources. Based on my research, some of them make sense and some of them don't. In writing an accurate portrayal of Lincoln's life through food, I'll put these suggestions in perspective. The real meat of the menu—a look at the foods, or even diet, of his time and place—presents trickier mysteries to figure out.

There is one excellent, comprehensive source—*Herndon's Informants*. Shortly after Lincoln was assassinated, his law partner and friend, William Herndon, set out to talk or write to everyone who knew Lincoln, especially during his youth. These interviews, finally published in full in 1998, began to point my way. As I read these primary source interviews in their entirety instead of excerpts quoted in Lincoln biographies, I found enough clues to focus my research. Others who knew Lincoln, quoted in Rufus Wilson's book, *Lincoln among His Friends*, and the work for *McClure's* magazine by Ida Tarbell, brought more ingredients into the mix. I happened upon a wonderful book that put me less than seventy-five miles from Lincoln's Indiana farm in 1820, three years after his family began homesteading. James Woods wrote *Two Years' Residence on the English Prairie of Illinois* for his friends in London to give a comprehensive explanation of his farm life in the New World. The book transported me as well with detailed descriptions of crops, wildlife, and American customs.

Yet, we must take even these voices with a grain of salt. Memory, especially when linked to an important event or martyred president, can be seasoned with an intrusive personal perspective. Communications theorist Dr. James Carey wrote of the inclination people have to put meaning, or themselves, into the narration of events: "They say what they say because they have purposes in mind. The world is the way it is because individuals want it that way." These evocative first-person narratives need to be sifted, mixed with other voices and with other period primary sources, tempered with reason or leavened with insight.

It is the same with recipes. I've worked with nineteenth-century recipes long enough to develop my own ways of translating their imprecise measurements, unwritten methods, and sometimes unfamiliar or unobtainable ingredients into a form that works in a modern kitchen. I try to get as close as I can to experiencing the flavors and textures of the past without driving myself—or anyone else—to distraction.

The best parts of these journeys through time are the fabulous flavors I've rediscovered. Even though ingredients and mixing and cooking methods may be essentially the same, the flavors are not. Wonderful, unexpected tastes and textures from the recipes of the past—molasses lemon cake, apple ketchup, and beef à la mode, to name a few—have surprised me time and time again. I am delighted with the dishes I've found from this adventure in the land of Lincoln: corn dodgers, almond cake, pumpkin butter, slow-cooked barbecue, and many more.

So, please, pull up a chair at my kitchen table. Its old round oak top is littered with notes; photocopies from agricultural journals, newspapers, grocery account ledgers; and stacks of old cookbooks. *Herndon's Informants* and biographies of Lincoln are here, too, along with my ring binder filled with pages of once neatly typed recipes now covered with penciled corrections and spatters of batter, the results of sampling and experimentation. Although this is a culinary exploration of Lincoln's life, not a cookbook, I've adapted the period techniques and recipes for cooking in today's kitchens and noted the sources. There is value in seeing the original recipes as historical documents, but I believe that value is outweighed by the enjoyment of preparing and eating foods that come as close to these culinary-heritage dishes as our stores and stoves can bring us. A biscuit made with soured milk and baking soda is a world of difference from one that pops out of a refrigerated tube. It profoundly changes the perception of what a biscuit can be.

I want readers to enjoy these foods. I've spent years figuring out how to make them from the scanty descriptions, incomplete measurements, and nonexistent instructions. In some cases, I've had to develop the recipe from just a description: you'll see "Re-created from period sources" under the titles of those dishes. For the recipes described as "Adapted from period sources," I've simply standardized the measurements to those used in today's kitchens, clarified the ingredients and put them in proper order, and written the method for preparation.

This book is organized generally as a biography following Abraham Lincoln's life from his childhood through his presidency. In some of the chapters, I describe my process for unraveling the historical clues to get to the flavors and textures. In others, I delve more deeply into Lincoln's biography and show how food brings new considerations to an understanding of his life, marriage, and time as president. All of the chapters have recipes at the end so you can undertake these explorations in your own kitchen. I promise these dishes are unlike anything we eat today. Delicious, evocative, and well worth the small efforts to prepare.

Come along. We'll see what directions food can take us as we travel to capture the flavor of Lincoln's times.

ABRAHAM AND MARY LINCOLN
CORN DODGERS AND EGG CORN BREAD

Both Abraham Lincoln and Mary Todd ate corn bread as children. He ate it from necessity; she ate it from tradition. The circumstances of their childhoods produced very different recipes. As adults, they continued to enjoy corn bread. Abraham relished it, eating corn bread and corn cakes "as fast as two women could make them," and for Mary there was no food more comforting. Years after Lincoln's death, in 1879, she was recovering from an illness during her four-year stay in Europe and wrote from France to her Springfield nephew of her longing for "a taste of ... good food—waffles, batter cakes, egg corn bread—... all unknown here."

As in colonial states, corn was the predominant crop in pioneering Kentucky, Indiana, and Illinois. It provided food for the people who lived on farms and for the horses, cows, and pigs as well. Although tedious to plant by hand, it grew reliably. The Lincolns grew mostly corn on their Indiana farm with some wheat. Beans or pumpkins commonly shared the corn patch, so farmers could get two, or even three, crops from one cleared acre. The pumpkin vines ran freely on the ground between the cornstalks and helped keep the weeds down by shading the soil to limit germination. Beans climbed the cornstalks for support. And corn, made into whiskey in a backyard still, could be turned into cash or used as an important barter good.

Abraham's father, Thomas Lincoln, did raise successful corn crops. When the family moved to Indiana, he had to leave behind forty bushels of corn stored in a neighbor's loft. Some biographers suggest Thomas took several barrels of whiskey to Indiana as well. Corn mash converted into whiskey through the alchemy of the still magically transformed corn into a desirable, highly portable cash crop.

I've worked with a lot of old cornmeal recipes over the years. Most of them are fairly straightforward and easily adapted to our kitchens and ingredients. From the Pilgrim days, our corn was referred to as "Indian" corn to differentiate it from wheat, which the English settlers called "corn." Many nineteenth-century recipes use that name. Despite their value and good taste, cornmeal dishes fall out of favor and are "rediscovered" as good food just about every generation. I've read articles in scores of nineteenth-century ladies' magazines, travel narratives, and agricultural journals preaching cornmeal's benefits. As Henry Andrews testified on the value of cornmeal in the March 1842 edition of the leading farming magazine of the day, the *Union Agriculturist*:

> I believe it is generally admitted that there is no grain grown in the U.S. of more value as to its general usefulness for both man and beast than the Indian corn, and yet with what contempt it is treated by many when it is occasionally placed on our tables in the form of bread. How many have I fallen in with in my travels among northern people particularly those who are unaccustomed to the mode of living in the middle and southern states who exclaim against corn bread or its usefulness any farther than for [live]stock. I think the cause of dislike is more from the want of knowledge how to prepare it for the table, than any thing else.

Preparing it for the table was a labor-intensive process and one that Abraham Lincoln would have known well. Corn keeps its own calendar with jobs for farmers at every stage. After the ears start to set kernels, farmers would remove the leaves below them, "pulling fodder" to feed their animals. In the fall, corn just shuts down, stops growing, and begins drying. The leaves wither to tan, the silks brown while the kernels harden and begin to dry on the faded ten-foot-tall stalks still standing in growing rows or after being cut and gathered into shocks. Although pioneers ate some of their corn crop in the "green" state—ears of corn boiled or roasted, as we do—they consumed most of it from the dried kernels transformed into cornmeal or hominy.

Settlers often turned the next step of the harvesting process into a social event. Indiana neighbors remember Lincoln at corn shuckings, neighborly gatherings where the husks were removed from the dry ears of corn amid joking, storytelling, and music. Sometimes the farmers divided the group down the middle in teams, and neighbors raced to see which side could shuck the most ears before placing them in the corn-crib or loft for storage. It was a perfect setting for the young Abraham to listen and practice his own storytelling skills.

Stripping the ears from the stalks, shucking them, and then shelling the kernels off the cob was hard work. It took one hundred ears of corn to make one bushel of corn kernels. Moderately successful corn crops in the 1820s yielded between sixty and eighty bushels from an acre. Mechanical picker-wheel or disk-type shellers appeared as early as 1815, but no one knows if the Lincoln family had one. They were so simple a child could operate them. Just hold an ear of corn against the spiked disk and crank away. The whirling spikes removed the dry kernels from the cob. These kernels then dropped into a container carefully placed under the sheller and were ready for the next cooking step.

Converting the kernels into cornmeal was work, too. The Lincolns may have made small batches of cornmeal by grating corn still on the cob across an oval piece of tin punched full of holes with a common nail and tacked on a board. We do know that young Abraham's chores included taking the corn to the mill so it could be ground into meal.

In 1818 Noah Gordon's horse-powered mill was just about two miles away from the Lincolns' Indiana home. Each farmer would hitch his horse to the mill and drive it around in a circle, powering the grinding stones. Various versions of a story about Abraham's accident at the mill exist, but the simplest is in the 1860 campaign autobiography in which Lincoln described himself using the third person: "In his tenth year he was kicked in the head by a horse and died for a time." Other stories provide more details. The horse was balky, Lincoln switched it one too many times on the flanks, and it kicked back. According to some neighbors' reports, he had been talking at the time. Abraham fell to the ground unconscious and when he woke up after more than a few minutes, he finished his sentence as though nothing had happened.

As to foods made from that ground meal, Lincoln's cousin Dennis Hanks described one of Abraham's more reliable snacks: "Seems to me now I never seen Abe after he was twelve that he didn't have a book in his hand or in his pocket. He'd put a book inside his shirt an' fill his pants pockets with corn dodgers an' go off to plow or hoe. When noon came he'd set under a tree an' read an' eat."

Judge John Pritcher, another neighbor, writing in 1888 recalled the dodgers in not-quite-appetizing terms: "I have eaten many corn dodgers made from the meal from that old mill—It would make good chicken feed now—but we were glad to get it then. Abe used to bring me my meal regularly."

So, a recipe for corn dodgers seems like a good place to start cooking. This is one of the archetypal images of the boy Lincoln, sitting under a tree absorbed totally in his reading. Hanks's description provided some recipe guidance as well. The dodgers needed to be sturdy enough to withstand being tucked into a pants pocket. Granted, pioneer pants were likely loosely fitted homespun, so the dodger wasn't jammed into the side of a pair of tight-fitting Levi's. Still, tender corn bread would not do the trick.

After dozens of test corn dodgers, I discovered two keys to making them: coarsely ground cornmeal—stone ground if you can find it—and patience. A nonstick skillet helps, too. Lincoln's mother and stepmother would have had a very well-seasoned cast-iron skillet. Although I have one, my modern nonstick skillet worked just fine. Corn dodgers are essentially cornmeal and hot water with the tiniest bit of fat and salt added. I tried making them with regular cornmeal, but they turned out hard and, as Judge Pritcher allowed, just fine for bird food. After working with the coarsely ground meal a couple of times, I developed a feel for the mix that is a cross between a batter and a dough. I was able to form the corn dodgers in the palm of my hand and slip them gently into the pan. Some modern recipes suggest frying the cakes in deep fat. I don't think the pioneers would have done that. Cooking fat, whether lard or butter, was a precious ingredient on a frontier farm. Using more than the bare minimum to cook meats or breads would have been wasteful.

The names of cornmeal breads that the Lincoln and Todd families ate in the 1820s and 1830s—corn dodgers, cornpone, Johnnycakes, egg corn bread—are familiar. The recipes I found in agricultural journals and cookbooks of the era, however, are definitely and deliciously different, as you will see in the recipe section at the end of the chapter. However, one ingredient, or dish, almost got the better of me: hominy.

About the only thing you can say for sure about hominy is that it comes from dried kernels of corn. After that, there are as many meanings for hominy and directions for making it as there are decades between now and the Pilgrims, regions of the country, and cooks in the kitchen. The hominy we buy in stores today is either canned, large white exploded kernels or finely ground hominy grits. Both of these products frequently have had the outer hull and the small hard germ removed. The germ, the part of the corn kernel where growth begins, looks like a small seed the size of a pencil point at the base of the kernel.

I was somewhat bewildered as I first tried to understand the nineteenth-century recipes with this twenty-first-century hominy perspective. When I looked at the period recipes after reading the *Union Agriculturist*, they made much more sense. The full name of the newspaper is the *Union Agriculturist and Western Prairie Farmer*, and it was one of a number of early monthly newspapers written for and by farmers. The *Union Agriculturist* began its first issue, published in January 1841, with a plea for information from the people who were working the western land, breaking the prairies, and who had the firsthand information for success. "Upon you we must rely for the matter that is to make this paper interesting and valuable."

And they got lots of answers on a great many subjects: breeds of cattle suited to the West, how to make a beet pie, best way to preserve butter, how to cure gapes in chickens were some of the pieces published from readers in 1841 and '42. Making hominy was a "Household Department" topic of interest in 1842. Three correspondents sent in their hominy-making thoughts to the paper. In March *Union Agriculturist* printed Putnam County (possibly Indiana) resident Henry Andrews's letter. In April, the paper published one from A. B. Gordon of Cold Bend, Warren County, which could have been in any number of midwestern states, and in June, the last piece was from a "Kentucky Farmer." Their letters thoroughly explained the early-nineteenth-century process and product while singing its praises as a delicious food.

Making hominy is a country task and opportunity. Though the ingredients would have been available to city residents, the mechanical apparatus to break the kernels was constructed and used in the farmyard. Hominy making was an all-day operation, and, as I discovered, one that is well worth the effort.

Abraham Lincoln would not have had my hominy problem. Pioneer children grew up in the kitchen, as the large fireplace that heated their one-room cabins served also as the cook stove. Not only did they, by necessity, work in the fields and garden to raise the crops and manage the chickens, pigs, cows, and horses, but they were also constant observers of kitchen tasks, even if they were not involved in the preparation of the food. On a pioneer farm, labor was constant. Every morning and evening someone needed to milk the cow. Milk was set aside so it could separate, and then someone skimmed off the cream that rose to the top and churned it into butter. Eggs needed to be gathered before they could start turning into chickens under the sitting hens. Fresh garden vegetables needed to be picked before they rotted on the vines or stalks. And in a one-room cabin, cooking took place in the space that was living room and bedroom as well as kitchen.

Every frontier child knew where his food came from and probably how to cook it. Lincoln, like many others, would have had to help even more. When his mother, Nancy, died from milk sickness, he was nine and a half, and his sister, Sarah, was eleven and a half. The homemaking fell to these two children. Even though Dennis Hanks minimized Abraham's indoor activities when he reminisced that all he and Abe did to cheer hardworking Sarah was to bring her a turtle as a pet, I strongly suspect Lincoln would have done more than wander in from the woods and fields. In the reality of rural life, he would have helped at the very least with common male chores: chopping wood, carrying water from the stream, and making hominy.

In the Lincolns' farmyard, the first step in making hominy would have been to make lye, essential to removing the hulls from the kernels. So let's look at the letters in the *Union Agriculturist* for the best ways to proceed. First the dried corn kernels must be soaked for fifteen to twenty minutes. Henry Andrews suggested using just boiling water, but the others insisted on a lye solution made by dumping a couple of shovels full of wood-fire ash into hot water and waiting for the ash to settle to the bottom of the pot. The resulting lye liquid, "strong enough to float an egg" or "sharp enough to bit the tongue," is dipped off and into a large pot. As the Kentucky Farmer said, this solution will "save half the labor." He also reported that a six-gallon pot could hold up to five quarts of corn for soaking. After the corn has soaked, remove it from the pot and "commence beating," using a mortar and pestle.

These few minutes of soaking loosened the hull but did not significantly soften the kernel. Settlers made large mortars to process both dry corn kernels for regular cornmeal and those soaked for hominy. They started with a log standing about thirty inches high. Next the hominy makers turned the top few inches of the log into the mortar bowl by chopping or burning a hole in it. Or they could use the method described by Mr. Andrews, the clever Putnam County farmer. He built up the mortar basin using boards nailed onto a tapered shape he chopped out of the top of the log so that it looked like the flared outside of a wineglass bowl. As he said, you could build this almost as fast as you could read about doing it. To add even more oomph to the pounding, the pestle had an iron wedge driven into the pounding end, secured by an iron ring. Some suggested that farmers could devise a "sweep" to make the job even easier. Attach the pestle to a light tree branch and then use its natural upward spring to lift the pestle before pulling it down to pound the kernels.

After the corn was sufficiently pounded, as the Kentucky Farmer said, "This beating is perfected when the grains are divested of the skin and each grain is cracked. We do not admire it beat fine." Then the rinsing and cooking began. Several rinsings in clear water were needed to float off the released hulls and some of the germ, as well as the lye residue. Next, simply cook the corn with a little salt and a lot of water for three to four hours in a large pot until "anyone can easily discover when it is well done by its greatly swelled appearance and by the rich savory done taste." One writer suggested: "It is a very nice dish served up hot out of the boiling kettle taken with butter or eaten with milk like mush."

But most of the nineteenth-century experts in the *Union Agriculturist* advised putting the cooked hominy away, as the Kentucky Farmer summed up, "in wood or stone vessels in a cool place to be used as occasion demands.... When wanted for daily meals it is either simply warmed in a skillet with a little butter or lard or fried or baked until a brown crust envelopes the whole mass. It is best taken with good butter."

Hominy, as cooked in the South and Midwest in the nineteenth century, was a fall and winter dish. Corn harvest, shucking, and drying finished up in October and November. The hominy-making process was not taken lightly, even by folks used to working with caustic lye, rigorous pounding, and long simmering over a wood fire. As one writer explained, "But the boiling is too serious a job to be performed as often as hominy is relished and that is at breakfast and dinner at least. It is therefore boiled say once or twice a week. Except in cold weather but a small quantity should be boiled at a time as it soon sours unless the temperature is low. Indeed, it is not used except in the cold months and would be neither relished nor deemed seasonable at any other time."

I am compelled to make the following warning: it is no longer safe or even possible to soak corn kernels in lye in a home or farm setting. Food-grade lye is no longer sold. Even if it were still available, lye is highly dangerous and no one should go near it. I've done some adventuresome cooking in my days, and I would not attempt soaking corn or cooking with lye. You can purchase a substitute, "culinary lime," in some stores or online, but it, too, is a caustic substance, and working with it can be tricky.

However, you can buy kernels of corn that have been treated to the pre-pounding hominy stage. I turned my attention southwest and discovered an online resource for "posole," kernels soaked in an alkaline solution to remove the thin, transparent outer hull. Gourmet stores and markets serving Mexican American customers carry the product sold as dried kernels. Mexican cuisine calls for cooking these "nixtamalized" kernels so they swell up to popcorn size. They are left whole in tasty soups and stews or ground and formed into tortillas.

I was more interested in the pioneer version, kernels shattered into "rice-size" pieces and then cooked. Like any modern cook, I turned to the food processor and quickly learned that modern isn't better. I experimented with a variety of pulsing techniques. No matter what I tried, the resulting pieces were either too big or too small. The processor's action chops or slices but doesn't shatter. And, worse yet, the hard germ, or the seed-to-be, was processed along with the rest of the grain.

Time to rethink, consider the pioneer experience, and search the garage. I found an old metal mixing bowl, a couple blocks of wood, and our old eight-pound sledgehammer. After a bit of steel-wool cleanup, I had the equipment to try the nineteenth-century pounding method. I just needed the right place. Then I remembered the tree stump.

A couple of years ago, a storm took out the top two-thirds of an old basswood tree. We cut it off about three feet from the ground, thinking it might make a nice, natural outdoor table. The inside had hollowed out a bit, just the right size to hold the mixing bowl. I put two-by-fours in first to support the bottom of the bowl and to provide an opposing hard surface for the sledge blows. I poured in about a cup of posole-treated kernels and began pounding. Mimicking the pioneer-described pestle technique, I lifted the sledge up and down, rather like operating a dasher on a butter churn, striking the corn with the top of the hammer instead of the normal striking face. At first the kernels had a tendency to jump. Some of them even landed out of the bowl. As more of them cracked, the mass tended to stay in the bottom. After about five minutes, I had enough to pour into a large mesh strainer, and sifted out the corn that was the desired size of a grain of rice. A good bit more remained. More pounding. More sifting. After about fifteen minutes I had it all pounded.

I put the hominy grains in a large bowl and filled it with water. I stirred the grains with my fingers and watched the cracked-off germ bits rise, if not completely to the surface of the water at least to the top of the sinking grains. I was able to whoosh and pick out most of the germ. Now, time to cook!

There are two cooking steps: swelling the grains and then frying them. I coaxed the hominy to plumpness in a slow cooker, covering the cup of grains with three cups of water and setting it on low. Several hours later the shattered hominy shards were almost back to the size of the original whole kernels. I drained off the remaining water and patted the hominy dry between paper towels. I couldn't wait to taste. I put some in a bowl with a bit of butter and shared with my husband. He had the best description of its somewhat elusive, delicious flavor and texture: "It's like liquid popcorn."

Frying the hominy in butter until it turned golden added a nice crisp layer to the slightly chewy grains. The flavor is mild and certainly corn-like. There is a subtle sweetness. It is easy to see why pioneers hungered for this hominy and why city folk who happened upon it wrote of its fine qualities.

Still, making hominy this way is a lot of work. I looked at the sack of coarsely ground cornmeal I used for my corn dodgers and wondered if I could skip the pounding. Would this easily available corn product work? A few hours later I had my answer. By golly, it did. I did have some preparation work to do, however. The cornmeal I use is ground with the hulls on and the germ attached. I sifted the cornmeal through a fairly fine kitchen sieve to remove particles smaller than about one-quarter the size of a grain of long-grain rice, smaller than the cracked corn Lincoln, other pioneers, and I made, maybe half or even quarter the size, depending on how much pestle "oomph" was applied.

I put the more finely milled cornmeal that had come through the sieve to the side for use the next time I made corn bread or Johnnycakes. I then put about a half cup of the corn remaining in the sieve into a two-quart bowl, filled the bowl with water, and stirred gently with my fingers as I had done with my home-pounded version. The hull chaff and some of the germ floated to the top. I tipped the bowl slightly and whooshed it off. Then I let my slow cooker, filled with water, do the rest of the work. After four hours or so, the grains had swollen up about four times, to about the size of a grain of rice. I drained them and put them in the refrigerator after taking a forkful to test. This version had the same nice light corn flavor, but it had a bit of a bite to it. The texture was starchier, so instead of cooking up easily into individual grains, it could be made into a corn cake that would hold together when carefully flipped. Definitely not mush.

On Christmas morning I put a dab of butter into my frying pan and patted out a flat cake of my newly made hominy. Crusted golden brown after about ten minutes over a slow fire, I gently flipped it over and browned the other side. It was, indeed, a delight ... and the beginning of a new holiday breakfast tradition. As to gifts under the tree, I might just spend some summer afternoons pounding up some posole grains to package for an authentic experience.

In the fourteen months between Nancy Lincoln's death on October 5, 1818, and Thomas Lincoln's marriage to Sarah Bush Johnston on

December 2, 1819, Abraham and his sister, Sarah, probably made many pots of hominy as well as other common cornmeal dishes, Johnnycake, hoecake, cornmeal mush, owendow, and various types of simple corn breads made largely from cornmeal. Sometimes, depending on the seasonal produce from the farm, they might have made the bread with eggs, milk, and butter, but seldom would they have used wheat flour. Dennis Hanks reported that on the farm the family raised corn and "sum wheat enuf for a cake on Sunday."

Life was very different in the Lexington, Kentucky, household of the Todd family as it faced the same tragedy, the mother's death. Children had died in both families as well. Lincoln's younger brother lived three days. Mary's younger brother died at the age of two, when she was four years old. Two year later, in 1825, Mary's mother died within days after giving birth to George, her seventh child in twelve years of marriage. In the motherless Todd household, the remaining six children didn't have the responsibilities that had fallen to Abraham and his sister, Sarah. Mary's eight-year-old brother, Levi, didn't have to do chores. Her two older sisters, Elizabeth, age twelve, and Frances, age ten, didn't have to manage the household or watch over the younger children—Mary, then six, Ann, age one, and the baby.

The Todd household was affluent and owned slaves. Mary's maternal grandmother lived in a large house on the same block. By most accounts, Robert Smith Todd, Mary's father, was largely absent from home. The job of raising his children fell to their grandmother, his sisters, and the slaves who kept the house running. Mammy Sally, as she was called by the family, was part nursemaid and part disciplinarian. A woman called "Old Chaney" was the cook, Nelson served at table and did the marketing, and Jane was another member of the household. Details of life in the Todd household are scarce, but it is not hard to imagine that the children might wander through the kitchen and sit for a spell watching Old Chaney prepare food. There is one suggestion of such closeness. When Mary was thirteen, she rode her new pony out to the home of renowned Whig politician Henry Clay on a lark. Clay had been a visitor to the politically connected Todd home. She is quoted as saying, "Mammy will be wild! When I put salt in her coffee this morning she called me a limb of Satan."

Corn-based breads would have been different in the Todd household as well. In a thriving city with fancy bakeries turning out elaborate cakes for society parties and political events, wheat flour would have been a common staple in most upper-class kitchens. As a recipe for "Superior Johnny-Cakes" from Goshen, New York, printed in the *Albany Cultivator* and reprinted in the *Tennessee Farmer* in 1836 noted, "The addition of wheat flour will be found to be a great improvement in the art of making these cakes. Those who have not eggs will find it will do very well without."

Similarly, the recipe for cornmeal rusk from *Farmer and Gardener*, also reprinted in *Tennessee Farmer*, is described as "among the many delicacies in the form of bread, which render the enjoyment of breakfast so acceptable, we know of none more deserving of notice than the one prepared according to the following recipe."

Mary's father eventually remarried. His second wife had all she could do raising her own eight children born between 1828 and 1841. Willful Mary went to a local boarding school and a French academy in Lexington, coming home for the weekends and holidays. Her oldest sister, Elizabeth, was the first to head to Springfield after her 1832 marriage to Ninian Edwards, son of the governor of Illinois, who had come east to study at Lexington's Transylvania University. The other three daughters from the first marriage, Frances, Mary, and then Ann, joined Elizabeth in the free state and married Illinois men.

Some of the recipes from Old Chaney's kitchen may have followed them there to become part of the comfort of home.

CORN DODGERS

• • • • • •

Texture and taste set the corn dodger apart from ordinary corn bread. When made with stone-ground cornmeal, true dodgers have a crisp crust with a tender interior. The satisfying deep corn flavor makes them wonderful alongside a bowl of soup, or enjoyed just plain.

CHOOSE STONE-GROUND CORNMEAL: "Stone-ground" cornmeal is ground between two stones, a traditional process that produces a coarser meal with the kernel's hull and germ mostly intact. Most cooks find that stone-ground cornmeal has a more pronounced "corn" flavor than regular mass-produced cornmeal, which is ground with metal rollers. The nutritious hull and germ have been removed from regular cornmeal and the texture is usually finer. Stone-ground cornmeal is more perishable and should be stored in the refrigerator or freezer.

> **2 cups coarse cornmeal, preferably stone-ground**
> **1/2 teaspoon salt**
> **1 tablespoon melted butter or bacon drippings, plus more for cooking dodgers**
> **1 1/2 cups boiling water**
> **1/3 cup regular cornmeal, optional**

Mix the coarse cornmeal and salt in a mixing bowl. Make a well in the center and pour in the butter or drippings. Pour the boiling water over the fat and stir carefully and thoroughly. Set aside to cool, 20 to 30 minutes. This should make a loose dough that you can form into dodgers shaped like ears of corn. Cornmeals vary, so you may need to add a bit more water or, if the mixture is too wet, add up to 1/3 cup regular cornmeal. In making these additions, begin by adding less than you think necessary.

TO COOK ON THE STOVETOP: Form the dodgers by placing about 2 tablespoons of dough in the palm of one hand and gently press the dough into an oval about 2 inches long and 1 inch wide. Put an 8- to 10-inch skillet over medium-high heat. When hot, melt about 1 tablespoon butter or drippings in the pan. Carefully place 6 of the formed dodgers in the hot skillet; don't crowd them. Lower the heat and cook until the bottoms are browned and the tops are firm and dry, about 8 to 10 minutes. Turn over carefully and finish cooking until browned on both sides, another 5 to 7 minutes. Repeat these steps with the remaining dodgers.

TO BAKE: Preheat the oven to 425°F. Grease a baking sheet well. Form the dodgers as described above. Bake until firm throughout, about 15 to 20 minutes.

TIP FOR SUCCESS: You can't rush corn dodgers. Patience will produce better results. You have to allow time first for the cornmeal–hot water mixture to cool and swell and then for the dodgers to cook through in the skillet. I've had them take as long as 12 minutes on a side.

Makes about 18 corn dodgers

RE-CREATED FROM PERIOD SOURCES.

EGG CORN BREAD

• • • • • • •

This corn bread emerges with a slightly crinkled crust and a moist, yet crumbly texture. The rich, egg taste rounds out the hearty corn flavors for the kind of bread Mary Lincoln would have remembered fondly from her childhood.

> 3/4 **cup water**
> 1/4 **cup coarse cornmeal, preferably stone-ground**
> 2 **large eggs, separated**
> 1 **cup milk**
> 1 **cup regular cornmeal**
> 1/2 **teaspoon salt, or less to taste**
> 1/4 **teaspoon baking soda**
> 1 **tablespoon butter, melted**

In a saucepan, bring the water to a simmer. Gradually stir in the coarse cornmeal and cook over low heat until it thickens, about 10 minutes. Set this cornmeal mush aside until cool, 20 to 30 minutes.

Preheat the oven to 350°F. Generously grease a deep, 9-inch round baking dish. Transfer the cooled cornmeal mush to a mixing bowl. Combine the egg yolks and milk and stir into the mush with a whisk or fork until the mixture is smooth. Add the regular cornmeal, salt, baking soda, and melted butter. Mix well. Beat the egg whites until they form soft peaks and fold into the batter. Pour the batter into the prepared baking dish.

Bake until the bread is firm in the center and starts to pull away from the sides of the pan, about 40 to 50 minutes. Loosen the edges from the pan while still warm. Cool before slicing.

Makes 1 round loaf, to serve 6 to 8

ADAPTED FROM PERIOD SOURCES.

2

LINCOLN'S GINGERBREAD MEN

In all of his writings, Abraham Lincoln didn't say much about food, but his evocation of gingerbread men may well have set his national political career on the right path.

At the first debate with Stephen A. Douglas in 1858, Lincoln used a childhood incident to partially defuse the very ugly Senate campaign tactics. A boisterous and partisan crowd of ten thousand, two-thirds of them hearty Lincoln supporters, filled Lafayette Square in Ottawa, Illinois, on August 21. Douglas spoke first for sixty minutes, then Lincoln for ninety, with Douglas returning to the platform for a thirty-minute rejoinder. As each man spoke, the audience interrupted with "cheers and laughter" and shouts of "yes, yes" and "Go get him." Douglas addressed the crowd using his typical unctuous style, praising his opponent for his accomplishments to the point of near mockery and then turning the rhetoric to a harsh and misleading attack on Lincoln's policy positions. When it was Lincoln's turn to address the crowd, he strongly defended his policy stance but then began telling a gentle anecdote that turned out to be a verbal assault on Douglas with an artfully vigorous "wink and a nod" to the audience so they were in on the joke, too.

Douglas had misrepresented Lincoln's stance on slavery, suggesting that he would "set the states at war with one another" over the issue. Rather than counterattack, Lincoln feigned bewilderment that the well-regarded Douglas would so misstate his positions and so he had been blindsided by the compliments Judge Douglas had heaped upon him. "I was not very accustomed to flattery and it came the sweeter to me. I was rather like the Hoosier, with the gingerbread, when he said he reckoned he loved it better than any other man, and got less of it."

Reportedly this story about his Hoosier friend wanting to eat gingerbread men charmed that Illinois audience, and also impressed the thousands of readers of the newspaper accounts. Six years later in the White House, Lincoln expanded the gingerbread story, giving a personal context as he recalled an incident from his Indiana boyhood.

Once in a while my mother used to get some sorghum and ginger and make some gingerbread. It wasn't often and it was our biggest treat. One day I smelled the gingerbread and came into the house to get my share while it was hot. My mother had baked me three gingerbread men. I took them under a hickory tree to eat them. There was a family that lived near us that was a little poorer than we were and their boy came along as I sat down.

"Abe," he said, "gimme a man?"

I gave him one. He crammed it in his mouth in two bites and looked at me while I was biting the legs from my first one.

"Abe," he said, "gimme that other'n."

I wanted it myself, but I gave it to him and as it followed the first I said to him. "You seem to like gingerbread."

"Abe," he said, "I don't suppose there's anybody on this earth likes gingerbread better'n I do." He drew a long breath before he added, "and I don't suppose there's anybody on this earth gets less'n I do."

Lincoln's anecdote gives great clues not only to how his mother would have made gingerbread men, but also about life in the early days of Indiana statehood.

The Lincolns moved to Indiana two months before Abraham's eighth birthday and just about the time the state was officially admitted to the Union on December 11, 1816. His father, Thomas, had scouted and claimed 160 acres that fall, probably marking the corners of his new farm with piles of brush, as was the custom, and quickly building a lean-to shelter before heading back about fifty miles southeast to fetch his family.

The move assured that Thomas Lincoln would own this farm in a state newly admitted to the Union. Titles to the two different farms he had purchased in Kentucky had been disputed, with Lincoln ultimately losing the land. Thomas and his wife, Nancy, must have felt that owning land with certainty in a free state was worth uprooting their two children, Sarah, almost ten, and Abraham, nearly eight, from school and community. Lincoln also left behind forty bushels of corn harvested from his productive Knob Creek land near Elizabethtown, Kentucky. It would be some time before the Indiana crops would be as bountiful. The new land was forested. The family even had to cut their way through saplings, trees, and tangles of wild grapevines the last few miles to the farm from the path-like township road.

Thomas Lincoln's family was among the first in that section, then two counties east from the southern tip of Indiana, although family would soon follow. Vincennes, sixty miles northwest, was the nearest big city. It would be two years before James Gentry settled two miles west of the Lincoln farm, opening up his store. Eventually the town was named for him—Gentryville. Troy, about fourteen miles southeast on the Ohio River, served as the Lincolns' market town for the first few years. They took corn there to be ground and traded for supplies they could not make or grow.

In October 1818 Nancy Lincoln went to help care for her aunt Elizabeth Sparrow, who had become sick on their neighboring farm. While there, Nancy, too, drank the poisoned milk, contaminated when cows grazed on toxic white snakeroot. She died in a few days from the "milk sickness," as did her aunt and uncle. A year later Thomas traveled back to Kentucky and returned with his new wife, Sarah Johnston. The two families had known each other in Elizabethtown. Sarah's husband had died just before the Lincolns moved north. She had three children, two of them about the same ages as the Lincoln children, Sarah and Abraham, now almost thirteen and eleven. It made sense in the pioneer days of the 1810s to combine the families.

The gingerbread parable is appealing whether Nancy or Sarah made Abraham's treat. He referred to them both as "mother." But I'm willing to bet that Nancy made those men. There were just two children during her days at the kitchen hearth. After Sarah moved in there were six children in the household including Dennis Hanks, a twice-orphaned Lincoln cousin whose guardians had been the Sparrows.

There is a poignancy to the vision of a small boy running to get his share that doesn't fit as well with an eleven-year-old who was, by most accounts, doing nearly a man's work in the forest and fields.

Lincoln's gingerbread recipe is one Nancy would have known in her heart and her hands. Abraham would have known it, too. Growing up in a one-room log cabin he was, essentially, raised in the kitchen. Not only would young Lincoln have watched food being cooked, he would have harvested and prepared some of the ingredients and probably learned to cook for himself, too.

However, I did need a recipe, so I consulted several period cookbooks, using Lincoln's description as a guide. I have three cookbooks by Miss Eliza Leslie of Philadelphia, perhaps the most well-known early- to mid-nineteenth-century cookbook writer. Some of her books are available as modern reprints or online. I do have two original volumes, one the same 1845 edition Mary Lincoln purchased. Mrs. Lettice Bryan's *The Kentucky Housewife*, published in 1839, has recipes with their origins right in Lincoln country. I pulled other resources off my bookshelf and from the stacks of photocopies of magazine and agricultural journal pages dating from the 1830s through the 1860s.

The ingredients Lincoln didn't mention are as important as the two he did. We're used to gingerbread as a mixed-spice cake. I usually make gingerbread flavored with ginger, cinnamon, and cloves. Some gingerbreads have nutmeg or mace; even allspice may turn up in the recipe. Almost all have molasses as the syrupy sweetener. I had hoped to find a period recipe using just ginger and sorghum. I did find a couple that were simply spiced with ginger, but none called for sorghum.

Miss Leslie's 1828 recipe for "Common Gingerbread," from her first cookbook, seemed like the best one to try. It is closest to the time period, uses very simple ingredients, and is spiced only with ginger. She made her gingerbread with flour, butter, milk, a hint of brown sugar, ginger, pearl ash, and molasses.

Lincoln specified sorghum, which is different from molasses. The flavor it brings is subtle, sweet, and aromatic without dominating. As my southern friends say, it is "truly fine." Sorghum would nicely balance the single spice, ginger.

Sorghum syrup, which you can usually find next to molasses in larger grocery stores, comes from the tall, broad-leafed sorghum plant that looks somewhat like corn when it is growing in the fields, only without the ears. For someone with a bit of time and a very big kettle, the syrup is relatively easy to make. Sorghum stalks are crushed, releasing the juice, which is strained to remove impurities and then cooked down in large kettles, evaporating excess water much like maple sap is made into syrup. It takes about twelve hours to make syrup from the juice. An acre of sorghum can produce 150 gallons of syrup.

Although sorghum is a farm product, it was rare in the United States before the 1850s. Farmers grew some sorghum in the South beginning in the 1700s, when seeds were imported from Africa. In 1850 a new strain was imported from France, and the crop took off. I've not seen it mentioned in recipes published through the 1850s; they all call for molasses. So Lincoln's mother's use of sorghum would have been unusual for the era. *The Kentucky Housewife* even specifies, "West Indian molasses, not sugar house" for its gingerbread. Most molasses is a by-product of sugar processing. As the juice extracted from the sugarcane is boiled, the pure white sugar crystallizes. In the 1800s the crystals were molded into a cone shape for sale. As the process continues, brown sugar crystallizes, with dark brown sugar having a higher molasses content than light brown. Finally, the remaining molasses is poured off. The last bit of molasses left in the bottom of the barrel, called "black strap," is the strongest.

The other ingredient Lincoln said his mother "used to get" was ginger, a product of the Caribbean. Ginger is grown for its tuberous root, used fresh or dried and then ground to make the spice. The first shipment of ginger from Jamaica to northern Europe was in 1585. Recipes for gingerbread published before the 1840s, including the recipe I used from Miss Leslie, require a lot of ginger. "Large spoonful" or a "third of a tea cup" were common measurements. By the 1850s, cookbooks call for far less, more in keeping with today's amounts measured in teaspoons. One explanation can be found in the instruction Miss Leslie wrote in the 1845 edition of her cookery book: "Ground ginger loses much of its strength by keeping. Therefore, it will be frequently found necessary to put in more than the quantity given in the receipt." As I was using modern ginger, I adapted the recipe by using a smaller quantity of the spice.

Pearl ash is a period-specific ingredient in Miss Leslie's recipe, but it has a readily acceptable substitute—baking soda. I've always simply substituted modern baking soda for pearl ash or saleratus, the substance that followed it. These powders react with acidic ingredients, such as molasses or sour milk, to make the batters bubbly and cakes bake up light.

No one knows if the Lincolns made pearl ash on their farm, but they could have. The raw material, clear-cut trees, was all around them. Six generations ago, before the Revolutionary War, my Scots-Irish relatives emigrated from Donegal, Ireland, settling on the western Pennsylvania frontier. Then in 1840, great-great-grandparents John and Mary Fails moved farther west to the Pennsylvania-Ohio state line. There, like the Lincolns, they settled on a heavily wooded farm. And there the Fails made "black salts," the first step to making pearl ash.

The process for clearing a forested farm hadn't changed much from colonial days. Whether it was the Lincolns or my Scots-Irish ancestors, the job started with the cold, sharp blade of an ax and finished with fire. Abraham and his father cut down trees and set aside logs for building their cabin and outbuildings, turning into furniture, chopping for firewood, or splitting into fence rails. The remaining branches, logs, and stumps were burned. For the Fails family and others of their time, the ashes from those fires were an important source of revenue.

I have a yellowed and tattered newspaper clipping from the 1920s in the family album describing their pioneering efforts some seventy-five years earlier. "It is a tradition in the family that after a log heap had burned, if even in the night a storm threatened, the family would hasten to gather the ashes least they should become wet and leached and in this way lose their value."

As my great-greats in Pennsylvania knew and as the Lincolns in Indiana would have known, the ashes from all those fires held the keys to making fat congeal into soap and cakes rise. Soaking the ashes in hot water leached out the lye essential for turning leftover rendered pork or beef fat into soap. Two more steps produced pearl ash for leavening purposes. Pioneers turned the liquid lye into solid black salts by boiling it until the water evaporated. Further refining the black salts in a very hot fire, perhaps even in a kiln, burned off all the dark carbon bits, leaving a pure, white ash. Fortunately, we can just dip our measuring spoons into the little orange-and-red box of baking soda.

I felt confident that Miss Leslie's 1828 recipe was the right gingerbread to test, but I was still struggling with the best way to make the gingerbread men. I was familiar with two kinds of nineteenth-century gingerbread, what cookbooks sometimes labeled "hard" and "soft." Hard gingerbread is the kind you get in Colonial Williamsburg, rather flat and baked on a sheet like a cookie. That's a fine process for a settled community with large brick ovens to put baking sheets into. But I didn't think the frontier Lincoln cabin would have had a brick oven for the first struggling years. I was skeptical, as well, that Nancy would have had a tin cookie cutter. I also figured she might not have taken the time to cut around the shape with a knife.

Nancy would certainly have had the essentials of cast-iron cooking equipment—in addition to a regular frying pan, she would have had a "spider," which was a frying pan that had legs so it could stand over hearth coals. She would have stewed meats or vegetables and baked bread, cake, or pies in a Dutch oven. This covered pot may also have had legs. Its cover has a raised rim to hold hot coals in place on top of the pot so foods cook surrounded by heat. Pioneer cooks rarely had reflector ovens, where the foods rested on a rack facing the fire. Mostly used for roasting meats, a polished piece of metal curved around the back of this rack, reflecting and concentrating the fire's heat on both sides of the cooking food.

Soft gingerbread is cake-like and could be baked easily in a Dutch oven or on the hearth. But how would Nancy make a man from that more liquid batter for hearth baking? Would she have carefully poured the batter into a frying pan, drizzling it off a spoon to form arms, legs, body, and head for a pancake-like version?

Lincoln's description of how his friend ate the gingerbread men provided more clues. These gingerbread men had to have the strength to hold their shape while Abraham carried them to where he could sit under the tree, and they had to be soft enough so his friend could cram one "into his mouth in two bites." I felt like the Three Bears—the pancake version was too soft, the hard gingerbread too tough. Once again, Miss

Leslie had an answer that was just right. Her directions for common gingerbread suggested that it was somewhere between the soft cake and the hard gingerbread man cookie. It is a deceptively simple solution for the frontier or modern kitchen. "Put some flour on your paste-board, take out small portions of the dough, and make it with your hand into long rolls. Then curl up the rolls into round cakes or twist two together or lay them into straight lengths or sticks side by side."

Or make them into men!

I found this dough as easy to work as children's clay. It was very simple to form into men three or four inches high. Perfect for pocket, hands, and mouth. The method Miss Leslie specified for mixing the dough was unexpected as well. Rather than creaming the butter and sugar together, she tells us to cut the butter into the dry ingredients. This is just like making piecrust or biscuits. The flour surrounds the small pieces of cold butter, and, as the food bakes, the melting butter forms a pocket, producing a flaky crust, biscuit, or gingerbread. Simply perfect for baking in a reflector oven, Dutch oven, or even a skillet with a lid to hold in the heat.

I think this approach is about as close as we can get to Lincoln's gingerbread men. This recipe fits his description of a gingerbread man sturdy enough to stuff into a pocket and soft enough to gobble up in a couple of bites.

As delicious as this gingerbread is, it still is a bit understated for the kinds of desserts we're used to. I wondered how it stacked up to other typical treats of the era and the region. I found a recipe for a more rustic cake I've taken to calling "Tennessee Cake," as the recipe appeared in *Tennessee Farmer* in 1835. It relies on farm products even more than a gingerbread recipe does, with brown sugar as the only purchased ingredient. Eggs, butter, flour, and cornmeal combine with that bit of brown sugar for a cake that tastes best with a sauce. Once you taste the two of them, it is easy to see why Lincoln's gingerbread would make a lasting impression on flavor alone.

GINGERBREAD MEN

• • • • • • •

Discover the delicate, mellow taste of sorghum. You'll find the recipe has just enough sweetness to complement the ginger. This easy recipe is perfect for a delightful afternoon of parent-child baking.

SORGHUM SYRUP: The amazing sorghum plant looks like corn, but without the ears. A native of China and Africa, sorghum or "broom corn" may have been first brought to the United States by Benjamin Franklin in 1757 for, well, making brooms. Nearly fifty years later, John Skinner described the plant's productivity in the July 2, 1824, issue of *American Farmer*. "Cultivated in almost every part of the United States ... the seeds are made into nutritious flour for feeding people and pigs.... The stalks are crushed to produce a delightful syrup."

A decade before the Civil War, a newer variety of sweet sorghum, "Chinese Amber," was introduced into the United States with the hopes of reducing the nation's reliance on imported cane sugar. Sorghum syrup production peaked in the 1880s and declined in the twentieth century in the face of competition from cheaper, less labor-intensive sweeteners. Sorghum syrup tastes like fruity honey with a touch of molasses. Pour sorghum syrup over pancakes and waffles; use it to sweeten baked beans or to replace honey in favorite baked goods. You can usually find a few bottles tucked in among the molasses, corn, and maple syrups in grocery stores.

- ½ **cup milk**
- ½ **cup sorghum syrup or light or dark molasses**
- 3 ⅓ **cups unbleached all-purpose flour**
- 2 **tablespoons packed brown sugar**
- ½ **teaspoon baking soda**
- 1 **tablespoon ground ginger**
- ½ **cup (1 stick) cold salted butter**

Preheat the oven to 325°F. Lightly grease 2 baking sheets. Pour the milk into a glass measuring cup. Add the sorghum syrup and stir the two together. In a mixing bowl, combine flour, brown sugar, baking soda, and ginger. Slice the butter into small pieces and cut into the flour mixture with a pastry cutter or 2 knives until the mixture looks like coarse cornmeal. Add the milk-and-sorghum mixture and stir well with a fork or spoon.

To make gingerbread men about 4 inches high, break off a piece of dough a little larger than a golf ball. Place it on the work surface and roll it lightly under your palms to form a pencil-thin rope of dough about 12 inches long. Break off a 4-inch-long piece and set aside; this will become the arms. Fold the remaining rope in half to form a narrow, upside-down *V.* Grasp at the folded top, pinch together 1 inch down from the top and twist, forming the head and neck. Place the arm piece across the back under the neck. Gently press to secure. Place on the prepared baking sheet. Repeat these steps with the remaining dough.

Bake until the cookies are lightly browned, about 15 to 20 minutes. Watch closely as the sorghum or molasses in the dough tends to burn quickly.

Makes about 18 gingerbread men

ADAPTED FROM "COMMON GINGERBREAD," MISS ELIZA LESLIE,
SEVENTY-FIVE RECEIPTS FOR PASTRY, CAKES, AND SWEETMEATS, 1828.

TENNESSEE CAKE

· · · · · · ·

Wheat was a rare crop in pioneer days because it was harder to grow than corn, a grain that provided food for people and farm animals. This lovely yellow cake stretched precious wheat flour with twice the amount of cornmeal.

4 large eggs, separated

4 tablespoons (¹/₂ stick) salted butter, at room temperature

¹/₂ cup packed brown sugar

¹/₂ cup unbleached all-purpose flour

¹/₂ cup coarse cornmeal, preferably stone-ground

¹/₂ cup regular cornmeal

Vinegar Sauce (see opposite)

Preheat the oven to 350°F. Grease and flour a 7 x 11–inch baking pan. In a large mixing bowl, using grease-free beaters, beat the egg whites until they form stiff peaks; set aside.

In a medium mixing bowl, cream the butter and brown sugar. Add the egg yolks and mix well. Combine the flour and cornmeals, then add to butter-and-sugar mixture. Gently fold one-quarter of the beaten egg whites into the batter to lighten it, then fold in the remaining beaten egg whites.

Pour the batter into the prepared pan. Bake for 20 to 25 minutes or until a toothpick inserted in the center comes out clean. Let cool. Cut into squares and serve with vinegar sauce.

Makes 14 servings

ADAPTED FROM "CAKE,"
TENNESSEE FARMER,
MARCH 1835.

VINEGAR SAUCE

• • • • • • •

Sauces were common in the nineteenth century to serve over typically firm, slightly dry cakes or with boiled or baked puddings. This thin sauce tastes like lemons, but is made from easily available pioneer ingredients.

- 3/4 cup sugar
- 2 teaspoons flour
- 1 1/2 cups water
- 1 tablespoon cider vinegar
- 1 tablespoon butter
- 1/4 teaspoon freshly grated nutmeg

In a small saucepan, whisk together the sugar and flour. Slowly add the water, whisking constantly. Bring to a boil and cook over medium heat for 10 minutes, stirring from time to time. Remove from the heat and stir in the vinegar, butter, and nutmeg. Let cool. Store in the refrigerator for up to 3 days.

Makes about 1 ¾ cups sauce, enough for fourteen 2-tablespoon servings

ADAPTED FROM "A VERY CHEAP SAUCE,"
MRS. LETTICE BRYAN, *THE KENTUCKY HOUSEWIFE*, 1839.

3

LIFE ON THE INDIANA FRONTIER
PAWPAWS, HONEY, AND PUMPKINS

My childhood's home I see again,
    And sadden with the view;
And still, as mem'ries crowd my brain,
    There's pleasure in it too....
[*last verse*]
The very spot where grew the bread
    That formed my bones, I see.
How strange, old field, on thee to tread,
    And feel I'm part of thee!
       —ABRAHAM LINCOLN, 1846

More than any other president, Abraham Lincoln was a son of the soil. Most of the first fifteen presidents farmed or owned plantations, as did 80 percent of the nation at the time. Millard Fillmore and James Polk were born in log cabins in what could be considered frontier settings—Fillmore in New York and Polk in North Carolina. Only Lincoln took an ax in his hands and helped chop the family homestead out of the forest.

The Lincolns lived on their farm near the southwest tip of Indiana for almost fourteen years, arriving from Kentucky in December of 1816 and leaving for Illinois in March 1830. Abraham grew up there. He was nearly eight when they arrived and twenty-one when they left. This was the land that formed him. He wrote a long poem, excerpted above, after a visit to his old neighborhood almost twenty years after the family had moved to Illinois. The sight of that land moved him to consider his past. It moved me, too.

Lincoln's farm field is still there. From mid-April through September, the National Park Service works the family's farm as an 1820s interpretive site. In the early afternoon, two days after Christmas, I was the only visitor. When I walked on the farm 162 years after Lincoln's visit, I was alone with the spirit of the place. There are a great many stories in this land. Standing there in silence, the wind whispered faintly, seemingly calling to me: notice, remember, consider, and imagine.

It was an unusually warm day, even for southern Indiana. The rich loamy smell of damp soil, not yet mud slick, lingered in the air. Light filtered through the leafless trees densely foresting much of the site. None of the pictures in the scores of Lincoln books adequately convey the sense of the place.

I walked away from the visitor center across the large open mall toward the American flag flapping on a tall pole. It didn't take long to climb the gentle flight of steps to the top of the hill. A quick step left onto the path through the trees and I was next to the pioneer cemetery, on what used to be a neighbor's farm, where Lincoln's mother, Nancy, is buried. Years after the president's death, the handsome marble marker was placed over what was thought to be her actual gravesite. Young Abraham and his sister, Sarah, wouldn't have needed a marker; they would have known just where she lay. Although Sarah (also called Sally) Johnston came to be their warm, kind, and generous stepmother just fourteen months later, seeing the relationship of the cemetery to the farm reinforced in my mind that Lincoln's "angel mother" was never far from his thoughts.

It took me just six minutes to walk down the fairly steep slope, across a small gully and onto Lincoln's land, the cabin reconstruction, and the farm fields. The cabin is on the high point of the land, situated nicely to capture the lightest summer breeze, yet protected from sharp, scouring winds of winter by the cemetery hill. This reconstructed cabin is just a few yards from the original cabin site. Workers for the WPA found the hearthstones in 1931. Today bronze replicas of those stones glimmer faintly at one end, assembled to represent the hearth of the spectral cabin. Others inside the high stone wall outline the footprint of the Lincolns' 22-x-16-foot home.

On an early winter day, the historic site is far enough off the beaten tourist path and highways to almost shut out the mechanized hum of modern life. But this silence is misleading. The Lincoln farm was not a shrine frozen in time. There would have been smells and sounds and people. And it was a dynamic place, changing rapidly during the years the family lived there.

For all the thousands of pages written about Lincoln's life, the Indiana and earlier Kentucky years are not well documented. Lincoln wrote less than half a page in a seven-page 1860 autobiography, giving scant details beyond his work with an ax and a bit about hunting. Neighbors' memories collected by William Herndon, Jesse Weik, Ida Tarbell, and others describe daily life, including foods. I've resigned myself to the realization that, with the exception of those few specifics mentioned in memoirs, I will never know what Abraham Lincoln ate for the more than fifteen thousand meals cooked on those hearthstones.

Certainly he would have been eating a lot. As his cousin John Hanks remembered, "Abraham was a hearty eater. Loved good eating. His own mother and step-mother were good cooks for the day and time."

My visit to the cabin site was one of those times I really wished I had a time machine. I got so close to feeling the sense of the place while I was walking there alone. I could almost smell the wood fires from neighborhood fireplaces and smokehouses curing meat, hear the thwack of an ax splitting logs, the laughter of children, the voices of cows, horses, chickens—the noises of settled farm life. But wishing alone isn't enough.

I began considering as I walked toward the cabin reconstruction. The setting looked well civilized. The cabin and small barn are set neatly near the kitchen garden patch and close to a six-acre field ready and waiting for spring planting. There are other outbuildings in the yard, a clear indication of self-sufficiency and prosperity: smokehouse, corncrib, and a carpentry shop, especially important for Thomas Lincoln's work as a skilled carpenter who built homes and crafted fine furniture for the Little Pigeon Creek neighborhood. This is the successful farm of 1824 to 1830, near the end of their time in Indiana, "when the Lincolns planted ten acres of corn, five of wheat, two of oats and an acre left to meadow," as Dennis Hanks told Herndon.

The trees of "unbroken forest" they encountered in 1816 were gone. So were the "many bears and other animals still in the woods." Life for the Lincolns on the Hoosier frontier was a time of rapid change. I wanted to find a food approach that would help explain those changes. I have a great many recipes from pioneer sources. Though pioneer cabin cookery is important to understanding the period and the dishes are delightful to taste, there is a much larger story from those fourteen years in Indiana than a set of recipes from hearth and home alone could convey.

On the way back to the car and the twenty-first century, I considered what I had read in the Herndon memoirs, nineteenth-century agricultural journals, and cookbooks. I realized that three foods—pawpaws, honey, and pumpkins—tell the story of growth from frontier life into established settlement. Each presents a key aspect of the way settlers interacted with nature and how the community and Lincoln grew.

When the Lincolns hacked their way through the vines and saplings to reach the small clearing and lean-to shelter Thomas had prepared, they were the first settler family on that section of land and one of the first in what would become Spencer County.

The Lincoln and Hanks families had settled on new land before. Ancestors on both sides arrived in America during the seventeenth century. They had known the challenges and hardships of breaking new territory. Later, as children in Kentucky, both of Lincoln's parents lost their fathers. Thomas continued to live with his widowed mother. He learned carpentry and farming skills while working for friends and relatives. In 1803 he purchased his first farm. He was twenty-seven years old. Three years later he sold 2,400 pounds of pork and 494 pounds of beef in Elizabethtown trade. Clearly he had learned his lessons well.

After Nancy's father died, her mother remarried, and Nancy was raised in the "pleasant and comfortable" home of her elderly maternal uncle and aunt, Richard and Rachael Berry, going to school and learning how to spin and weave. Upon their deaths, she continued to live in the household then headed by her cousin, Richard Berry, Jr. The elder Berry's tax records and will showed how successful he had become. He had six hundred acres of land, horses, cattle, furniture, and kitchen goods—plates, dishes, pots, kettles, and a Dutch oven. He also owned three slaves—a woman named Nan, her daughter, Hannah, and a boy, Fill.

So, when Thomas and the family moved into the new state of Indiana, they were drawing upon their own successful pioneering heritage to gain a foothold in a free state of limitless promise. In another poem, "The Bear Hunt," written about the same time as the lines beginning this chapter, Lincoln described the wildness of that early settlement:

> When first my father settled here.
> 'Twas then the frontier line:
> The Panther's scream, filled the night with fear
> And bears preyed on the swine.

Nancy Lincoln's aunt and uncle, Elizabeth and Thomas Sparrow, with their ward Dennis Hanks, arrived sometime in the fall of 1817. These new Hoosiers, descendants of hardworking farmers, had skills and knowledge to live off the land before their farms were in production. When they left Kentucky for the Indiana frontier, they left behind the possibility of shopping in Elizabethtown, Nancy bartering her eggs for flour, her peaches for spices, or Thomas buying sugar or molasses with coins received for furniture he made and sold. For the first months on the Indiana farmstead, the Lincolns, Sparrows, and their few neighbors would have been pretty much self-sufficient, by necessity living a real lesson in eating locally and seasonally until they could clear farmlands and plant their crops. In short, they were gathering and hunting their food, rather than planting and growing it.

But what food it was! Reading early Hoosiers' lists of wild fruits, game, and fish, I was struck by the diverse and healthful supply of food and how much of it I've had the luck to eat. Some of the meats common in Lincoln's forest, such as bear, are virtually impossible to find, and even if you do, according to recent Centers for Disease Control research, bear meat is infested with parasitic trichinous and unsafe to eat. However, you can find rabbit and duck, along with pheasant and venison, even if you aren't friends with someone who hunts or fishes. Markets carry those meats and a few of the fish as well, especially in the Midwest. Among those freshwater fish listed by Hoosier neighbors were catfish, perch, carp, bass, skipjacks, black fin, suckers, pike, garfish, shovel fish, sturgeons, minnows, sunfish, eels, and soft-shelled turtles.

Certainly there was plenty of protein in those first years. Various neighbors recalled Abraham's skills obtaining it. A. H. Chapman, a neighbor, told Herndon that Lincoln "never cared much for hunting or fishing yet when a youth was successful as a hunter and a fine shot with a Rifle." E. R. Burba, a neighbor from Kentucky, recounted settlers' memories of Lincoln and reported that he combined his hunting and woodsman skills. Burba said that Lincoln had a "fondness for fishing and hunting with his dog & axe. When his dog would run a rabbit in a hollow tree he would chop it out." Transplanted Londoner James Woods described the same behavior. "Rabbits are tolerably plentiful.... They do not burrow in the earth, but when hunted run into the hollow trees so that an axe is necessary in rabbit hunting."

J. W. Wartmann, an old Lincoln neighbor, wrote a list of the fruits of the forest there for the gathering: mulberries, hickory nuts, hazelnuts, chestnuts, black walnuts. Elizabeth Crawford, another neighbor, expanded the list: winter grape, fox grape, wild plums, wild cherry, black haw, red haw, crab apple, blackberry, raspberry, gooseberry, dewberry, strawberry, persimmons, and the pawpaw.

The pawpaw, sometimes called the "Hoosier banana," is an unusual fruit with a complex, rich, and fragrant flavor, packed with vitamins, minerals, and even amino acids. Pawpaws ripen over a four-week period from August to October depending on where they grow. Ripe fruit is soft and keeps for only two or three days. I've tried to imagine the impact this richly flavored fruit would have on a pioneer's taste. It is the only fruit Dennis Hanks mentioned in his interviews.

Certainly there were other sweet fruits. Peaches were grown in southern Indiana orchards. Pineapples had been used as the welcome sign in cities along the Gulf and Atlantic coasts since the colonial period. Miss Leslie of Philadelphia has a recipe for preserving pineapple in her 1828 receipt book. Other tropical fruits flourished in Florida in the 1820s as one southern traveler described: "The banana, the plantain, the pine apple [sic], the cocoanut [sic] and most of the tropical fruits flourish.... Figs, oranges, limes, lemons and all varieties of citrons ... thrive." For all this bounty, I've not seen any evidence that those fruits could have been common, or even known, in the Mississippi and Ohio River valleys in the 1820s.

The imperative chorus of an old folk song demonstrates the joy of pawpaws—children run "way down yonder to the pawpaw patch ... pickin' up pawpaws, put 'em in your pockets." Beyond nutrition, exotic flavor, and delight in eating, I see the pawpaw as a horticultural metaphor for pioneer settlement. One plant's success becomes the foundation for many more. A single pawpaw sends out runner roots, matting the sub-surface of the soil. These roots send up new trees (technically branches from the same original tree), and soon the single pawpaw has become a patch.

One settler, James A. Little, wrote in 1905, "We can never realize what a great blessing the pawpaw was to the first settlers.... Well do I remember sixty or more years ago my father would take his gun and basket and go to the woods and return in the evening loaded with pawpaws, young squirrel, and sometimes mushrooms of which he was very fond. There will never be a recurrence of those which were the happiest days of my life."

Abraham Lincoln expressed yet another view of pioneer life. He wrote succinctly, "I was raised to farm work, which I continued till I was twenty-two." He also wrote that his father put an ax into his hands when they arrived in Indiana. Fellow Hoosiers remembered his skill. "His ax would flash and bite into a sugar tree or sycamore, down it would come. If you heard him felling trees in a clearing, you would say there were three men at work."

Dennis Hanks recalled those early days, too. "In the winter and spring we cleared ground, made a field of about 6 acres on which we raised our crops. We all hunted pretty much all the time. Especially when we got tired of work—which we did very often, I will assure you. We did not have to go more than 4 or 5 hundred yards to kill deer, turkeys & other wild game. We found bee trees all over the forests."

Honey from those bee trees stands in my mind as symbolic of the second stage of settlement. Gathering pawpaws and other fruits and nuts simply made use of nature's gifts. Harvesting honey from bee trees marked the intrusion and impact of settlers on the land. Honey bees were not native to the United States. Early colonists brought beehives over from Europe. As settlements advanced away from the Atlantic coast, bees flew ahead, staking their own claims, protected from natural predators, in the hollows of dead trees. To reach the honey, bee tree hunters simply chopped the tree down. They shattered and destroyed months, even years, of work by the bee colony in just a few strokes of an ax. Some bee hunters captured the bees as well to establish farmyard hives to pollinate gardens and provide a handy honey harvest.

I wondered what the honey from those wild and later farm-tended hives tasted like. For years the only honey I ate came from the grocery store. Highly filtered and heated during processing, it's sweet and almost cloying. I have to confess it has not been my favorite sweetener. Certainly the honey the Lincolns and their neighbors enjoyed would have been different. Then two summers ago my neighbor, Tim, set up a hive in his backyard. Now bees harvest pollen and nectar from my flowers, pear tree, and even the basil plants. I see them all summer long. Sometimes the rubber mat outside my back door is covered with bees harvesting the morning dew. Tim says they need a lot of moisture in the spring and fall. You could say that unheated, lightly filtered honey from Tim's bees has vintages. Summer honey is light and beguiling, almost with a hint of mint from the linden tree pollen and clover. End-of-season honey is dark and rich with heady floral overtones. The Lincolns must have enjoyed these kinds of honey. And they could have had a lot of it, too. Tim gets about eighty pounds a year from his hive. Those eighty pounds yield twenty-six quarts. Bee trees would have yielded much more.

Washington Irving wrote about wild bees in an essay published in 1848. He asserted that the "Indians consider them the harbinger of the white man, as the buffalo is of the red man; and say that, in propor-tion as the bee advances, the Indian and buffalo retire. We are always accustomed to associate the hum of the bee-hive with the farm house and flower garden and to consider these industrious little animals as connected with the busy haunts of man, and I am told that the wild bee is seldom to be met with at any great distance from the frontier."

The Lincolns' Little Pigeon Creek community in Spencer County did grow quickly, pushing back the frontier forest. In 1818, newly married to Thomas Lincoln, Sarah Johnston and her three children moved to Indi-ana. She brought furniture and household goods from her Elizabethtown city home to civilize this "country that was wild and desolate."

By the 1820 census, four years after the Lincolns arrived, there were nine families, including the Lincolns, living within a mile of their farm with forty-nine children: fifteen boys and thirteen girls under seven, and twelve boys and nine girls between seven and seventeen. In another mile radius there were six more families with thirty-four more children.

That's nearly 120 people in the neighborhood, with more and more arriving every year. In 1818 James Gentry moved to the county and set up the first store in the Little Pigeon Creek community. The market community was starting to build, too.

As the neighborhood changed, so would the food. Farm-produced surpluses of milk, butter, and eggs meant ingredients for baking and extra to barter or trade with merchants for foodstuffs—sugar, spices, coffee, tea—that could not be produced on the farm. Importantly, the community grew by socializing, a national trait that intrigued Englishman Woods:

> Americans seldom do anything without having [a frolic]. They have husking, reaping, rolling frolics. Among the females they have pickling, sewing, and quilting frolics. Reaping frolics are parties to reap the whole growth of wheat etc. in one day. Rolling frolics are clearing wood land when many trees are cut down and into lengths to roll them up together so as to burn them and to pile up the brushwood and roots on the trees. Whiskey is here too, upon request, and they generally conclude with a dance.

Lincoln neighbor Elizabeth Crawford recalled some of the foods served at church celebrations. "In the wintertime they would hold church in some of their neighbors houses at such times they were always treated with the utmost kindness. A bottle of whiskey, pitcher of water, sugar and a glass, or a basket of apples or turnips or some pies or cakes."

Crawford's list of special foods told me what was highly prized as a sign of hospitality: whiskey, possibly made in the host's or a neighbor's backyard still from local corn mash. Sugar was definitely a purchased item, and the glass used to serve it and the whiskey was a very special piece of tableware, quite a change from hollowed-out gourds or tin cups for everyday drinking. Apples were rare in the early Indiana settlement days. It took three to five years, or longer, for an apple tree to bear fruit. The crisp white flesh of a peeled mild turnip is not that different from a tart apple, if you think about it. Then there were the pies and cakes. Not only were apples in short supply, wheat flour was, too. Cornmeal and corn breads were common, and cake recipes used a mixture of wheat and cornmeal.

As more and more forest fell to ax and plow, there was less area for wild fruits and nuts to thrive and more people vying to gather them. Game animals would have retreated farther away from the danger of man. Now that the farms were established, the Hoosiers depended upon their cultivated lands to supply food for themselves and their animals. The pumpkin was one of those important foods. Lincoln even recalled that it was his job on the Kentucky farm to plant the pumpkin seeds in every third hill of corn his father planted. Pumpkin vines running among the corn hills gave two crops on the same land.

This was a new vegetable for Englishman James Woods and one that, for me, is indicative of the maturing of farm life from the wilds of the frontier. Woods wrote for his readers back home, "Pompions are another highly prized production of this country. They often grow to an immense size and weigh from 40 to 60 pounds." As Woods explained, "Cattle of all descriptions, pigs, poultry are fond of them, but they prefer the inside and seeds to the outside."

Once, settlers had simply turned cows and hogs out to feed in meadows and forage on the forest mast of fallen leaves, fruit, and nuts, a practice with great risk, as Lincoln said in his poem, of the bears feeding on the swine. More important, open grazing was a risk to the health of the community. Milk from cows grazing on wild white snakeroot poisoned Abraham's mother and many other settlers. Now farm animals, too, needed sustenance from farm-raised food such as pumpkins, rutabagas, and corn. Leaves pulled from still-growing cornstalks were used to feed livestock. To pay a neighbor for a copy of Weem's *Life of Washington* borrowed and accidentally damaged in a rainstorm, Lincoln "pulled fodder," spending three days stripping those leaves.

Of course, people enjoyed pumpkins. Yet, as anyone who has ever kept a jack-o'-lantern on the porch steps past Halloween or through a freeze knows, pumpkins do not keep for very long. As Woods explained, "They make good sauce and excellent pies and are much eaten here; they are sliced and dried for winter use for pies and sauce." Some sources say that the children would eat the dried pumpkin as a kind of fruit leather.

The way pumpkin pie or sauce was prepared depended on the affluence of the cook. I've made simple pumpkin butter, sweetened with honey or molasses and just sharpened with a dash of vinegar. The recipe included here calls for a bit of cinnamon or nutmeg. Though the pumpkin, honey, and vinegar would have been readily available, Hoosiers would have had to purchase molasses and spices. As the community grew, those ingredients probably would have been accessible, if not common, and good cooks like Abraham's stepmother, Sarah Lincoln, would have sought them out. Pumpkin pie recipes in cookbooks of the era are not all that different from the ones we make today.

Fortunately we can start with canned pumpkin, saving the time to cut up the pumpkin, stew it in a pan with a little water, and pass it through a sieve for a smooth puree, or to soak dried pumpkin to soften it before making it into the paste. Period sources also have recipes for corn bread where the stewed pumpkin stands in for a large part of the liquid in the recipe. I've included versions for both pumpkin butter and pie in the recipe section.

In a relatively short time, the farms of Spencer County would have come to look like the one farmed today by the Park Service. Lincoln's neighbor A. H. Chapman provided a succinct description. "Lincoln's little farm was well stocked with hogs, horses, and cattle and ... he raised a fine crop of wheat, corn, and vegetables." Chapman also reported that Thomas had planted apple trees.

Woods provided a comprehensive description of the vegetables he saw planted on Indiana and Illinois farms. "I've seen no sweet potatoes, but Irish or common potatoes grow tolerable in wet season ... very few parsnips or carrots, but they are said to do well in wet season ... small beans of the kidney kind are cultivated by the Americans. They are generally planted to climb on the corn and are many sorts and different colors ... cabbages grow well." He continued his list: "Onions and shallots, cucumbers grow well. Parsley and radishes thrive and lettuce. We found many morels [mushrooms] in the spring."

Another source for varieties of vegetables grown in the United States is the first American cookbook, written in 1789 by Amelia Simmons. She includes recipes for turnips, peas, green beans, beets, spinach, squash, and cooked tomatoes as well as those vegetables mentioned by Woods.

I was really glad to come across Woods's list of plants cultivated for seasonings. Capsicum, a member of the hot red pepper family, topped his list for use in soups and stews, followed by "fennel, coriander, peppermint, spearmint—the last two are scarce, sage is extremely plentiful."

This was the stuff recipes were made of, and the period cookbooks are full of them. I'm tempering my recipe selection with a goodly dose of common sense. As with the recipes for baked goods, I prefer to work with simple recipes, recognizing that the earliest American cookbooks were published on the Atlantic coast where women had better cooking facilities and more varied ingredients. Woods's simple listing and the indication that red pepper was "used in soups and stews" may be recipe enough. Sage complements pork and fowl. Fennel leaves and seeds have a wide range of traditional uses from sausage to sauces for ham and pork to giving a sweet accent to vegetables such as potatoes, cucumbers, and cabbage, as well as seasoning vegetable soups. Coriander flavors pea soup, vegetable soup stocks, spinach, sausage, and even biscuits.

The Lincoln women were considered "good cooks." They did what anyone who cooks 365 days a year does: they looked at what was in the garden or pantry and pulled together a simple dish that made the best of their local ingredients. It seems sensible that preparation would have been simple, too. Fruits would have been eaten out of hand, simply stewed for a sauce, possibly sweetened with wild honey, or dried to preserve them for winter use. Meats and fish could be roasted, grilled, boiled, or made into a soup or stew.

Knowing the wild and cultivated foods and even having some recipes from the period gets us close to the flavor of the era. But here, too, a time machine would come in handy, for even if the ingredient names are the same, the flavor of those foods would have been different. I've been lucky enough to gather some from the wild. Although specialty markets in big cities may have some of these delicacies from field and forest, even they can't come close to treasures freshly plucked from secret and not-so-secret places. The pencil-eraser-size wild raspberries I pick each July from a high lake bank are sharper flavored than the ones I grow in my garden or even the ones from the farmers market. Tiny wild strawberries are jewels compared to the huge plastic-wrapped grocery-store varieties. As to mushrooms, you can't match even the fanciest to a freshly gathered, spongy-looking morel. Hard-traveled red or purple plums from California or Chile can't stand up to small, flavor-packed wild plums plucked from a creek-side tree. Wild asparagus is a slender, flavorful, condensed version of the cultivated varieties.

Lincoln's Indiana neighbors attest to times when the bountiful surroundings and successful farms fell on hard times. Elizabeth Crawford
used food in her interviews with Herndon to bring those hard times into
focus. She remembered a tale that Lincoln himself may have related. It
seems one day there were only roast potatoes for dinner. Thomas Lincoln
offered grace, thanking the Lord for these blessings. "When he sat down to
eat, Abraham put on a long face and said I call these very poor blessings."

Potatoes play a role in Mrs. Crawford's second remembrance, too:

> It was nothing for people to go 8 to 10 miles for a [church] meet-
> ing. In the winter time they would put on their husband's old
> over coats and wrap up their little ones and take one or two of
> them up on their one beast and their husbands would walk and
> they would go to church and stay in the neighborhood til the
> next day and then go home. Apples were very scarce them times.
> Sometimes potatoes were used as a treat. I must tell you the
> first treat I ever received in old Mr. Lincoln's house was a plate
> of potatoes washed and pared very nicely and handed round.
> It was something new to me for I never had seen a raw potato
> before. I looked to see how they made use of them. They took a
> potato and ate them like apples…. They were glad to see each
> other and enjoyed themselves better than they do now.

Another verse from Lincoln's poem brings my experience on the
land and in the kitchen full circle. Every time I make the recipes from
this chapter, I have in my hands the stuff of dreams and understanding.
I can let myself flow onto the stream of memory from pioneers, Lincoln,
and even my own past. It is a magical window with a delicious pumpkin
pie sitting on the sill, just waiting for me to see, smell, taste, touch, and
take a sweet bite out of history.

> O memory! Thou mid-way world
>   'Twixt Earth and Paradise,
> Where things decayed, and loved ones lost
>   In dreamy shadows rise.

PAWPAWS: Fresh pawpaws can be found in late summer and early fall at some eastern, mid-Atlantic, and southern farmers markets. Alas, they don't grow in Minnesota. Fortunately a Missouri friend of a friend was kind enough to ship me a few of the fragile fruits carefully wrapped in paper towels and plastic bags and placed in a cooler. My backyard thermometer was close to 100°F the afternoon the package arrived. The outside of the box was hot to the touch and I feared I'd find only fermenting mush inside. But when I lifted the cooler lid, an almost-tropical sweet fragrance filled the kitchen. Fortunately the cooler had done its job. I chilled the pawpaws for a couple of hours and then it was time to taste.

Perfectly ripened pawpaws have a rich custardy flesh you can eat with a spoon. Cut down the center and lift out the row of hard, large black seeds before digging in. You can slice the orange flesh of slightly underripe pawpaws and enjoy it like a mango.

Like fresh apricots, pawpaws are more aromatic than flavorful. When I opened one of the protective bags, the aroma was nearly overpowering. I smelled banana, mango, pineapple, apricot, even brandy. The taste, however, was far subtler, with some of those same fruity flavors. Pawpaws have a pumpkiny richness, but they're not as earthy. And, although sweet, they are not nearly as sweet as berries.

As to how the pioneers enjoyed them, the memoirs are as elusive as the flavors. They may have mashed the flesh into a sauce sweetened with a bit of honey or sugar. Or, as the old song suggests, they simply ate them during the short season. Frozen pawpaw puree can be ordered from several online sources. Missouri State University in St. Joseph, Missouri, and Kentucky State University in Frankfort, Kentucky, both have pawpaw propagation projects. Though the Internet is loaded with recipes using pawpaws in a variety of cooked dishes, I think the fruit is best discovered as the pioneers would have enjoyed it, eaten out of hand or as a simple sauce.

ENJOYING OTHER WILD FRUITS: You may be fortunate enough to live in an area where you can forage for wild berries, grapes, plums, or even mushrooms. My husband remembers picking wild gooseberries growing in the patch of woods behind his boyhood home in northern Iowa. His mother baked them into a pie that he recalls as "very tart." Luckily gooseberries are one of the heritage fruits that can be purchased. The simple recipe for gooseberry pie printed on the label of Oregon brand gooseberries is very nice—and very tart.

GOOSEBERRY PUDDING

• • • • • • •

Nineteenth-century puddings are not like the sweet, milk-based desserts we enjoy. A Lincoln-era pudding resembles a thickened fruit cobbler in some versions or a dense cake. As with many hearty pioneer recipes, a little serving goes a long way. If you can't find fresh gooseberries, green grapes make a good substitute.

- 1 ½ **cups fresh green gooseberries or green grapes, or one 15-ounce can gooseberries, drained**
- ½ **cup sugar**
- 2 **tablespoons butter, at room temperature**
- 3 **large eggs**
- 1 ¼ **cups fresh breadcrumbs made from grated stale, homemade-style bread**

Preheat the oven to 350°F. Generously butter a 1-quart baking dish. Slice the gooseberries or grapes in half. If using fresh fruit, put in a microwavable container, cover with plastic wrap and cook at half power until tender, 2 to 4 minutes. Set aside to cool. (If using canned gooseberries, continue recipe from this point.)

Mix the fruit and ¼ cup of the sugar in a bowl. In a separate bowl, cream the butter and the remaining ¼ cup sugar. Add the eggs 1 at a time, beating well after each addition. Stir the sweetened gooseberries and the breadcrumbs gently into the batter. Pour the batter into the prepared baking dish. Bake until the top is golden brown and a knife inserted in the center of the pudding comes out clean, about 65 to 75 minutes. Store any leftover pudding in the refrigerator.

Makes 4 to 6 servings

ADAPTED FROM "GOOSEBERRY PUDDING," MISS ELIZA LESLIE,
SEVENTY-FIVE RECEIPTS FOR PASTRY, CAKES, AND SWEETMEATS, 1828.

PUMPKIN BUTTER

• • • • • • •

I've adapted this recipe using readily available canned pumpkin. If you have home-cooked pumpkin puree, it will be even better. The pumpkin butter is good on corn bread or even as a not-too-sweet topping for pancakes. It is also quite nice as a relish alongside roast pork or turkey.

- **1 15-ounce can pumpkin or 2 cups homemade pumpkin puree (see Pumpkins for Pumpkin Puree, page 50)**
- **½ cup honey, molasses, or sorghum syrup**
- **¼ cup cider vinegar**
- **¼ teaspoon ground allspice**
- **⅛ teaspoon ground cinnamon**

Combine all ingredients in a heavy saucepan. Cook over low heat until the mixture has thickened, about 20 minutes. Stir frequently to keep the butter from scorching. Cool. Ladle into a clean jar. Store in the refrigerator for up to 3 weeks. For longer storage see pages 160–61 for home-canning directions.

Makes about 2 cups pumpkin butter

ADAPTED FROM PERIOD SOURCES.

PUMPKIN PIE WITH HONEY

· · · · · · ·

Easy-to-grow pumpkins played a variety of important roles in pioneer kitchens. Served fresh as a vegetable, dried into a kind of fruit leather as a winter treat, simmered into a long-lasting butter, or blended with honey and treasured spices for a pie, pumpkins were praised by farmers and travelers alike. This pie is rich with pumpkin flavor. A small slice is very satisfying.

PUMPKINS FOR PUMPKIN PUREE: Choose the smaller pie or sugar pumpkins for making pies and pumpkin butter, not the large, fibrous jack-o'-lantern pumpkins. Cut a 3- to 4-pound pie pumpkin into quarters. Scrape out seeds. Place the pumpkin pieces in a baking dish and sprinkle with 2 or 3 tablespoons apple cider or water. Cover with aluminum foil and bake at 350°F until tender, 60 to 75 minutes. Let cool and scoop out the cooked pumpkin flesh. Mash to a smooth puree. You should have about 4 cups. Pumpkin puree can be frozen for several months.

- **1/2 of the Double-Crust Pie Dough recipe (opposite)**
- **2 cups homemade pumpkin puree or one 15-ounce can pumpkin**
- **1/2 cup milk**
- **1/4 cup honey, molasses, or sorghum syrup**
- **1 large egg, lightly beaten**
- **1 teaspoon ground cinnamon**
- **1/2 teaspoon ground ginger**

Preheat the oven to 425°F. Line an 8-inch pie plate with the pie dough. In a mixing bowl, combine the pumpkin puree, milk, honey, egg, cinnamon, and ginger and whisk until smooth. Pour into the unbaked pie shell. Bake for 15 minutes at 425°F. Then lower the oven temperature to 350°F and continue baking until a knife inserted in the center comes out clean, about 45 to 55 minutes longer.

Makes an 8-inch pie to serve 8

RE-CREATED FROM PERIOD SOURCES.

DOUBLE-CRUST PIE DOUGH: Although fancy puff pastry is mentioned in some recipes, the basic piecrust described in Lincoln-era cookbooks is not very different from the one I learned from my mother and she learned from hers. It is a short crust, where the flour is "shortened" as fat is cut into it. Some of the period recipes specify lard; many others call for butter, which would have been the more readily available, year-round fat on the farm or in the city.

- **1 1/2 cups unbleached all-purpose flour, plus extra for rolling out the dough**
- **1/8 teaspoon salt**
- **1/2 cup (1 stick) cold unsalted butter or 1/2 cup lard, cut into small chunks**
- **4 to 5 tablespoons ice water**

Combine the flour and salt in a mixing bowl. Using a pastry cutter or 2 knives, cut the butter or lard into the flour until the mixture looks like uncooked oatmeal. Stir in 3 tablespoons of ice water with a fork. Gradually add more water until the mixture just begins to come together. Divide in half and pat each half into a ball. Sprinkle the work surface and rolling pin with flour. Dust a ball of dough with flour and roll from the center out in all directions to make a circular crust. Repeat for the second crust.

TIP FOR SUCCESS: For single-crust pies, such as the pumpkin pie, make the full double-crust recipe and put the remaining half piecrust dough in plastic storage bag. It will keep refrigerated for up to 2 days, or freeze for up to a month.

Makes enough dough for 1 double-crust pie
or 2 single-crust pies or tarts

4

JOURNEYS OF DISCOVERY
NEW ORLEANS CURRY AND NEW SALEM BISCUITS

The great difference between Young America and Old Fogy, is the result of *Discoveries, Inventions,* and *Improvements.* These, in turn, are the result of *observation, reflection,* and *experiment.*

—ABRAHAM LINCOLN
LECTURE ON "DISCOVERIES AND INVENTIONS,"
FEBRUARY 11, 1859

In the spring of 1830 the entire extended Lincoln family picked up stakes from their established Indiana community and moved to central Illinois to establish a new farm. Moving must have been bittersweet for Thomas and Abraham. They sold the farm they had carved out of the wilderness along with animal stock and crops for more than five hundred dollars. But the pioneering had come at a price. Nancy Lincoln had died from milk sickness and, in 1828, Abraham's sister, twenty-one-year-old Sarah Lincoln Grigsby, died during the birth of her first child, who did not live.

The three-family group of thirteen packed up two oxen carts and moved west, settling on the north fork of the Sangamon River about ten miles southwest of Decatur. There, the land was said to be even better for crops. Although now twenty-one years old, the age when most young men were released from obligations to their parents, Abraham stayed at home for another year, helping his father, stepbrother, and cousins clear land and splitting hundreds of rails to fence their new farms.

In 1831, he set off to find his own place in the world. Abraham Lincoln was more than ready to pick up his own journey to self-education. Over the next eighteen months, from March 1831 through September 1832, he would see and experience more than many Americans of the era. He would begin this journey as an impressionable young man and emerge a budding politician. The foods he encountered underscore the possibilities of the expanded worlds he was discovering. His journey began perhaps unexpectedly when somehow he connected with Denton Offutt, an entrepreneur from Kentucky, who was accumulating a flatboat-full cargo of agricultural products from area farms to take down the Mississippi River to sell in New Orleans.

It is hard to imagine the magnitude of the river of food that connected Lincoln's central Illinois world to New Orleans. During the 1830s travelers wrote home from the bustling delta city, telling of hundreds of flatboats choking the levee at this "most wonderful place in the world." One observer wrote that, as far as the eye could see, the Mississippi River bank was "lined with flat-boats, come from above, from every part of the Valley of the Mississippi. Some are laden with flour, others with corn, others with meat of various kinds, others with live stock, cattle, hogs, horses, or mules." In 1831, one of those flatboats was built and piloted by Abraham Lincoln.

The plan was for Lincoln, his stepbrother John Johnston, and cousin John Hanks to take the boat down to New Orleans and sell the goods. Offutt would travel aboard as a passenger. But when the three crewmen met up, as planned, with Offutt in Springfield in early March, he had bad news. The man he had hired to build the flatboat over the winter hadn't shown up. So the flatboat crew instantly became boatbuilders.

Lincoln had built boats before. Back in Indiana days, he had built a small scow to ferry travelers across the Ohio River and sometimes just halfway out, hailing passing steamboats that would then pause in mid-river for the passengers to come aboard. On one trip, his two customers each tossed a silver half-dollar into his boat. He recalled that "the world seemed wider and fairer" now that he had earned a whole dollar.

Lincoln had made an earlier flatboat trip down the Ohio and Mississippi Rivers, too. In 1828, when he was just nineteen, he and Alan Gentry, the son of the local Indiana merchant, built a flatboat for a similar trade journey. Gentry no doubt had a store filled with the agricultural products he acquired bartering with area farmers. He needed to convert them into cash so he could restock the store with goods he would purchase in New Orleans, St. Louis, or other cities to the south or east. What was on Gentry's flatboat? Indiana newspapers reported on the cargoes shipped from the area just two years earlier: bushels of corn, bacon hams, barrels of [salt] pork, barrels of cornmeal, live cattle, live chickens, bushels of oats, beeswax, beans, and venison hams.

Did Lincoln spend much time in New Orleans on this first trip? It is hard to say. He wrote in his 1860 campaign biography that the nature of the cargo "made it necessary for them to linger and trade along the Sugar coast." This region south of Baton Rouge including Iberville and Ascension Parishes was the most densely populated, most cultivated hundred-mile region of the Mississippi River. Here Lincoln and Gentry presumably sold most of their goods trading directly with plantations along the river. They may have spent just a few days, possibly more, in the city before boarding a steamboat to hurry back home.

Now, three years later, in the spring of 1831, Lincoln planned to go all the way to New Orleans. Some writers suggest he was considering relocating there and spending the winter gainfully employed cutting wood. But before he and the others could do anything, they had to build the flatboat. Lincoln, Johnston, and Hanks set up camp at Sangamo Town on the Sangamon River, northwest of Springfield. Hanks explained in an interview with William Herndon, "We made a shantee shed. Abe was elected cook" during the four weeks it took to build the boat.

No one knows exactly what Lincoln's flatboat looked like—how long it was or how wide. Most flatboats were set up with a house-like structure above the cargo decking. The crew would stand on its roof and steer the way downstream with a rudder at the back and substantial poles, or sweeps, as long as twenty feet or more, attached on the sides. Hanks did give a hint of a description to Herndon: "We kept our victuals & in fact slept down in the boat—at one End—went down by a kind of ladder through a scuttle hole."

Neither do we know what cargo Offutt loaded aboard to make his fortune in New Orleans. Hanks told Herndon, "I saw it loaded with bacon, pork and corn." But we don't know if that corn was still on the cob, loose kernels, or even cornmeal. One report suggested they carried barrels of salt pork, flour, and cornmeal from Bogue's Mill. Hanks also mentioned that live hogs were along for the journey. Flatboats could carry an impressive amount of cargo. Filled with barrels of goods weighing between one hundred and two hundred pounds, the total load could be somewhere between twenty-five and one hundred tons.

No one really knows the experience Lincoln and the others had on the river. Today's Mississippi, transformed and tamed by the Army Corps of Engineers, is no match for the wild, uncontrolled river of the 1830s with its treacherous snags of half-submerged trees, sunken wrecks of exploded steamboats, and flood-shifting shorelines.

As a modern-day traveler, on trips to Iowa from the east, I drive across the river on the high I-80 bridge at the Quad Cities of Illinois and Iowa. From the vantage point of the bridge, I can look down and see barges loaded with grain pushing gently along downriver, pausing to pass through the locks and dams. The occasional tourist steamboat paddles along upriver. Recreational motorboats create glistening wakes going in both directions and sometimes bank to bank.

The 1830s river traffic was dramatically different. Then, the only mechanical sounds would have come from steamboats heading north and south, "dashing through the water with the noise of thunder and vomiting forth columns of smoke." The downward course of the river was crowded with many more boats, and most of them were simply carried along at three or four miles per hour on their way south.

How do you capture the experience of this on-the-water community? Surrounded by homemade flatboats of all sizes and descriptions, Lincoln and his boat-mates would have seen, heard, and smelled all the cargoes. Cattle, pigs, and chickens would have been lowing, squealing, and clucking their way to market. It took a month to six weeks for the Sangamon, Illinois, and Mississippi Rivers to carry Offutt's crew and goods to what was then America's most sophisticated city.

The trip would have been an adventure. Lincoln, Hanks, Johnston, and Offutt eased into the Mississippi by first navigating the more lightly traveled Sangamon and Illinois Rivers. These waterways provided the men with a chance to hone their boat-handling skills. The winter of 1830–31 had been particularly harsh. Old-timers referred to it as the "winter of the deep snow." Spring melted the snow into torrents of water, and all the rivers were at flood stage, spreading out over forest and farmland. Currents would have been strong when the flatboat swept into the Mississippi from the Illinois and even more turbulent when other large rivers joined the Mississippi, especially the Missouri from the west and the Ohio from the east. Lincoln, Johnston, and Hanks would have been pulling hard on the sweeps to keep from being dashed into the shore or colliding with another boat.

Having been "elected cook" for the meals on shore, it makes sense that Abraham continued to cook during the journey. Their meals in camp and on board were probably simple, quickly cooked from cheap ingredients that were easy to carry along or get as they traveled—corn dodgers, catfish caught with a line dangled over the side of the boat, biscuits. They may have dipped into a barrel of apples taken along to sell or even had a bit of smoked ham. Local boys had helped build the flatboat, and maybe one of their mothers took pity on the crew and sent along some tasty gingerbread as a treat.

Both the steamboats and the flatboats traveling on the river needed to buy, or barter for, fresh food. Fortunately it was readily available. As one steamboat passenger reported: "Provisions are very good—fresh eggs, butter, and milk are got every day on the banks of the river at the stopping places for wood." Most boats pulled in for the night, too, as river travel was dangerous in the dark. They stopped either along the shore or at town landings, where travelers could step off and even eat at restaurants or gamble and dance at the nineteenth-century versions of honky-tonk halls.

As the Mississippi River carried the flatboat closer and closer to New Orleans, more and more vessels crowded into the widening river. By the time Offutt and his crew reached the levee, the river was nearly paved with flatboats, tied up three and four deep and ready to sell their cargo.

More than any other American harbor in the 1830s and '40s, New Orleans was the dynamic and profitable nexus between the products of the Old World and the agricultural riches of the New. The skyline to the south of New Orleans was forested with the masts of scores of sailing ships bearing spices from the Far East, fresh and exotic fruits from Cuba and the West Indies, and fancy goods from England and Europe. Cargoes from around the world were harbored just outside the city crescent.

Steamships, which had only come into widespread, practical use in the previous decade, were the powerful connection that made this exchange of riches and resources possible. Flatboats drifted down the river and, because they could not float back upstream, were sold for scrap lumber. Sailing vessels needed a fair wind and enough open water to tack toward their destination, and they did head back across the seas, their holds filled with cotton for English textile mills. But the steamboats, loaded with prize cargoes of sugar, molasses, spices, china, and manufactured goods—all paid for by the sale of upriver crops and foodstuffs—could set and keep a time schedule, steaming northward against the current at five to eight miles per hour.

Abraham Lincoln stepped off the flatboat sometime in May of 1831 with his pay in his pocket and ready to explore. So now, we're at the meat of his coming-of-age experience, and that's all we know. Lincoln never wrote or said a word about his time in New Orleans.

Luckily, some other young men, just about Lincoln's age, did write about their adventures on the Mississippi and in New Orleans. Local boosters described the wonders of the city to entice travelers. And we can see the influence the sights and experiences had on Lincoln in his first campaign presentation to the "People of Sangamon County," written just a year after he made the trip. He speaks of the need for transportation improvements including railroads. One of the first rail lines in the country opened up between New Orleans and Lake Pontchartrain in the month before he arrived.

Still, we'll just have to imagine how New Orleans affected Lincoln and make some educated choices from the menu of options the city had to offer. Stand next to the statue of Andrew Jackson in the square that bears his name. Turn your back to the levee and look at the Cathedral of St. Louis. Squint your eyes to blur the modern world from view. You will begin to see the New Orleans that Abraham Lincoln saw: the cathedral, built thirty years before Lincoln's visit; the essential New Orleans architecture; and the French Quarter's narrow streets and alleys. Close your eyes and stand in front of an open-air restaurant. Feel the atmosphere, the heavy air perfumed with alluvial and fishy river aromas, sweet flowers, and the delightful seasonings of some of the best cooking in the world. Breathe in New Orleans.

As complex as this atmosphere is, I think Lincoln's would have been even richer. In your mind, try to subtract the sharp smell of gasoline that hovers over our modern age and add the rich, heavy aroma of manure from horses on the streets and livestock on the flatboats, the cooking smells from the backyard ovens and smoky fires from scores of surrounding households, all cloaked in the clinging, rising dust from partially unpaved back streets. Eternal, essential New Orleans is here. One youthful traveler wrote in 1830: "No city contains a greater population. Inhabitants from every state in the union, and from every country in Europe mixed with the Creoles, and all the shades of the colored population, form an astonishing contrast of manners, languages, and complexions."

Conversations in the streets were a Babel of all those native tongues: French, Spanish, Portuguese, German, English. Complexions were even more varied than the languages. All shades of people walked the streets, and it is here that Lincoln must have had an immediate and stunning immersion into a slave society. Several sets of statistics during the period represent the population of just under thirty thousand as roughly one-half white, one-quarter free persons of color, and one-quarter slave. It would have been hard for Lincoln to miss slave auctions. James Stuart visited New Orleans in March and April of 1830, the year before Lincoln's trip. He reported the sales of nearly one thousand African American men, women, and children forced to exchange one experience of slavery for another.

Slave labor, from street sweepers to household helpers, would have been a constant presence, too. Ever-observant Lincoln would have had the opportunity to see all manners of relationships between slaves and their owners. Slave hands prepared much of the city's food.

What was the flavor of Lincoln's time in New Orleans? Did he stay on the flatboat eating catfish and corn dodgers, or did he decide to spend some of his earnings (Offutt had paid him more than twelve dollars) to take a room in a boardinghouse on the American side of the canal, west of the French Quarter? I can't help but think that he got off the river as soon as he could and began wandering wherever his long legs would take him.

Certainly Lincoln would have explored the public markets. The city vegetable-market building was finished just a year before he arrived. Open on the sides, the building fronted on Old Levee, St. Philip, and Ursuline Streets and the river. Handsome plastered brick columns supported its tiled roof. Inside, vendors sold all manner of vegetables and fruits from local farms—peas, strawberries, cabbages, sweet potatoes, onions, rice, carrots, lettuce—as well as tropical fruits from the West Indies. The open-air meat market had been completed in 1813. Its "rusticated Doric order" columns supported a slate-covered roof on the levee between St. Ann and Main Streets. In addition to the usual beef, mutton, lamb, chickens, turkeys, wild game, and pork of all varieties, Lincoln may have discovered another local ingredient: "The barred owl is very often exposed for sale in the New Orleans market. The Creoles make a gumbo of it and pronounce the flesh palatable."

Those were some of the raw ingredients. Seafood would have been abundant, too. Maybe Lincoln had his first taste of oysters in New Orleans. He ate them later in Illinois. Discarded oyster shells were found in buried trash areas around his Springfield home. They were famously served to celebrate the success of the Sangamon Long Nine—a group of very tall state legislators, including Lincoln, from Sangamon County— upon their success in passing legislation to move the state capital from Vandalia to Springfield in September 1837. At a party hosted by the Long Nine at Capp's Tavern, other members of the legislature were treated to oysters, almonds, raisins, cigars, and eighty-one bottles of champagne.

Today's classic New Orleans cuisine is a mix of Cajun and Creole. You can't go to a New Orleans restaurant without having a delicious choice of gumbo and jambalaya. Rich coffee and beignets, too. Recipes for gumbo and okra begin to appear in published cookbooks in the 1830s. Midwestern agricultural writer Solon Robinson shared a recipe for "Hopping Johnny or Jambalaya" in the May 1845 *American Agriculturist.*

The foods and dishes Lincoln sampled would have been as varied as the cultural opportunities before him. Aromas from the cuisines of the French, Spanish, Germans, Portuguese, and other nationalities who made New Orleans their home would have perfumed the streets. We know that in his Indiana youth Abraham had tasted ginger and probably cinnamon and nutmeg. Sage and red peppers were commonly grown and used to season meat dishes even on pioneer farms. But what about oregano, basil, tomatoes, okra, turmeric, cumin, coriander? Oranges, lemons, and pineapples were as common in New Orleans as wild plums were in Illinois. Would fruit-loving Lincoln have tasted his first piece of citrus?

Rich cultural opportunities and the latest in technological advances were there for Lincoln's eyes and mind to feast upon, too. The first railway west of the Allegheny Mountains had recently started its run between New Orleans and Lake Pontchartrain. It used a horse-drawn locomotive to make the four-mile trip, but there was a demonstration model of a steam engine very near the levee. Certainly Lincoln, with his abiding interest in "discoveries, inventions, and improvements," would have spent time looking at that. The American Theater was performing. Would he have seen his first real play? He had enjoyed a magician's show in Sangamo Town during the time he and his crewmates were building the boat. New Orleans was filled with news. It had several local newspapers and a free public reading room with newspapers from around the country and overseas, as well as books. Surely knowledge-hungry Abraham could have visited. Restaurants, bars, taverns, bakeries, and other shops lined the streets. Lincoln must have taken it all in.

The dish I've pulled from the countless possibilities may surprise you. I've not picked one of the Creole traditions, but rather a curry. This is a meat-stretching dish a boardinghouse cook seeking to please English and American guests might serve. Poured over a base of Louisiana rice, curry would be cheap and filling. And it represents to me the amalgam of Lincoln's experience here. Exotic seasonings and tropical fruits combine with homegrown chicken and rice to make a wonderful dish.

After a couple of weeks, sometime in June, the men decided to return to Illinois. Lincoln, Johnston, and Offutt boarded a steamboat to make the journey home at a speedy eight miles per hour. John Hanks had left the flatboat earlier when they stopped in St. Louis to scout for new Lincoln/Hanks farm locations in southern Illinois. Lincoln and Johnston certainly traveled as deck passengers, riding along on the sheltered top deck of the boat instead of in staterooms. "Deck passengers" paid the cheapest fare. They were "bound to give assistance carrying wood aboard" and cooked on a "small stove" up on the top deck, using provisions they brought or bought. Lincoln probably cooked again, at least his own food if not for Johnston and maybe even Offutt.

Whatever the uncertain vision of the future had been when the crew set out back in early April, there was a specific plan in place on the trip home in June. Offutt decided that Lincoln would be the ideal person to operate a general store and that New Salem, Illinois would be a good place to set up shop. Offutt stopped in St. Louis to purchase stock for the store and arrange shipment of the goods to New Salem. On July 8 in Springfield, Offutt paid a five-dollar licensing fee indicating the stock in the store would be worth one thousand dollars. Lincoln had had enough of farming. He was ready to settle in a dynamic community and see what he could make of his life.

The flatboat crew had made quite an impression in New Salem on the way downriver, and the community had good cause to remember the tall, gangly young man for his quick-minded innovations. Even though the water in the Sangamon had been unusually high all spring, by the time the flatboat was ready at the end of April or early May, the river had started to drop. Somewhat dramatically, the Lincoln flatboat got stuck on the New Salem milldam. That mishap could have meant the end of the journey and Offutt's investment, save for Lincoln's quick thinking.

As the boat teetered on the dam, crew and community began removing the cargo barrels. As the load shifted, the stern gradually started to tilt backward under the weight of the splashed-on water. Lincoln realized that this water could be the engine of their progress off the dam. He quickly stopped the unloading process and shifted several barrels to the front of the boat. He cut a branch into a wooden peg. Then, borrowing an auger from the town's cooper, he bored a hole in the front of the boat and quickly shifted the remaining barrels to the front. The water flowed from the stern and out of the hole in the bow. Just before the boat was ready to slide off the dam, Lincoln hammered the peg home, stopping up the hole, and they continued on their way. From the sound of it, this adventure was the talk of New Salem residents for years.

In 1830 New Salem was still a very new community. Millwrights John Cameron from Georgia and his uncle James Rutledge from North Carolina arrived in 1828. They planned to anchor the new village with combination grist-and-saw mill. In their vision New Salem would be a commercial village serving the needs of the rapidly expanding farm community. Here, farmers from Wolf, Sugar Grove, Concord, Sandridge, Little Grove, Athens, Irish Grove, Indian Point, Rock Creek, and Clary's Grove could barter farm produce or purchase manufactured goods, sugar, spices, molasses, and even brandy or whiskey.

To engage the power for the mill, Cameron and Rutledge enlisted the help of these neighbors to dam the Sangamon River. They built pens out of logs and lowered them into the river. They began filling the pens with rocks. A year and a thousand wagonloads of rocks later, the mill stood on log and rock pillars out into the river, fully enclosed and ready to grind corn or wheat and saw lumber. Rutledge also operated a tavern and inn for the comfort of travelers along the beaten path to Springfield, Peoria, and other communities. Others in town took in boarders.

More merchants and tradesmen moved to the area and set up shop along the L-shaped Main Street ready to do business serving the extended community of settlers and farmers. In 1829 Samuel Hill and James McNamar opened the first store selling groceries such as tea, coffee, sugar, salt—essential for preserving meats—and whiskey. They also stocked dry goods such as blue calico, brown muslin, men's straw hats and ladies hats, too, homemade jeans and gloves, and other items of "ornamental feminine apparel."

Cooper Henry Onstot moved from Sugar Grove and built a residence and shop to make barrels, essential for storing and shipping farm produce. Philamon Morris set up a tannery. Shoemakers Alexander Ferguson and Peter Lukins and hatmaker Martin Waddel, who worked with wool, rabbit, and other animal furs, filled some of the clothing needs of the community. Robert Johnston, wheelwright and cabinetmaker, built the means for area residents to make their own clothes, spinning wheels and looms, as well as furniture. Samuel Hill installed a mechanical wool-carding mill, turning sheep shearings into wool. Dr. John Allen, graduate of Dartmouth College Medical School, came west to seek a better climate for his health and set up practice from his home on Main Street.

Other merchants opened groceries, a nineteenth-century designation for stores selling liquor by the drink and bottle, and general stores. At one time between 1831 and 1833, there were four such stores. Lincoln was involved in two of them before they "winked out" in the competition and lack of ready money among the customers.

James McNamar summed up life in New Salem: "An abundance of the necessities of life, its luxuries unknown or uncared for. Lavish hospitality and brotherly love abounded and everywhere the latch string was hung out for all comers."

Just as steamboats bridged utility between the practical flatboat and the soaring tall sailing ship, market and resource towns like New Salem filled the middle ground of progress between farms and sophisticated cities. This was the spot where things happened; it was the hub of the wheel of commerce. It was the perfect place for an engaging young man to interact with people and information. Abraham was off the farm and in his own place of higher learning and vital experiences.

Today we pass right by towns on our highway journeys, hardly noting their existence beyond a quick stop for refueling. In 1830s Illinois, travelers became part of the community for a few hours or a night at a friendly break in the prairie and forest. Those from the east came to town on the ferry across the Sangamon, while those from communities to the south, west, and north rode horses, stages, or wagons or even walked.

New Salem stores were designed as gathering spots to talk politics or engage in a game of checkers or cards. Covered front porches provided shelter from the sun. The long main street was the perfect spot for horse racing. Old-timers remembered the barbecue pit behind Hill's store and the cock-fighting pit located on the hillside outside of town.

Modern archaeology has revealed a site that suggests the footprint of a whiskey-making still. Another area where community, and possibly even commercial, hog butchering took place showed its footprint, too. One old-time New Salem resident remembered a large hog-stationing pen near the area. Three distinctive sections of the uncovered site reveal this complex fall activity, and the importance of "using everything but the squeal." After the hog—often weighing more than two hundred pounds—was dispatched, its carcass was plunged into a trough of scalding water to loosen the bristles from its hide. After the bristles, useful for making into brushes, were scraped off by hand, the carcass was hung up by its hind feet. Then, men cut it into pieces sorted for packing into barrels for salted "pickled pork" or rubbing with dry seasonings to be hung up in the smokehouse. This was such a profitable enterprise that Dr. Allen asked his farmer patients to pay him in butchered hogs, which he would "cure into hams and bacon, pack in hogsheads, and ship via Beardstown to the St. Louis market."

Those modern excavations have uncovered other important tangible shards of evidence from the community's past. Although the homes and stores were log cabins, they had whitewashed, plastered interior walls. Families ate off of shell-edged Queensware plates and drank from glassware as well as tin cups. Storekeepers' families grew their own vegetables and had fruit trees. They raised chickens and stabled cows and horses.

Abraham quickly became a valued member of the community. He slept in the store and took his meals boarding with a number of different families, but there are few details of what he ate. N. W. Branson reported to William Herndon that Lincoln "was a fast eater, though not a hearty one," and that he liked "bread and honey." Another old New Salem neighbor agreed. "He was not very particular in what he Eaten [*sic*] he was fond of Pop Corn I remember."

Lincoln was always ready with a story or joke. And because he could read and write, neighbors called upon him to write up agreements or to witness legal documents. Among the people of New Salem Lincoln found an academy of learning. He borrowed their books, read their old newspapers—and as postmaster he knew which papers came into town and when—and he peppered them with questions. Lincoln took full advantage of these New Salem resources to study and achieve an education in literature, poetry, grammar, mathematics, surveying, and the law. When business was slow in the Offutt store and then the market he owned in partnership with William F. Berry, Lincoln stretched out on the counter and poked his nose into a book. He discussed Robert Burns's poetry and William Shakespeare's plays as he cast fishing lines with Jack Kelso; he was a character who was more at home in field and stream than any man, but who could "recite Shakespeare and Burns by the hour." Justice of the Peace Bowling Green loaned law books and encouraged Abraham in his studies. When Lincoln was appointed deputy county surveyor, schoolmaster Mentor Graham is said to have helped him work through the problems in Flint's *System of Geometry and Trigonometry Together with a Treatise on Surveying* as he mastered the skills essential for his new profession in just six weeks. He took part in the Debating Society organized by James Rutledge.

Denton Offutt wasn't around New Salem much; it appears he spent his time chasing opportunities in Springfield and other towns. Always looking for a way to make more money, he hired the exclusive use of the Cameron-Rutledge grinding mill. Lincoln spent time overseeing the operation of the mill as it ground corn and wheat. In the spring of 1832, Offutt gathered up what cash he could and, leaving his creditors in the lurch, simply disappeared. Lincoln managed the declining store until the stock was sold to pay off the debts, and then it "just petered out."

In March 1832, Lincoln declared his candidacy for representative to the Illinois General Assembly. In his "Communication to the People of Sangamo County," he addressed the need for "internal improvements"— roads, cleared waterways, and "rail roads." He drew upon the year's experiences, making a comprehensive analysis of the situation. "I have given as particular attention to the state of the water in this river, as any other person in the country." Lincoln, twenty-three years old, was poised for the possibility of loss. "Every man is said to have his peculiar ambition ... I have no other so great as to be esteemed by my fellow men ... I am young and unknown to many of you.... If the good people in their wisdom shall see fit to keep me in the background, I have been too familiar with disappointments to be very much chagrined." Losing this election, he was elected for the next term in 1834.

A few years ago I happened on a lively little book printed in 1927. *Lincoln at New Salem*, commissioned by The Old Salem Lincoln League, is a collection of all the memories from New Salem residents and their descendants. One of the first pages is a charming hand-drawn bird's-eye view of New Salem. Two dozen houses or other features are illustrated, and they just hint at the complexity of life in the bustling community. Missing are the barns, smokehouses, and privies. It looks simple, but it's not.

You can't see the books in people's homes or the newspapers from Springfield, Lexington, and St. Louis arriving at the postmaster's. Understanding life in New Salem, Lincoln's rapidly developing intellect, the world that opened up before him, and the experiences he sought requires some serious chewing.

Innovations, inventions, and information continued to follow the north-to-south river path that the young Lincoln took. By the 1840s the Springfield newspapers advertised the arrival of "barrels of fresh oranges and lemons." "Internal improvements," canals, and railroads pushed westward, and by the 1850s railroad tracks crossed the rivers.

The saleratus biscuit recipe that follows is the perfect edible metaphor for New Salem and Lincoln's dynamic change during the six years he lived there. The recipe looks basic: flour, a bit of butter, some boiling water. Yet combined with the magic alchemy of baking saleratus (baking soda) and sour milk, these simple ingredients are transformed into a chewy, delicious biscuit. It is complex and unforgettable—kind of like Abraham Lincoln.

Oh, and one more thing. The New Salem milldam incident with the flatboat remained in Lincoln's mind. In 1849, eighteen years after the incident, he received a U.S. patent for his device for "buoying vessels over shoals." Lincoln is the only U.S. president to receive a patent for an invention.

NEW ORLEANS CURRY POWDER

• • • • • • •

Before steamships, canals, and railroads, residents of coastal cities from New England to New Orleans enjoyed a complex variety of foods and seasonings unavailable in the developing center of the nation. There are scores of recipes for curry powder in period books and magazines. This curry powder is mild and goes well with chicken, lamb, or vegetables.

- 2 **tablespoons ground turmeric**
- 2 **tablespoons ground coriander**
- 2 **tablespoons ground cumin**
- 2 **tablespoons ground ginger**
- 2 **tablespoons freshly grated or ground nutmeg**
- 2 **tablespoons ground mace**
- 2 **tablespoons ground cayenne pepper**

Mix the spices together. Store in a sealed jar. Curry powder will keep in a cool, dark place for weeks. Use as you would any curry powder.

Makes 1 scant cup curry powder

ADAPTED FROM "CURRY POWDER," MARY RANDOLPH,
THE VIRGINIA HOUSE-WIFE OR, METHODICAL COOK, 1824.

NEW ORLEANS CHICKEN CURRY

• • • • • • •

    3 tablespoons flour

1 to 3 teaspoons Curry Powder (see page 66)

    2 cups low-sodium chicken broth

    2 tablespoons butter or olive oil

    **2 pounds boneless, skinless chicken
    (breast and/or thigh meat), cut into 2-inch pieces**

    2 cloves garlic, minced

    Juice from 1 lemon or orange

    2 cups prepared rice, to serve

Put the flour and curry powder in a pint jar with a lid. Add 1 cup of the chicken broth, tighten lid, and shake well to blend. Set aside.

Heat the butter or oil in a large frying pan over medium heat. Add the chicken pieces and cook until browned on one side, about 5 minutes. Turn the chicken pieces over and add garlic. Continue cooking until the chicken is browned and garlic is tender, about 5 minutes. Shake the jar of curry/broth blend once again and pour slowly into the frying pan. Add the remaining 1 cup chicken broth and stir until sauce is thickened. Cover and simmer about 10 minutes until meat is fork tender. Stir in lemon or orange juice. Serve over rice.

Makes 6 to 8 servings

ADAPTED FROM "TO MAKE A DISH OF CURRY AFTER
THE EAST-INDIAN MANNER," MARY RANDOLPH,
THE VIRGINIA HOUSE-WIFE OR, METHODICAL COOK, 1824.

NEW SALEM SALERATUS BISCUITS

· · · · · · ·

As pioneer settlements became villages and towns, farmers began planting more wheat. Wheat breads and biscuits took their place on tables where just a few years earlier cornmeal was the primary bread grain. Saleratus, an early form of baking soda, worked with the sour milk to make a light, chewy, and delicious biscuit.

- 2/3 **cup milk**
- 2 **teaspoons white vinegar**
- 2 **cups unbleached all-purpose flour**
- 1/2 **teaspoon baking soda**
- 1/8 **teaspoon salt**
- 1 **teaspoon butter**
- 1/4 **cup boiling water**

Preheat the oven to 400°F. Lightly grease a baking sheet. Combine milk and vinegar in a glass measuring cup and set aside to sour, about 5 minutes. Mix the flour, baking soda, and salt in a mixing bowl. Add the butter to the boiling water to melt and then stir into the flour mixture. Then stir in the sour milk. Stir with a fork and then knead briefly. You may need to add a bit more milk or flour to make a dough that is firm enough to work and not sticky. Break off pieces about 1 inch in diameter and place on the prepared baking sheet. Bake until browned, about 15 to 20 minutes.

Makes 16 biscuits

RE-CREATED FROM PERIOD SOURCES.

5

BACON AND BLACK HAWK

n April 1832, Abraham Lincoln was just twenty-three years old. After about nine months in New Salem, Denton Offutt's store was nearly out of business. Soon Lincoln would be out of a job. Frontier events provided an opportunity. Like every able-bodied man, Lincoln was required to drill in the militia twice a year or pay a fine of one dollar. So, on April 19, when word reached the folks in New Salem that Governor John Reynolds called for volunteers to protect the citizens from a feared massacre at the hands of aggrieved Winnebago chief Black Hawk, Lincoln was ready to go.

Later, during his only term as a U.S. congressman, Abraham Lincoln used fighting words on the floor of the U.S. House of Representatives to describe his military career. In a July 27, 1848, speech he confronted General Lewis Cass, the Democratic Party candidate in the presidential campaign, on the extension of slavery, the overuse of the presidential veto, and the waging of an unnecessary war, unleashing his strongest volleys on Cass's claimed military successes. The Lincoln-supported Whig candidate, General Zachary Taylor, had a proven army career; Cass apparently spent some of his time during the War of 1812 foraging behind the lines. Using his skill at turning personal anecdote toward sharply honed argument, Lincoln compared his own service in the Black Hawk War to Cass's battle experiences.

"If General Cass went in advance of me in picking huckleberries, I guess I surpassed him in charges upon the wild onions. If he saw any live, fighting Indians, it was more than I did, but I had a good many bloody struggles with the mosquitoes and although I never fainted from loss of blood, I can truly say I was often hungry."

This was one of the few times Lincoln publicly mentioned his military service. History is fortunate that George M. Harrison served with him as an Illinois Militia volunteer during the Black Hawk War, and we are equally fortunate that William Herndon, Lincoln's Springfield law partner, wrote to everyone he could think of as he documented Lincoln's life in the years immediately after his death. Herndon received three lengthy letters from Harrison, filled with chatty details. Harrison described meals and cooking methods so well he could have written a cookery book. Harrison even recalled their shared culinary adventures in a letter he sent to Lincoln in May 1860, congratulating him on the Republican Party presidential nomination. Harrison wrote of their friendship forged "when we ground our coffee in the same tin cup with the hatchet handle—baked our bread on our ramrods around the same fire—ate our fried meat off the same piece of elm bark."

As to the cooking, Harrison impressed upon me the value of bacon prepared from nineteenth-century fatty hogs. In the early 1800s, "bacon" referred to all pork cured by salting and smoking, not just the slices from the hog's flank or belly we call bacon. Legs could be called "hams" as we call the bone-in ham today. Period agricultural sources talk about the economics of "making bacon" from the whole hog.

Bacon is a wonderful food for an army on the move. Rendered carefully and with consideration, the slab of basic streaky bacon yields meat, seasoning, frying medium, and an essential ingredient for campfire bread. I spent the better part of a morning working with thick-sliced bacon, cooking it slowly in my cast-iron skillet over a low wood fire built in our Weber grill. I needed the bacon grease to test some of Harrison's cooking methods and wanted the meat for other dishes. I pushed the pieces to the side of the pan as they began to crisp. Bacon fat continued to melt into the pan, and the next strips added to the accumulating fat. The result: nearly a cup of clear fat and a pile of perfectly lean, chewy meat. It was a revelation.

Enveloped in smoke and bacon perfume, I considered that the service Lincoln rendered in the three-month-long Black Hawk War in 1832 had converted him as well. In April, Abraham Lincoln was a raw young man. Although he never saw battle, by the time he returned toward the end of July, he was a man who had begun to find his path toward leadership and public service. Harrison described Lincoln's impact: "The whole company, even amid trouble and suffering received Strength & fortitude, by his buoyancy & elasticity."

Lincoln modestly wrote that he experienced the "ordinary hardships of such an expedition." He and Harrison were mustered out, along with the last of the volunteer militia, just two weeks before the final engagement. His election to captain of his troop of fellow Sangamon County volunteers at the beginning of the war was, as he wrote in 1860, "a success which gave me more pleasure than I have had since."

Lincoln's connection with Native Americans began before he was born. His father was just six years old when he witnessed his own father's death. As Abraham described it, "my paternal grandfather, Abraham Lincoln, emigrated from Rockingham County, Virginia, to Kentucky about 1781 or 1782, where a year or two later he was killed by the Indians, not in battle, but by stealth, when he was laboring to open a field in the forest."

Twenty years later, the various treaties signed between the U.S. government and the Shawnee, Miami, Pottawatomie, Sauk, and Fox—the tribes of lands that would become Indiana, Ohio, Kentucky—granted them the right to "be at liberty to hunt within the territory and lands which they have now ceded to the United States, without hindrance or molestation, so long as they demean themselves peaceably, and offer no injury to the people of the United States." As the white settlers encroached, those who had lived in the land for generations, roaming and hunting in its forests, slipped back into the margins, in most cases trying to coexist with newly declared property owners.

No one really knows how much Lincoln interacted with Native Americans in his youth and young adulthood. When asked by Herndon, Lincoln's cousin Dennis Hanks simply wrote back, "No Indians there when I first went to Indiana. I say No ... Nun." Shawnee had lived in the area, so it seems probable that Abraham would have unearthed arrowheads as he worked in newly cleared fields. During the same time, John James Audubon wrote of seeing Native Americans hunting in the forests while he scouted subjects for his *Birds of America*. He described a lone Indian hunting bear in the Kentucky woods within a hundred miles or so of Lincoln's home in that state. Audubon felt sorry for the Indian's condition, a dilapidated gun and ragged blanket for his clothing. But he admired the man's skill at hunting, killing two mallards with one shot, and the grace with which he prepared them over a campfire for his dinner.

Not all interactions were so peaceful. Families like the Lincolns and, on his mother's side, the Hankses, who had pioneered their way from Virginia through Tennessee or Kentucky up into Indiana and Illinois, had personal history of Native American attacks. In this letter to Jesse Lincoln, a distant cousin, Abraham Lincoln wrote that the story of his grandfather's death at the hands of the Indians and of his Uncle Mordecai, a fourteen-year-old, then killing one of the Indians was "the legend more strongly than all others imprinted upon my mind and memory." His father fought in several skirmishes during his service in the militia. Abraham's mother, Nancy, named their daughter, Sarah, after her cousin who had been kidnapped and held captive by the Pottawatomie for five years.

So, in April 1832, when Illinois Governor Reynolds called for volunteers to respond to the threat from Chief Black Hawk's band of five or six hundred warriors near present-day Rock Island, the young men in the New Salem area, including the men from Clary's Grove three miles away, were ready to sign up. By all descriptions it was a rag-tag bunch. Although the state militia quartermaster issued "muskets & bayonets" along with flints, powder, and lead, each man was responsible for providing his own clothing and horse. They would have taken their own food, too, for traveling to Beardstown where they met the rest of the army of nine thousand on April 22.

It was about forty miles from New Salem to the enlistment point at Beardstown—a decent day's journey for men and horses. Years later, journalist Ida Tarbell reported the details that Lincoln was elected captain at Richland, about thirty miles southeast from Beardstown on what is now Illinois Highway 125, the day before the group reported for duty. So the company must have left New Salem on April 20, traveled south to Richland, and spent the night there before joining up.

I was curious about the sixty-eight men who served under Captain Lincoln during the first month of the war. The Illinois secretary of state website lists them all. Using the 1830 census for Sangamon County and helped by unusual nineteenth-century names, I identified fifteen of the men as heads of household and figured that another eight were older sons in families who were living in the area in 1830. Lincoln didn't arrive in New Salem until 1831. I had expected to find the company comprised of young single men, the type who would be rowdy and looking for adventure. Certainly there were those young men among the ones I couldn't place. But the men I could identify in the census from two years earlier were family men. Most were between twenty and thirty years old, but four were between thirty and forty, one was older than forty. Among them they had thirty-eight children, twenty-eight under the age of five, eight children between five and ten, and two older than ten.

Residents of New Salem were not scurrying off into the forts for protection the way northwestern Illinois settlers were. The families stayed in town and on the surrounding farms. Would they have gathered on the morning of April 20, 1832, for a ceremony in the center of New Salem where the main street bends, separating the shopping street from the town's homes? Would cups of last fall's cider have been raised in a salute? Did any of the twenty little boys under five chase after his father with a play wooden musket over his shoulder or a flag in his hand as the band of fighters rode out of town?

Perhaps New Salem wives and mothers would have provisioned their brave volunteers with foods for the two-day road trip and to hold them over until the group received army rations. I can't imagine it any other way. The women would have had to hurry, too. News of Black Hawk's threat and the governor's call for troops arrived in town on April 19. Smokehouses and barrels would still have had fall-cured and smoked pork cuts including bacon. Those meats would normally need to supply the tables through the end of summer, but this was an emergency. Home-dried apples or peaches might have been packed into saddlebags. Gingerbread certainly would have traveled well, too. Bacon, ham, cornmeal, and maybe even some expensive coffee seem likely victuals for the volunteers.

But what could the women prepare to send along as a special taste of home? Mid-April is a time of husbanding resources in midwestern farming communities. The spring of 1832 was damp and cold. The first fresh garden crops of spinach, peas, lettuces, and radishes were weeks away. So was fresh meat. However, certain foods were plentiful. Chickens lay more eggs in the spring than any other season. Cows with newly weaned calves have plenty of milk. There should have been good supplies of milk and eggs. The ladies of town could have sent their soldier boys off with a sturdy boiled pudding as a special treat. Steamed or boiled puddings have less fat and sugar than cakes, so they would have been more affordable. They also have the advantage of quick mixing and cooking without the need for constant monitoring, most helpful for women who probably had to mend clothing, perhaps even quickly sew up a spare shirt for the adventure.

Maria Eliza Ketelby Rundell offered some puddings in her 1823 *American Domestic Cookery*. Her recipes are clearly written for city-dwelling cooks with ingredients such as rice, oatmeal, lemons, orange-flower water, and "a two-penny loaf" of bread. Still, from the title, her "Puddings in haste" looked like a possible candidate, but as I considered the ingredients and method, it seemed less likely. In pioneering Illinois, suet, or beef fat, would have been a precious ingredient, suitable for Christmas plum puddings and possibly not even available in the spring. Other ingredients, such as grated wheat bread, currants, and lemon peel, would have been similarly rare. The method of forming egg-size balls and dropping them in boiling water certainly would have produced a pudding in haste, but would have required careful watching.

I turned to Miss Leslie's 1828 receipt book. Although hers were eastern recipes, it was not too hard looking at the ingredients to pick dishes much more suitable to central Illinois cooking conditions. I found two possible candidates, "Batter Pudding" and "Indian Pudding." Miss Leslie's recipes for a boiled wheat and a corn batter pudding were economical desserts more like a very damp cake than the custard dessert we commonly call pudding. The recipes look simple but, as I discovered, are downright tricky to make the old-fashioned way. Miss Leslie's method sounds easy enough. Have a large pot of boiling water. Take a sturdily woven cloth, wet it, and then dust with flour. Pour the pudding batter into the cloth and tie it shut, making sure to "leave room for the pudding to swell." Then just boil it for one to three hours. "Serve up hot with sauce made from drawn butter, wine and nutmeg."

Her "Batter Pudding" recipe called for six eggs and a quart of milk with eight "tablespoons" of flour. Clearly that was not a measuring tablespoon. A look twenty-five years ahead into Eliza Acton's cookbook, *Modern Cookery in All Its Branches*, which was revised for the American market by *Godey's* editor Sarah J. Hale, gave a proportion of half a pound of flour to four eggs.

I made adjustments and have included an adapted recipe of the batter pudding at the end of this chapter. I started with a quarter recipe. Several indigestible, sticky, doorstop puddings later, I had discovered the huge problem with boiling: there isn't an easy way to check progress. My boiled puddings had a terrible tendency to come out way too damp. Seems as though mid-nineteenth-century cooks may have had the same problem and advanced to cooking the batter in molds. Mrs. Acton scolded that though "modern taste is in favor of puddings cooked in moulds … they are seldom as light as those boiled in cloths." Be that as it may, I figured it was worth a try. The advantages of being able to easily check doneness outweighed the possible change in lightness. Much to my delight I found that, in my kitchen, the baked-in-the-mold version was much better. Light and somewhat plain, but good.

This description at the end of Miss Leslie's recipe for "Indian Pudding" caught my attention: "When cold it is very good cut in slices and fried." Sounds perfect for men out on a military campaign even though the "Indian" refers to cornmeal, not a possible enemy. Miss Leslie was right. That lightly spiced molasses pudding is very good served that way. I figured the camping soldiers might enjoy the plain batter pudding served just that simple way without a sauce. You could add a half teaspoon each of cinnamon and nutmeg to the Tennessee Cake on page 32 to sample a cake similar to Indian Pudding.

Another recipe I found in Miss Leslie's book worth considering is a sturdy cracker called "Apee." I've made these for years and was delighted to find them in an 1828 source. They are somewhat like an English "digestive biscuit," a cross between a cookie and a cracker. The caraway seeds actually do have a soothing effect on digestion. Perhaps the Rutledge family would have prepared these cookies in their tavern kitchen. As the leading family in town with two sons marching off, they may have made a couple of batches as a farewell—and "eat well"—contribution to the war.

But even better than these cookbook recipes was a treasure I found on microfilm. I was reading the *Sangamo Journal* newspaper, and there in the November 3, 1832, edition was a column of recipes. Although the date was six months after the men marched off—and five months after many of them came home—and published in the relatively more urban city of Springfield, it is hard to get closer time and place than this. The eighteen recipes are for cakes and cookies. Two of them fit nicely into this soldier-provisioning story. Pint cake is a variation of several styles of early cake that are simply bread dough enriched with sugar, dried fruit, additional butter or eggs, and some spices. With housekeepers making loaves of bread on a daily basis, it was an easy matter to pull out a "pint" of bread dough and turn it into cake. The second recipe that jumped right out and demanded to be made is a jumble. This version is different from Mrs. Jemison's jumbles, the very first historical recipe I researched and cooked. This recipe is just as tasty but has less butter and sugar and uses caraway seeds instead of exotic mace for flavoring. Given that the cook would have to form the cookie rings individually, it probably wasn't a recipe that the ladies of New Salem had time to bake as the men set off, but maybe it would have been a good treat to serve when they returned. I just know I couldn't resist.

As to what the New Salem militia men actually ate in camp, government documents and memoirs helped me to figure out some of the possibilities. Once in Beardstown, the Sangamon County troops joined others from around the state. Steamboats brought provisions upriver for the regular army troops and volunteer militia. Scattered records of provisions for the New Salem company survive. On the 25th, Lincoln signed for corn, pork, salt, one barrel of flour, and five-and-a-half gallons of whiskey. On the 28th, the company was formally enrolled in state service, and Lincoln again drew supplies including candles; soap; a fifty-pound gridiron; four tin buckets; seven coffee boilers; seven tin pans; sixteen tin cups; more corn, pork, flour, and whiskey. He also signed for fighting materiel: lead, powder, and thirty muskets and bayonets. On May 17, he drew ten pounds of cornmeal and ten pounds of pork. Certainly the Sangamon County volunteers would have had more to eat than this. Rations for the regular army included fresh beef and vinegar.

Memoirs from Lincoln's company's thirty-day enlistment are limited, too. As the volunteers moved northeast through Illinois on the track of Black Hawk, they witnessed the grim results of battle and encountered one Indian. William Greene recounted that an "old Indian" stumbled into their camp. Although he had a pass from General Cass stating that he was a "good & true man," some of the army soldiers were intent, saying, "We have come to fight the Indians and by God we intend to do so." According to Greene and others, Lincoln stood between the soldiers and the Indian, protecting him from harm and letting him go along his way. By the end of May, the volunteers and their horses were exhausted and their calico clothing torn to shreds by continually tramping through brush and brambles. Royal Clary explained the governor's release statement: "The men's times were up—horses jaded & worn out—men naked etc and they must be discharged and so we were."

The New Salem area men were mustered out on May 27. However, Lincoln reenlisted for two more terms of about twenty days each. First he joined Captain Elijah Iles's company, this time as a private. When that enlistment was up, he joined an independent spy company under the command of Captain Jacob M. Early. And, more important to me, he was in the company of George M. Harrison, who later told Herndon a good deal about actual food in the campaign. According to Harrison, bacon was an important part of the army diet. "The government furnished four raw articles from which we prepared our diet; bacon hams and shoulders, pickled pork, flour and beef cattle." Harrison explained they always had plenty of bacon, unless they failed to carry enough.

Cooking equipment was similarly limited. "A frying pan with a short handle, a tin water bucket furnished by the government, pocket knives, bowie knives, hatchets, tin cups, a coffee pot and elm bark for dishes, kneading tray furnished by ourselves." It is unclear what happened to the fifty-pound gridiron Lincoln had signed for a few weeks earlier. The life of the volunteer troops had changed over the brief course of the war. Earlier on, men described camp life that included singing, card games, and various sports. Now the commanders moved troops quickly following the movements of Black Hawk and his band, which included warriors and women and children.

As to the food the volunteer militia ate, Harrison's descriptions were more specific than many period cookbook writers. "The meat we could boil—when we could get a pot—broil, roast or fry; the latter was generally practiced in order to save all the grease for bread to shorten and to fry. The bread we could bake or fry, the latter mode was generally practiced, for it was the less trouble and the less time of the two modes; the former mode we usually practiced by wrapping the stiff, shortened dough in a spiral manner around our ramrods ... where it would bake into a most esculent bread."

"Shortened." Here is a recipe in an adjective. None of today's discursive language: "make a short crust." Just a single word. I knew what Harrison meant. A short crust is used for pies, where we combine butter, lard, or "shortening" with flour so that bits of the fat are encased in a flour envelope before the liquid is added. As this crust bakes, the fat melts, giving off its own bits of liquid, turned to steam, and the result is a flaky crust we all know from well-made pies or biscuits. This was, in fact, the first recipe and cooking method I learned from my mother. I had never really thought about the name. Recipe writers at least as far back as the middle 1600s used the same verb to describe this quickly made alternative to puff pastry. Back then, Sir Kenelm Digby described the piecrust made by Lady Lasson for her pie of "Neats-tongues": "Her finest crust is made by sprinkling the flower [*sic*] ... with cold water and then working the past[e] with little pieces of raw Butter in good quantity.... And this makes the crust short and light."

There was a slight hitch to adapting Harrison's flour and bacon fat to my usual short crust method that calls for ice-cold water and hard shortening. Harrison and Lincoln were eating in June and July. I took another clue from Harrison's description of their cooking equipment, "kneading tray furnished by ourselves," and figured the men simply mixed the fat with flour using their hands. Four tablespoons of bacon fat, cooled so it was just turning white, mixed perfectly with one cup of flour. As to cooking technique, I opted for a modification. I didn't have a rifle ramrod, but I did find an old auger in the back of the garage—an advantage of living in a 125-year-old house. This rusty two-foot-long piece of iron was about the right diameter—a half inch—to replicate Harrison and Lincoln's method. I covered it with aluminum foil and wrapped the snake of dough around it, then propped it up over the low wood fire and waited. And waited. And waited even longer. Harrison was right; this was a very slow method. I unwound the still slightly raw dough from the "ramrod" and placed it on the grill over the lingering coals. About fifteen minutes later, we did indeed have a most esculent bread.

As to main dishes, militia volunteers made use of what they could find as they moved through the land of small, panic-abandoned farms set in northern Illinois and southern Wisconsin forest clearings. Apparently, the men went hungry rather than engage in widespread hunting. Maybe lead to make bullets was scarce. Possibly they were under orders not to shoot as the retort might make others in the area think they were under attack. Or perhaps the wildlife abandoned the area as well as the farmers. Harrison made much of one hunting success: "Once in particular, after stretching our rations nearly four days one of our mess shot a dove, and having a gill of flour left, we made a gallon and a half of delicious soup ... this soup we divided among several messes that were hungrier than we were and our own mess."

Here was a recipe that demanded to be tried. The ingredients and the method are very clear. I substituted a Cornish game hen from the grocery freezer section for the dove and was pleasantly surprised at the result. There was more water to meat than I usually use when making chicken soup. The amount of flour, equal to a half cup, thickened the soup the slightest bit. The meat from the "dove" stretched farther that I thought. All in all, an edible soup even without benefit of salt, pepper, or other seasonings.

There were also bigger birds to prey upon. Harrison described the men raiding a chicken coop and capturing scrawny hens and roosters. The family who settled on this northern Illinois farm had "skedaddled for fear of losing their scalps." The hungry band of volunteers took advantage of the unfed chickens before them. They tried simply cooking them over the fire, but then took a notion to fry them in some grease rendered from a hog jowl Harrison had found up in the rafters of the smokehouse. It provided just enough to make the tough fowl as acceptable as "eating saddle bags." The chickens we get in the grocery are nowhere near as tough and skinny as those half-starved chickens were, but I wondered how the combination of grilling and then frying in bacon fat would taste. The result was quite good, but very messy to make. In the recipe at the end of the chapter, I've adapted the concept, pairing the chicken and bacon in a much more succulent dish than the men of Lincoln's mess would have had, but the flavor combination is very good, especially cooked over a wood fire.

Lincoln and Harrison were discharged from the army in July near Whitewater, Wisconsin. The trip home was slightly more than two hundred miles. The two made most of the journey on foot because their horses were stolen the evening before they departed. They were not the only men of the company who walked home. Members of their company did share rides from time to time, but Harrison reported that the horses' backs were "too sore from constant riding." In Peoria, the company split up and Lincoln and Harrison bought a canoe. Taking up a new mode of travel for "a novelty," they paddled along on the slow current of the Illinois River. At one point they overtook a raft and were invited aboard for a feast of "fish, corn bread, eggs, butter and coffee; just prepared for our benefit." They sold the canoe in Havana, Illinois, and walked the rest of the way, with Harrison stopping at Petersburg and Lincoln continuing on to New Salem and his first election campaign for a seat in the Illinois legislature.

BATTER PUDDING

• • • • • •

This has been the trickiest recipe in all of my Lincoln cookery research. With just five ingredients, batter pudding is simple to mix. But it can be challenging to cook successfully. I wrote of my frustrations with the traditional boiling method in the text. When baked in the oven, the pudding puffs up, rather like a popover. Patience is key for serving: if you cut it before it cools, the inside may be too damp and doughy. The compromise method of steaming works well, but you are stuck in the kitchen for the hour it takes the pudding to cook through. Yet for all the issues, this is a dessert worth trying. Its simple taste makes a lovely base for fresh berries or vinegar sauce (see page 33). Pumpkin butter (see page 49) would be tasty spooned over it as well.

³/₄ **cup milk**

1 ¹/₄ **cups unbleached all-purpose flour, plus extra for sprinkling**

¹/₄ **teaspoon baking soda**

¹/₈ **teaspoon salt**

1 **egg, lightly beaten**

Pour the milk into a mixing bowl and gradually stir in the flour, mixing with a fork. Stir in the baking soda and salt. Mix in the egg. Boil, bake, or steam the pudding following one of these methods:

TRADITIONAL BOILING METHOD: Fill a large stockpot about two-thirds full with water and bring to a boil. Meanwhile, dip a heavy pudding cloth or linen-like dishtowel in the boiling water and then sprinkle well with flour on one side: this will form a seal between the boiling water and the pudding batter. Shake off excess flour. Lay the cloth floured side up on the work surface. Pour the pudding batter onto the center of the cloth, gather up the edges of the cloth, and tie them up at the top securely with a long piece of kitchen string. Make sure you leave some room for the batter to swell inside the cloth. Lower the pudding into the boiling water, extending the end of the string outside the pot so you have a way to pull the pudding out of the pot. Wrap the end of the string around a wooden spoon and balance the spoon across the top of the pot. Keep the water at a strong simmer for 1 hour. Pull the pudding out to check if it is done. Press lightly on the side of the cloth; if the pudding rebounds, loosen the string and stick a skewer or thin knife into the pudding. If it comes out clean, the pudding is done. If not, tie it up again and return to the boiling water for as long as another hour. Remove from the water. Let cool before unwrapping and slicing.

MODERN BAKING METHOD: Preheat the oven to 350°F. Pour the batter into 2 lightly greased small loaf pans. Bake until firm in center and the pudding has just begun to pull away from the sides of the pans, about 45 to 55 minutes. The pudding will rise up and then fall when removed from the oven. Cool completely before breaking into serving pieces.

STOVETOP STEAMING METHOD: You will need: a 1-quart heatproof pudding bowl or casserole; waxed or parchment paper; kitchen string; and a deep pot with a lid large enough to comfortably hold the pudding bowl or casserole. You will also need a trivet to keep the bowl off the bottom of the pot. (I improvised with iron flower-arranging frogs.) Lightly grease the pudding bowl and add the batter. Lightly grease a piece of waxed paper, lay it across the top of the bowl, and tie in place with the string. Lower the bowl into the pot. Add enough boiling water so the water comes about halfway up the bowl. Maintain a strong simmer until the pudding is done, adding more boiling water as needed. Check the pudding with a skewer after about 45 minutes. (You can stick the skewer through the waxed or parchment paper.) If the skewer comes out clean, the pudding is done. If not, continue cooking until the skewer comes out clean. This could take another half hour.

Boiled pudding is best served with a sauce such as vinegar sauce, pumpkin butter, or fruit.

Makes 1 round pudding or 2 small pudding loaves, for 6 to 8 servings

ADAPTED FROM "BATTER PUDDING," MISS ELIZA LESLIE,
SEVENTY-FIVE RECEIPTS FOR PASTRY, CAKES, AND SWEETMEATS, 1828.

APEES

• • • • • • •

*Caraway seeds have long been known as digestive aids and breath
sweeteners. Combined with cinnamon and other aromatic spices in
this crispy treat, the resulting cross between a cookie and a cracker will
quickly become a family favorite. Apees are "good keepers," staying
delicious for weeks—assuming they last that long in your cookie jar.*

> **2 cups unbleached all-purpose flour,
>   plus extra for dusting**
>
> **1/2 cup sugar**
>
> **3/4 teaspoon ground cinnamon**
>
> **3/4 teaspoon freshly grated or ground nutmeg**
>
> **3/4 teaspoon ground mace**
>
> **1 1/2 tablespoons caraway seeds**
>
> **1/2 cup (1 stick) cold salted butter**
>
> **1/3 cup white wine**

Preheat the oven to 350°F. Combine the flour, sugar, and spices in a
mixing bowl. Cut the butter into the dry ingredients with a pastry cutter or 2 knives until the mixture looks like uncooked oatmeal. Stir in
the wine with a fork and then knead the dough with your hands. Roll
out the dough on a lightly floured surface to a 1/8-inch thickness. Cut
into 1 1/4-inch rounds. Place on ungreased baking sheets and prick the
tops with a fork two or three times. Bake until lightly browned, about
20 to 25 minutes. Apees shrink as they bake.

Makes about 7 dozen small cookies

ADAPTED FROM "APEES," MISS ELIZA LESLIE, *SEVENTY-FIVE
RECEIPTS FOR PASTRY, CAKES, AND SWEETMEATS*, 1828.

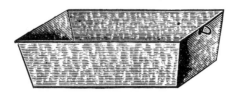

PINT CAKE

• • • • • • •

This cake is named for the "pint" of bread dough the baker would set aside from her normal multi-loaf batch to make the cake. Before chemical leaveners such as baking soda, cakes were made light with beaten egg whites, which must have been touch-and-go baked in the beehive or Dutch ovens of the day. The clever addition of sweet ingredients to already-in-progress bread dough gave the homemaker two-for-one results.

This cake is similar to Federal-era, yeast-raised cakes such as the "Election Cake" from Amelia Simmons's American Cookery, *recognized as the first American cookbook. The recipe appears in the 1796 second edition. Tradition has it that these sturdy, satisfying cakes were served to voters and those counting the ballots well into the night in Connecticut elections. Back then ballots from around the state were brought to the state capital, Hartford, for tabulation and the official announcement of results. Later cookbooks frequently called this recipe "Old Hartford Election Cake."*

This pint cake recipe appeared in the Sangamo Journal, *the Springfield newspaper Lincoln might well have read in New Salem.*

A WORD ON YEAST: Today bread bakers don't have to worry about keeping their supply of yeast happy and alive between bread-baking days. We can just tear open a packet of dry instant yeast. The rapid-rise variety is so reliable you don't even have to proof it by mixing it with warm water as the first step. If you are used to this method, you can certainly use it for this recipe. Call me old-fashioned, but I still like to proof my yeast. There's something about the yeasty smell as it develops that I enjoy, so I've written directions with that step in mind.

FOR THE BREAD DOUGH (JUST ENOUGH TO MAKE 1 PINT CAKE):

- **1 packet instant rapid-rise yeast**
- **1 tablespoon sugar**
- **3/4 cup warm water**
- **2 1/2 cups unbleached all-purpose flour**

FOR THE CAKE BATTER:

- **1 cup raisins, coarsely chopped**
- **3 large eggs, lightly beaten**
- **1 cup packed light or dark brown sugar**
- **1 teaspoon baking soda**
- **1 teaspoon ground cinnamon**
- **1/2 teaspoon ground allspice**

Combine the yeast, sugar, and warm water in a glass measuring cup. Let stand for about 5 minutes. The mixture should be bubbly and smell "yeasty." Pour the yeast mixture into a large mixing bowl. Stir in the flour with a wooden spoon. Knead lightly with your hands until you have a slightly sticky dough.

Grease two 8 ½ x 4 ½–inch loaf pans and line with parchment paper. In a mixing bowl, combine "cake" ingredients. Gradually knead the cake ingredients into the bread dough. This is a messy process. Or, use a large food processor fitted with dough blade or a standing mixer fitted with a dough hook to accomplish the mixing process. When the dough is thoroughly mixed, divide it in half and place each half in a prepared loaf pan. Set the pans aside in a warm place for about 20 minutes.

Preheat the oven to 350°F. Bake the cakes until they just begin to pull away from the sides of the pans, about 45 to 55 minutes.

TIP FOR SUCCESS: Don't skimp on the time it takes to mix the bread and cake ingredients. Make sure you don't have any unincorporated bits of bread dough, because it will rise to the top, bake faster, and form hard lumps in your lovely cake.

Makes 2 cakes, 8 servings each

ADAPTED FROM "PINT CAKE," *SANGAMO JOURNAL*, 1832.

JUMBLES

· · · · · · ·

Jumbles are doughnut-shaped cookies formed by rolling little snakes of dough and joining the ends. These cookies are a lot of fun to make. You can make them without the caraway seeds.

It was said that Lincoln read all the available newspapers. We can connect this recipe to him as it appeared in a Springfield, Illinois, newspaper during the time he lived about twenty miles to the northwest in New Salem.

1 1/2	cups unbleached all-purpose flour, plus extra for rolling
1/2	cup sugar, white or firmly packed brown
4	tablespoons (1/2 stick) cold salted butter
2	teaspoons caraway seeds
1	large egg
2	tablespoons milk or cream
	Extra white sugar for cookie topping

Preheat the oven to 350°F. Lightly grease 2 cookie sheets. In a large mixing bowl, stir together the flour and sugar. With a pastry cutter or 2 knives, cut the butter into the flour mixture until it looks like cornmeal. Stir in the caraway seeds.

In a small mixing bowl, beat the egg lightly and then stir in the milk or cream. Pour the egg mixture into the dry ingredients. Stir with a fork and then knead until you have dough that feels like child's play clay. If mixture is too dry, add more milk a teaspoon at a time.

Divide the dough into 12 equal pieces. On a lightly floured work surface, roll 1 piece of dough into a rope about 18 inches long and the diameter of a pencil. Break off lengths about 3 inches long, slightly taper the ends, and then join them into a ring. Dip the top of this jumble into sugar and place on a prepared cookie sheet. Repeat these steps with the remaining dough. Bake until firm and just beginning to turn golden, about 15 to 20 minutes.

Makes about 6 dozen jumbles

ADAPTED FROM "JUMBLES," *SANGAMO JOURNAL*, 1832.

BACON-BASTED MILITIA CHICKEN

• • • • • •

This adaptation captures the flavor of the troop's campfire roasted–fried chicken. Today's well-fed and grocery store–purchased fowl is considerably more tender than the bird the soldiers in Lincoln's Black Hawk War company managed to find.

1 whole chicken, about 4 pounds
4 slices bacon, diced

Preheat the oven to 300°F. Split chicken along the spine. Flatten and place skin side up in a roasting pan. Gently lift skin by sliding your hands between the skin and meat. Distribute the bacon pieces evenly over the entire chicken and pat the skin back down. Slow-roast the chicken, basting with the pan juices from time to time, until the skin is slightly transparent and the meat is well done, about 1 hour and 40 minutes. (An instant-read meat thermometer inserted in a thigh will register 165°F.)

Serves 4 twenty-first-century diners
(or 10 hungry men of the Black Hawk War company)

RE-CREATED FROM PERIOD SOURCES.

6

COURTSHIP AND CAKE
THE LINCOLNS' ROMANCE AND MARY TODD'S ALMOND CAKE

Mary Todd moved to Springfield, Illinois, in October 1839 from Lexington, Kentucky. Two months shy of her twenty-first birthday, Mary was starting a new life in the home of Elizabeth Todd Edwards, her married oldest sister, and, just maybe, looking for a husband among the politicians, lawyers, and strivers in the newly designated state capital. Abraham Lincoln had settled in Springfield two and a half years earlier. He arrived in the town of nearly 2,000 in April 1837 riding a horse borrowed from a New Salem friend. He was twenty-eight years old, a member of the Illinois State Legislature, and a lawyer in practice with John Todd Stuart, Mary Todd's cousin.

By the time Mary Todd arrived in town, the population had increased to nearly 2,500. The Stuart & Lincoln law practice was busy, and Lincoln spent his free time in a variety of activities. He presented serious lectures to the Young Men's Lyceum. He went fishing in the streams surrounding Springfield with friends and their sons, and he escorted their daughters and sisters to concerts, plays, and other social events about town. Lincoln encountered Mary Todd at a cotillion in December 1839. "Miss Todd, I want to dance with you in the worst way," he said asking for a dance. After the evening Mary told one of her cousins, "And he certainly did."

Todd family tradition suggests that Mary made an almond cake during their courtship and also after they were married. Lincoln is said to have called it "the best cake I ever ate." When I first saw a recipe for

"Mary Todd Lincoln Cake" in a book, I could readily see how the recipe had been adjusted over the years, adapted to newer ingredients, losing its period texture and taste.

As I read more and more about those early Springfield years and the lives of the Lincolns—thought about what was clearly reported, and what wasn't—I considered that the explanation of their courtship, like the almond cake recipe, has been adapted to modern interpretations. Here, too, the truth may have missed the essential ingredients.

In this case, the Todd family was largely silent on the ups and downs of the couple's three-year courtship. Springfield friends offered theories. Hints abound—broken engagement, flirtations with others, melancholy, and even a duel. There is much to be discovered about the truth of the cake recipe and the reality of Mary and Abraham's relationship. So I decided to weave the two together and explore their story while I tested cake recipes. By the end I hoped for something to chew on ... and some food for thought.

I first encountered the almond cake recipe attributed to Mary Todd while casually flipping through a cookbook of presidential favorites. I have to admit that I was surprised. The recipe didn't make any sense for an 1840s cake. Some of the ingredients were wrong, the method suspect, and the history tenuous.

I've spent countless days along with barrels of flour, bushels of corn-meal, several firkins of butter, gallons of molasses, and clutches of eggs, cooking from nineteenth-century recipes. I've learned a thing or two along the way, and when I saw baking powder listed as an ingredient in what would have been a pre–Civil War recipe, I knew it could not be the real deal.

Baking powder was invented before the war. Some sources date it to the late 1840s. But it wasn't commonly called for in cookbook ingredients until the 1870s. There may have been a lag between appearing in print and typical home use, but baking powder didn't show up in the lists of available products in midwestern grocery store newspaper advertisements either. Other commercial leavening ingredients—starting with saleratus, then baking soda, and finally cream of tartar—showed up with regularity beginning in the 1840s. When home cooks stirred the latter two ingredients together into their batters, they made the equivalent of baking powder.

Period cookbooks specified other homemade ways to make cakes light: yeast sponges left over from bread baking mixed in with sweet ingredients; pearl ash, made by filtering water through fireplace ashes and then concentrating it (as I discussed in Chapter 2); and the much simpler and faster technique of using well-beaten egg whites.

It is no wonder that baking powder in that ingredient list incited my curiosity. I looked in a few other modern presidential recipe collections and online. The same almond cake recipe kept showing up in the Lincoln section. Always with the same provenance. The recipe was one prepared by famed Lexington confectioner Monsieur Girard in 1825 when General Lafayette came through town. The stories said that the Todd family so enjoyed the cake that Monsieur Girard shared the recipe with them. Sorry, not even a French caterer in the sophisticated town of Lexington would have had access to baking powder in 1825. The recipes I kept seeing could not be authentic.

So, if Mary served such a cake to Mr. Lincoln, as she always called him in public, what would it really have been like? How could I make an authentic almond cake today?

After my disappointing foray into modern sources, I hoped my favorite early-nineteenth-century cookbook author would have the answer. Miss Eliza Leslie wrote several cookbooks. Of the three I own, one is a very handy reprint of Miss Leslie's first book, *Seventy-Five Receipts for Pastry, Cakes, and Sweetmeats*. Published in Philadelphia in 1828, it was just the right place to start. Miss Leslie offered two possible almond cakes. One of them was even called "French Almond Cake." For good measure I consulted Mrs. Lettice Bryan's 1839 *The Kentucky Housewife*. Mrs. Bryan offered an almond cake similar to Miss Leslie's version and an almond pound cake that seemed almost foolproof.

All four of these recipes are what we Minnesotans call "spendy." They use expensive ingredients and lots of them: sweet and bitter almonds, the finest loaf sugar. When I first looked at the recipes I was skeptical. One called for fourteen eggs, another used twenty-two, and neither one of them had a lot of flour. But then I realized these were essentially early versions of angel food or chiffon cakes. I also reminded myself of my cooking-from-period-sources mantra: Always trust the original recipe. I am certainly glad I did for these cakes.

These are rich people's cakes, just the sort of thing you would expect to find in the Edwards home. The stately home of Ninian Edwards and his wife stood with a few others on a hill overlooking the village of Springfield. These houses were described by an 1840 visitor as being "showy edifices, the principal expense of which seems to have been their decoration, standing rather proudly apart from the throng of neat but humble mansions." The Edwards family stood apart as well. Ninian, son of the late first governor of Illinois, was an attorney and a member of the Illinois State Legislature. His wife, Elizabeth, Mary's sister, was the eldest child of Robert Todd, a wealthy Kentucky banker and Whig party political activist. Both Elizabeth and Mary were well educated, encouraged to participate in the political functions that filled their childhood Lexington home and to speak their minds.

In Illinois the Edwards home was filled with the best of Springfield society. After the city became the state capital, Ninian and Elizabeth Edwards served as hosts for the legislators, judges, and state officers at four receptions a year. They regularly entertained friends, relatives, and everyone who was anyone in town.

As early as 1831, grocery stores in Springfield carried a wide range of luxury goods, just what the community needed to serve the very best at all those parties. Hosts could take their entertaining inspirations from national magazines. William Manning's bookstore sold subscriptions for magazines including the *Saturday Evening Post* and, all-important to the women in the Edwards/Todd family, *Godey's Lady's Book*. By 1835 mail from St. Louis arrived every day. By 1840 progress and prospects continued to improve. Springfield cooks had their choice of staples and fancy groceries from a score of merchants.

Even though the streets were paved in thick, sticky mud instead of gold every time it rained, people continued to pour into town. More than a hundred new buildings were built in the summer of 1840 and again in 1841. The air would have been filled with the sound of banging hammers and scented with sweet, fresh sawdust and acrid, drying plaster.

Springfield in the 1840s was a community of contrasts, and those differences complicated the Lincoln-Todd courtship. From their hilltop mansion Ninian and Elizabeth Edwards could look down on Springfield—literally and figuratively. And that lofty perspective may have created problems for Mary and Abraham. Mary could have known her plans for marriage lay with Abraham Lincoln and he could have seen in her a woman who could challenge him and be his intellectual partner. But the Edwardses might only have seen a backwoods legislator and lawyer who was not Mary's equal. She spoke French and loved fine things. He was reserved in society and his clothes seldom fit properly. Still, the attraction was evident and powerful. Elizabeth Edwards described their interaction when Abraham came calling on Mary. "I have happened in the room where they were sitting often & often Mary led the conversation. Lincoln would listen & gaze on her as if drawn by some superior power, irresistibly so: he listened—never scarcely said a word."

It appears that Lincoln came calling on Mary frequently, joining the other eligible men of Springfield society in the home on the hill. The quantity of letters she received during her 1840 summer visit with her Uncle David in Columbia, Missouri, amply demonstrated the diligence of many of her suitors. Lincoln was out of Springfield for much of the spring and summer of 1840, too. He traveled among the communities along the central Illinois court circuit and gave political speeches for Whig candidates in the southern counties of the state. Mary and Lincoln met once during the summer when he stopped in Columbia during his speaking tour, and reading between the lines of Mary's letter to her best friend, Mercy Levering, suggests that Abraham was one of her correspondents whose letters may have been unexpected as they "were entirely unlooked for."

The entreaties of various distinguished beaux introduced by relatives didn't sway Mary. She wrote Mercy, "My hand will never be given, where my heart is not." Elizabeth Edwards recounted another of Mary's opinions on the man she would marry. "I would rather marry a good man—a man of the mind—with a hope and bright prospects ahead for position—fame & power than to marry all the houses—gold & bones in the world."

In the fall, when the Illinois legislature opened its session on November 23, 1840, Lincoln and Mary were both in town and, the history suggests, keeping serious company, for by the end of the year the two were known to be engaged. Lincoln was nearly thirty-two and launched on his political and legal career. Mary, who had just turned twenty-two years on December 13, 1840, clearly demonstrated that she knew her mind, what she wanted, and how to get it.

Some writers have called Mary's almond cake a "courting cake." It may well be that the delicate texture and light almond flavor with a hint of lemon loosened Lincoln's tongue enough for him to speak of his deep feelings. If so, this was a cake that was definitely worth the expense and the time to make it.

Certainly the bakers in the Edwards household could have afforded and could have found the ingredients for a fancy almond cake such as Miss Leslie's French almond cake. Having the time and the energy to make it was another matter. In 1840 Ninian and Elizabeth Edwards were raising two children under five. There isn't any clear indication that Elizabeth had household help other than her sister Mary. There were not any live-in women other than family documented in the 1840 census. The 1850 census did show an Irish girl, Alice Fogerty, in the home. Mrs. Edwards may have had hired day help with laundry, cleaning, and other chores essential to keeping house and entertaining. Elizabeth was recognized as a good cook. I think she and Mary would have made this special almond cake.

Following Miss Leslie's almond cake recipe was a two-day process, beginning with preparing the almonds. Both the sweet and bitter almonds needed to be blanched by dipping them in boiling water, then cooling them so the brown skins could be slipped off easily. Next Miss Leslie instructs the baker to pound the nuts to a paste, preferably one at a time in a mortar and pestle. She suggests, "Prepare them, if possible, the day before the cake is made."

The Kentucky Housewife pound cake is easier to make as it is much like a standard cake recipe today: cream the butter and sugar, add the dry ingredients alternating with wet ones. But Miss Leslie's and the other egg-dependent recipe in *Kentucky Housewife* are for expert cake makers. For the 1840s novice baker, risks of failure were high. Miss Leslie cautioned, "Unless you are provided with proper and convenient utensils and materials, the difficulty of preparing cakes will be great, and in most instances a failure; involving disappointment, waste of time and useless expense." In short, if the effort of whipping the egg whites into stiff peaks didn't give you the vapors, uncertainty about baking temperatures and times was likely to result in a case of the fantods.

Reinforcing the precision and difficulty of these almond cake recipes, the ingredients are listed by weight, not cups, or by approximations commonly found in period recipes such as "butter the size of an egg." Both of these almond cake recipes specify types of baking pans, rare for cookbooks of this era. The French almond cake is to be baked in a turban mold, while *The Kentucky Housewife* version specified a square pan and a brick oven. One could bake the pound cake in a Dutch or reflector oven on the fireplace hearth, but the fancier versions relied on stiffly beaten egg whites to make a light, lovely cake. If this cake were hit by the slightest draft while baking, the egg whites would fall and cause the cake to collapse. Care was taken when cooling the cakes as well, or they would sink even though they were perfectly baked.

Clearly not only did the period cook need to be an expert baker with a set of scales, she needed a kitchen with a brick oven at the very least. The Edwardses might have installed one of the new cast-iron stoves that Springfield newspapers advertised. One old-time Springfield resident, Judge Samuel D. Lockwood, recalled these innovations in a letter written about this time. His family in the neighboring town of Jacksonville installed "a new invention today, my dear Mary [his wife], called a cooking stove; it is said to be a panacea for all evils, but in my opinion it will not work."

Fortunately, I have a lovely electric oven, can buy my almonds already blanched, and can use my food processor to turn them into a paste. Not having arms strengthened by beating carpets, riding horses, churning butter, or stirring up cakes, I use my electric mixer to whip egg whites and mix batters.

But what about those bitter almonds? I've watched enough mysteries to know that when the detective sniffs around the mouth of the murder victim, he is likely to mutter something along the lines of, "Aha! A faint smell of almonds. Must be poison." Bitter almonds are, in fact, poisonous and cannot be sold in the United States. Their flavor is much stronger than that of the sweet almonds we can buy. Extract companies do have a process to safely make flavoring from the bitter almond. I used pure almond extract when testing the recipes, while increasing the amount of sweet almonds to maintain the balance of wet and dry ingredients.

My friends have had to eat dozens of slices of almond cake in an effort to determine which one fits the description Abraham Lincoln gave Mary Todd's cake, "the best cake I ever ate." They didn't complain. In the end I couldn't decide and included recipes for Miss Eliza Leslie's French almond cake and Mrs. Lettice Bryan's almond pound cake at the end of the chapter.

Sometime in the late fall of 1840, Mary and Abraham had made their decision, too. They became engaged. But the engagement was short lived. Something happened on New Year's Day 1841 to change the course of their romance. In Springfield the New Year's Day custom was to exchange house visits of celebration. As their friends and neighbors gathered in the Edwards parlor, it would have been natural to announce wedding plans, or at least to toast the happy couple. Instead Abraham Lincoln was to call it "that fatal first of Jan'y."

The engagement was broken off, perhaps because of an insecurity on Lincoln's part that he could give Mary the life she deserved, perhaps because of Mary's possible flirtations with other suitors. Perhaps there was anger between them, or family pressure from Elizabeth, and especially Ninian Edwards, who was Mary's legal guardian. Mrs. Edwards suggested family concerns as the cause of the rupture in her terse interviews with William Herndon. "Mr. Edwards & myself after the first crush of things told Mary & Lincoln that they had better not ever marry—that their natures, mind—education—raising etc. were so different they could not live happy as husband and wife."

Lincoln became immediately despondent, so much so that his friends feared for his sanity. He soon apologized for his behavior, saying, "I have within the last few days, been making a most discreditable exhibition of myself." Lincoln returned to his responsibilities in the legislature after a week, although he continued in a melancholy state of mind.

We know less of Mary's true feelings. She seemed to have carried on, holding her head high through the winter social season. However, from her words in the letter she wrote to Mercy Levering in June, Mary suffered from the dissolution of the engagement, too. She wrote that she "was left in the solitude of my own thoughts, and some lingering regrets over the past, which time alone can overshadow with its healing balm."

Even though Mary and Abraham didn't see each other during all of

1841 and into the following year, they were aware of events in each other's lives. In March 1842, Lincoln was still deeply affected by the estrangement, but he expressed relief that Mary seemed, at long last, to be of glad heart. "I cannot but reproach myself for even wishing to be happy while she is otherwise. She accompanied a large party on the Rail Road cars to Jacksonville last Monday; and on her return, spoke, so I heard of it, of having enjoyed the trip exceedingly."

Springfield was a small town and the social circles of Mary Todd and Abraham Lincoln were even smaller. By the spring of 1842 mutual friends of the two decided it was time to bring them together again. Mrs. Simeon Francis, wife of the *Sangamo Journal* editor, cleverly invited both Abraham and Mary to her home without telling them, or anyone else, that they would meet. The couple must have picked up where they had left off eighteen months or so earlier.

More than twenty years later, six months into her widowhood, Mary Lincoln wrote about an incident during that secret engagement period. Josiah Gilbert Holland had sent her a copy of his book *The Life of Abraham Lincoln*. In it he had revealed very publicly the event the Lincolns had pledged never to discuss in public—the duel Abraham Lincoln nearly fought, in part, to protect Mary Todd. The event is instructive. It highlights Mary's political interest and involvement and Lincoln's devotion. It was a bit of youthful and political fun gone awry, and Lincoln's actions demonstrate both the consequences of his youthful, sometimes careless, wit and the price he was willing to pay to correct it.

In February 1842, the state bank of Illinois collapsed, making the paper currency it had issued worthless. When state taxes came due, James Shields, the Democratic state auditor, refused to accept that currency, saying the taxes must be paid in silver. Lincoln, a member of the opposing Whig Party, saw this declaration as an opportunity to make political points and to poke some fun at Shields, an intemperate dandy who also fancied himself as a ladies man.

Springfield newspapers commonly published letters written in the character of rural, unsophisticated voters to make political points. Lincoln, adopting the voice of "Rebecca," a semiliterate widow who lived in "Lost Township," sent in a letter to the *Sangamo Journal*. Writing of the troubles her farmer neighbor would have paying his taxes, Rebecca then attacked the character of Shields, ridiculing him as "a conceity dunce" for whom "truth is out of the question." In the letter Lincoln also "quoted" Shields's conversation with a group of young women. "Dear girls. It is distressing, but I cannot marry you all. Too well I know how much you suffer; but do, do remember, it is not my fault that I am so handsome and so interesting."

Mary Todd and her friend Julia Jayne, both ardent Whigs, submitted a "Rebecca" letter of their own continuing the ridicule as the backwoods woman. In the letter Rebecca even offered to marry Shields. He became the laughingstock of Springfield. His friends took to teasing him about it. Shields quickly demanded to know the identity of the letters' author.

Protecting Mary and her friend, Lincoln claimed authorship of the letters and hoped that would resolve the issue. In response, Shields escalated the incident. He demanded more than an apology; he challenged Lincoln to a duel. Such satisfaction was illegal in Illinois and so the men and their seconds agreed to meet on "Blood Island," a neutral territory on the Mississippi River near Alton, Illinois. As the one who was challenged, Lincoln had the right to choose the weapon. He selected broadswords, later saying, "I did not want to kill Shields, and felt certain that I could disarm him …; and furthermore, I didn't want the d—d fellow to kill me, which I rather think he would have done if we had selected pistols."

Once on the island, the men came to their senses and called off the duel. As Mary wrote to Josiah Holland in 1865, "the foolish and uncalled for *rencontre*, with … Shields … when Mr. Lincoln thought he had some right to assume to be my champion …. Mr L & myself mutually agreed never to refer to it & except in an occasional light manner, between us, it never was mentioned."

Mary and Abraham continued to meet in secret at the Francis home and made their plans to marry. Their decision to marry was so secret and sudden that it bordered on an in-town elopement. They would simply go to the minister's home and exchange their vows. Even Mr. and Mrs. Francis were kept in the dark until the morning of the wedding. When Ninian and Elizabeth Edwards learned on the day of the wedding that the couple planned to marry at the home of the minister, they hurriedly insisted that the marriage take place up on the hill. They also insisted that the wedding take place a day later and then scrambled to prepare for the event.

Three years after they met, Mary and Abraham did have a wedding cake, but it was not a fancy two-day-cooking version. Mary's other sister Frances Todd Wallace described the wedding-day flurry. "It was a hurly-burly day. How we hustled! I had a whole boiled ham which I took over for the wedding supper, and made the bride's and groom's cake. It was a very pretty and gay wedding. After the ceremony, congratulations, and the wedding supper, we danced until midnight." None of the thirty or so guests described what kind of cake was served. Some did recall that when it was brought out at the end of the ceremony, it was too warm for icing.

A week after the wedding, Lincoln wrote to a friend describing the event with an apt terseness of language that was the hallmark of his oratory. "Nothing new here except my marrying, which, to me, is a matter of profound wonder."

And so the Lincolns' marriage began.

FRENCH ALMOND CAKE

• • • • • • •

There are several Lincoln-era versions of this white almond cake. This adaptation is from an 1828 recipe, which advises the cook to allot two days to make the cake as the almonds need to be blanched, peeled, and pounded into a paste the day before baking. With modern kitchen equipment and ingredients, this cake is ready in an hour or so. The original recipe called for both sweet and bitter almonds. The former are the almonds we buy today. Poisonous bitter almonds are no longer sold. However, pure almond extract is made from those nuts, treated to be safe.

4 large eggs, separated

1/2 cup granulated sugar, pulverized

3/4 teaspoon pure almond extract

1/4 teaspoon pure lemon extract

3 ounces blanched slivered almonds, finely crushed or chopped into 1/16-inch pieces

1/4 cup unbleached all-purpose flour, sifted 3 times

Preheat oven to 350°F. In a deep, large (3-quart) bowl beat egg whites until they stand in stiff peaks, then set aside. In a second large bowl, using an electric mixer, beat egg yolks until they are thick and have turned into a light yellow color. This could take as long as 5 minutes. With the mixer running, begin adding the sugar about a tablespoon at a time. Continue beating until the sugar is fully incorporated and the batter is thick. Stir in the almond and lemon extracts and then the almonds. Stir in the flour. With a flexible rubber spatula, fold about one-third of the beaten egg whites into the egg yolk batter to lighten it up. Then gently fold this lightened batter into the remaining egg whites.

Pour the batter into an *ungreased* tube pan. Bake until the cake is firm and lightly browned on top, about 25 to 30 minutes. Invert the pan over a bottle to cool completely before removing the cake from the pan.

TIPS FOR SUCCESS: There are a few tricks to making this cake successfully. Nineteenth-century white sugar came in a compressed cone. Cooks snipped off what they needed with sugar shears and then pulverized it into fine crystals. For the French almond cake recipe, I put the ½ cup of granulated sugar in a plastic bag and pulverized it by pressing my rolling pin over it a few times. The resulting finer sugar blends more easily with the egg yolks. Stiffly beaten egg whites provide structure for this cake. It is lightest when baked until light brown in an ungreased angel food cake pan, then turned upside down until it is completely cool. I have also baked it in an antique tube pan with fluted sides. To get it out successfully, I greased just the bottom of the pan (top of cake), turned it upside down to cool completely, and then gently pressed against the cake, pulling it away from the sides. You can grease and flour the sides of the baking pan and cool the cake right side up. But the resulting cake, while delicious, will not be nearly as light.

Makes one 10-inch-diameter cake to serve 8 to 10

ADAPTED FROM "FRENCH ALMOND CAKE," MISS ELIZA LESLIE,
*SEVENTY-FIVE RECEIPTS FOR PASTRY, CAKES, AND SWEETMEATS,*1828.

ALMOND POUND CAKE

• • • • • • •

The same rich lemon-almond flavors infuse this cake as in the French Almond Cake. Both cakes are delicious. The pound cake structure is sturdier and some people like the buttery richness more than the light angel-food style.

- ½ cup (1 stick) salted butter, at room temperature
- ½ cup sugar
- 3 large eggs
- ¼ teaspoon ground mace
- ¼ teaspoon pure almond extract
- 1 teaspoon grated lemon zest
- 1 tablespoon freshly squeezed lemon juice
- 4 ounces blanched slivered almonds, finely crushed or chopped into ¹⁄₁₆-inch pieces
- 1 cup unbleached all-purpose flour
- ½ cup white wine

Preheat the oven to 350°F. Grease and flour an 8 ½ x 4 ½–inch loaf pan. Cream the butter and sugar. Add the eggs 1 at a time, beating well after each addition. Stir in the mace, almond extract, lemon zest and juice, and almonds. Stir in ½ cup of the flour, followed by the wine and then the remaining ½ cup flour, mixing well after each addition. Spoon the batter into the prepared pan. Bake until the cake is lightly browned and a knife inserted in the center comes out clean, about 40 to 50 minutes.

Makes 1 pound cake, for 10 to 12 slices

ADAPTED FROM "ALMOND POUND CAKE," MRS. LETTICE BRYAN,
THE KENTUCKY HOUSEWIFE, 1839.

7

EATING UP ILLINOIS POLITICS
BARBECUE, BISCUITS, AND BURGOO

Barbecue has long been the bread and butter of American politics. Today a political handshake or information often comes from a tweet over a smartphone, rather than a meeting over a plate of ribs or a hot dog. But picnic grounds and meeting halls can still pack in activists when the cause is important or the politician of interest.

Abraham Lincoln went to a lot of barbecues, picnics, and rallies during his thirty-five years in public life. He campaigned for the state legislature, his seat in congress, on behalf of other candidates, in the Lincoln-Douglas debates, and in 1859 as he began to think about running for the presidency. Many who saw him at these events and heard him address the crowds wrote about it. As I looked back at those long-ago gatherings, I found a clear understanding of the power of Lincoln's presentations and a not-so-clear explanation of the foods. It is a lot easier to get a feel for how Lincoln served up his ideas than it is to get a taste for the food that the crowd chewed.

Lincoln's good friend Joshua Speed attended many of his early speeches and wrote of their impact. He admired how Lincoln could present an idea and then support it when attacked by the opposition. "I have never heard a more effective speaker. He had all the party weapons of offense, and defense seemed to be entirely under his control. The large crowd seemed to be swayed by him as he pleased."

Lincoln's speeches often contained anecdotes in which "his own enjoyment was so genuine, his realization of a situation was so keen, that it exercised a power almost hypnotic over his hearers. Even the dullest saw the scene as he did. While describing it, his expressive face showing every emotion in turn. Then when the climax was reached he would lead the laughter with a heartiness that seemed to convulse his whole body."

Journalist Jonathan Birch described Lincoln's attire in 1858, the summer of cross-Illinois campaigning including the seven debates with Douglas. "He usually wore ... a linen coat, generally without any vest, a hat much the worse for wear and carried with him a faded cotton umbrella which became almost as famous ... as Lincoln himself."

A newspaper reported his speaking style at Cooper Union in New York. Lincoln began his speech in a high-pitched tone which lowered as he warmed to his topic, tossing his head with "vim this way and that." William Herndon, who witnessed many of Lincoln's speeches, said that although Lincoln stood still on the speaker's platform, not moving about or making broad gestures, as did most other orators of the day, "his little gray eyes flashed in a face aglow with the fire of his profound thoughts."

And, much to my delight, one man described what Lincoln ate at a pre-speech barbecue on September 24, 1858, during the Urbana, Illinois, agricultural fair. That fall was in the middle of the seven debates between Lincoln and Douglas held across the length of Illinois, and three months after he delivered his "House Divided" address accepting the Illinois Republican nomination to run for the U.S. Senate.

Years after Lincoln's assassination, James O. Cunningham, a well-known Urbana attorney, recalled the event:

> At the entrance to the grounds [Lincoln] was met by a committee of ladies and escorted to a seat at the head of the table supporting an abundance of barbecued food at which particular seat had been placed the best of the spread for the use of the honored guest. He took the seat prepared for him while the long tables were being assailed by his followers, and began eating his dinner. Looking around, he saw an old woman standing not far away looking intently at him. He at once recognized her as a waiter and dishwasher at the hotel in Urbana whom everybody knew as Granny. He said to her. "Why Granny, have you

no place? You must have some dinner. Here, take my place."
The old lady answered, "No, Mr. Lincoln, I just wanted to see
you. I don't want any dinner." In spite of her protestations, Lincoln rose from his seat at the head of the table and compelled
her to take his place and have her dinner, while he took his turkey leg and biscuit and seating himself at the foot of a nearby
tree ate his dinner apparently with the greatest satisfaction;
meanwhile Granny Hutchinson filled the place at the head of
the table and ate her dinner as he had insisted she do.

I am somewhat skeptical of the whole story, but I'll accept the food
detail. People of all classes did mingle at outdoor public celebrations and
political events. The Fourth of July in particular was a day when Lincoln
celebrated with the joyful, hungry hordes.

In 1839 Lincoln was the assistant marshal for the Springfield
parade that ended at the newly completed State House. The Globe Tavern accommodated a hundred people at a noon dinner. Six years later
the 1845 celebrations began with "reveille sounded from the state house
cupola followed by a 13 gun salute at 3 in the morning." Lincoln delivered
the oration of the day at two o'clock in the afternoon. Later he spoke to a
Sunday school picnic. "The fire-pit in which the sheep and the 'young ox,
tender and good' were roasting was uncovered, and the contents served
by ready and willing hands to the children and adults seated in long rows
on the grassy slopes that were made cool by the shadows of the trees and
the gentle breezes that played among the leaves."

Very few reports provide even as much of a menu as did the Sunday school picnic article. However, in the scattering of images and narratives, memories and reports, one phrase keeps repeating, "an old
fashioned Kentucky barbecue" or simply "an old fashioned barbecue." I
hadn't given the topic much thought until I read a modern book in which
the author extended the leap made in an 1870s newspaper article suggesting that the food served at these various 1850s events was burgoo, a
mixed-meat-and-vegetable, single-pot meal. Depending on the cook and
the region, burgoo can be the consistency of a good, rich stew, or thick
enough to stand the cooking spoon upright. I simply could not figure out
how such an inherently untidy dish could be fed to crowds of ladies and

gents before the era of paper napkins and disposable plates, so I started following the crumbs.

The barbecue celebrating the Kentucky wedding of Lincoln's parents, Nancy Hanks and Thomas Lincoln, on June 12, 1806, in Henderson sounded like quite a party. Hosted by Thomas Lincoln's family and John H. Parrott, who signed the marriage certificate as Nancy's guardian, although he may have just been the witness, it was described by former neighbor Dr. C. C. Graham in a letter written after Lincoln's death. The menu is long on meat and whiskey. "We had bear meat, venison, wild turkey and ducks, eggs wild and tame (so common that you could buy them at two bits a bushel), maple sugar strung on a string to bite off for coffee and whiskey, syrup in big goards [*sic*], peach-and-honey, a sheep that the two families barbequed whole over coals of wood burned in a pit and covered with green boughs to keep the juices in and a race for the whiskey bottle."

Graham's detail of the pit at the Lincoln nuptials, coupled with the Sunday school picnic article, turned on the light bulb and focused my thinking. I didn't see any mention of the huge cast-iron burgoo-cooking cauldrons, nor did it make a lot of practical sense to prepare a dish that must be stirred constantly or it will scorch. Of course! Those "old fashioned barbecues" were not the high-heat charcoal-briquette or gas-fired grilling we all do in our backyards. They would have been the slow, dug-deep-in-the-earth pit barbecue, where logs burn all night, transforming into a bed of long-lasting, consistent embers. The meat is slow roasted all the next day under some kind of wet, protective greenery to keep it from drying out as it cooks to slow, tender perfection. Pit barbecues involve a fair amount of set up, but then they cook themselves.

Even though I understood what it was, replicating it is another story. There are three major obstacles to a re-creation of these dishes: kind of meat, size of meat, and most important, cooking medium. The key question: How close to the experience can we get? There are pit barbecues and reenactments from time to time around the country where whole sheep or sides of beef are cooked all day in a simple pit. But I wanted to find a way to make this a more common experience. These events were things of legend, and the food might just be legendary, too.

It has been some time since I've cooked over a Girl Scout or Boy

Scout campfire, but I still remember those experiences. These recipes and methods would work for folks who go camping and are experienced cooking over a long-burning wood fire. There is a huge difference between the kind of heat produced from flaming logs and that from well-established embers. Embers hold a gentle, yet significant, heat for long periods of time, as anyone who has cleaned out a fireplace twenty-four hours after a weekend-long Yule-log fire knows … when he or she foolishly shovels the ash into a paper grocery sack.

I've done a lot of inventive backyard cooking over the years. I've built small wood fires in my Weber kettle and grilled over aromatic cherry, hickory, and apple branches. I've tantalized neighbors with the smells coming from pork, beef, chicken, and turkey cooked in a simple upright charcoal-fueled smoker. (I did share.) But Lincoln's barbecued meats were not smoked. Clear coals produce heat and maybe a bit of smoke caused by fat dripping into the fire. This is not the same as aromatic smoke made by damp wood or wood chips.

Not even I am adventuresome enough to dig a pit in the backyard to test these recipes, but I did the next best thing—dig into the period cookbooks. As providence would have it, Mrs. Lettice Bryan wrote how "to barbeque a shoat or beef" in *The Kentucky Housewife*. What better source for a Kentucky barbecue could I find? Even better, her method suits the home cook because it doesn't require digging a pit. Mrs. Bryan calls for cooking the meat slowly for several hours "on a large gridiron over a bed of clear coals."

The straightforward recipe looked simple, but I still had questions: the first, how big a piece of meat to barbecue? Here, too, *The Kentucky Housewife* differs from the period picnic descriptions of the "whole young ox" or "sheep." Mrs. Bryan called for a "shoat." A shoat is a pig on the way to becoming a hog, and it can be a fairly large animal. In one period source, examining the economics of fattening pork on corn, the farmer started with "a small-sized shoat weighing 92 pounds." Two months later the animal weighed 146 pounds and dressed out to 118 pounds of meat.

The other meat Mrs. Bryan mentioned in the recipe title—beef—is really vague. I can imagine anything from a five-pound rump roast to half a calf. Her cooking process does, however, give a few hints to the meat's size. She tells us to rub the meat with salt, pepper, and molasses, let it stand, and then rinse it off. She also has the cook baste the meat with only salted water and turn it as it "cooks slowly for several hours." The meat is cooked over coals on the ground, so the side not on the heat would cool while the other side is over the coals. A bed of coals would not retain heat like the walls of a pit. The only way I can think this method would be an effective way to cook would be to have some sort of flat piece of meat. A split carcass would work, especially if the cook had help with the basting and turning.

Considering Abraham Lincoln simply ate a turkey leg, according to Mr. Cunningham's account, and that I was doing this alone, I decided to start with chicken thighs. They are small and have a high bone-to-meat ratio, making them less dense and faster to cook than a boneless pork loin. I figured I could handle the vagaries of cooking them completely over a low heat in my covered grill. I set the usual grill and lid aside and began the experiment. I just had to get enough slow, long-lasting coals to do the job. After several experiments trying to make enough wood coals without taking all day, I developed a compromise method of building a fire with some large kindling-size sticks, about one and a half inches in diameter and small enough to fit in the basin of my grill. I mixed in a few old half-burned pieces of charcoal to help sustain the heat.

I built this fire in the center of the basin and propped two bricks on either side to support a "gridiron," in this case a flat, perforated sheet made for cooking vegetables on the grill. When the small bed of coals was hot enough for me to hold my hand about five inches above for about six seconds before it was uncomfortable, I placed the gridiron and chicken on the bricks and started cooking, turning, and basting. About ninety minutes later, I had some of the best chicken I've ever made. The significant difference between this and what we commonly call barbecue is that the meat cooks slowly without smoke, or barbecue sauce mopping and sopping.

Not everyone has a grill, and when it is ten below zero, I don't much like using mine. So I tried cooking another batch of chicken in the oven at 300°F. I also slow cooked a beef brisket in the oven following the same technique. Cooked on the grill, the meat is moist with a rich browned coating. The oven-roasted version is equally good but not quite as browned. Chicken, pork, or beef, the meat tastes simply wonderful.

Feeding barbecue to three hundred Sunday school children is one thing, but one report of a July 4, 1839, Springfield "old fashioned barbecue" raised another question. During "a gigantic Whig party rally" for the campaign of William Henry Harrison, barbecue was served to fifteen thousand people. Even though these barbecue meats were not dripping with sauce, I did still wonder how all the people at these various events ate it. After all, there weren't disposable plates or paper napkins. Luckily, I found a detailed newspaper account of a July 4, 1858, barbecue Lincoln attended along with hundreds of Springfield residents who made the trip on a special train. The celebration was held in Jacksonville, just a few miles down the tracks from Springfield. Lincoln was one of the dignitaries on the speaker's platform, although apparently he did not make any remarks.

As reported in the *Daily Illinois State Journal*, after the conclusion of the remarks:

Stephen Dunlap then announced that some refreshment had been provided for the occasion and that the ladies would take their seats at the tables first, the gentlemen after. This request was not strictly adhered to, for in less than five minutes hundreds of men and boys were congratulating one another with chunks of bread and meat in both hands, quite sufficient to fill a hungry belly. It was an old fashioned barbeque, and of course, we did not hear of any cups and saucers, or plates and dishes being broken; nor of any knives or forks being lost or stolen. But we did see numbers of boys carrying off four pound loaves. There was not a great variety of provisions, but it was *substantial!*... Everybody seemed satisfied, even the ladies agreed that "fingers were made before forks," and the gentlemen, as well as boys, admitted that "half a loaf was better than none."

The reporter answered my eating etiquette question within his definition of an "old fashioned barbecue" where plates, dishes, and silverware were not heard of and the meat was eaten out of hand with chunks torn from large loaves of yeast bread that were one part plate, one part napkin, and one part meal.

Back at the 1858 Urbana event, Mr. Cunningham described Lincoln as eating a biscuit with his turkey leg, and he also said that the table was "filled with an abundance of barbecued food." I am inclined to take at least this part of his description literally. This, too, was a meal heavy on a variety of meats and some bread. Having equivocated on the meat part of the barbecue preparations, I was eager to dive into the bread half of the menu.

Period yeast breads are not all that much changed from today's. Even though the yeasts themselves and the wheat flour may be slightly different, there isn't a radical alteration in recipe, flavor, or texture for a good, homemade-style loaf. Biscuits, on the other hand, are a lesson in food history. As leavening methods evolved from yeast to baking soda, biscuits began to rise in popularity. Period cookbooks and magazine articles I looked at all had pretty much the same collection of biscuit recipes. And these biscuits are as different as different can be from the overly fluffed, smacked-from-a-refrigerated-tube type many of us fall back on to get dinner on the table fast.

I was surprised to see the word "biscuit" used to describe a small yeast roll in a couple of my references, but most of the recipes from the 1830s through the 1860s skip the yeast and provide lessons in making breads light either with layers of butter, beating the biscuit dough until it crackles, or by employing the magic combination of baking soda and sour milk.

I thought I would be able to pick a favorite. I couldn't. Each of the recipes I tested had an appeal. As to what these biscuits looked like, if I had been the cook making biscuits for any of these mass events, I would have pinched off pieces of dough, as suggested in one of the recipes, rather than rolling and cutting with a circle-shaped cutter. (I wrote about this delicious soured-milk recipe and method in Chapter 4.) We also don't have a clue whether these biscuits were baked in bakeries in town or tossed over a rekindled fire once the meats had been removed. Either is possible and both would be filling and good.

Now that I'd wandered through the pits and gridirons, cookbooks and journals, I'd pretty much made up my mind that the "old fashioned barbecues" were simply cooked, unsauced meats served with bread or biscuits. Still, burgoo was cooked at public gatherings in Lincoln's time.

Today it is cooked in backyards, at church fund-raisers, and at civic celebrations in huge cauldrons, simmering for hours, and stirred constantly, often with a long, two-by-four piece of lumber. Some say the name harkens back to a bulgur wheat dish cooked on sixteenth-century English sailing vessels. Others say the name is from an eighteenth-century American corruption of "bird stew" or "Brunswick stew." The trusty *Kentucky Housewife* from 1839 has an elegant recipe for "Boulli Soup" calling for chicken, ham, and a variety of vegetables all cooked separately, diced, and combined just before serving. Gallons of burgoo were supposedly made during the Civil War by a Lexington, Kentucky, French-born chef for the Confederate Raiders under the command of General John Hunt Morgan.

There are scores of references to burgoo in culinary history books and online. Most all of them repeat the recipe from *322 Old Dixie Recipes* published in 1939 claiming to be from the 1850s. It makes 1,200 gallons and the list of ingredients includes 600 pounds lean game on the bone; 200 pounds fat hens, plucked; 2,000 pounds potatoes, peeled and diced; 200 pounds onion, peeled and diced; 5 bushels cabbage, chopped; 60 pounds tomatoes, pureed; 24 pounds corn, cut from cob; salt and pepper to taste; and Worcestershire sauce by the pint.

Dan Beard, one of the founding leaders of the American Boy Scout movement, wrote a history of burgoo in his *American Boys' Handbook of Camp-lore and Woodcraft*, published in 1920. Beard was born in 1850 and lived much of his life in Kentucky. He interviewed old-timers, gathering information about pioneer life and Native American lore, and wrote and illustrated several classic books for youth sharing that wisdom. His take on burgoo presents it as a "come as you are and bring your meat with you" kind of event: "In Kentucky in the olden times the gentlemen were wont to go out in the morning and to the hunting while the negroes were keeping the caldrons boiling with the pork and other foundation material in them. After the gentlemen returned and the game was put into the caldron, the guests began to arrive and the stew was served late in the afternoon; each guest was supposed to come supplied with a tin cup and a spoon, the latter made from a fresh water mussel shell with a split stick for a handle. Thus provided they all sat around and partook of as many helpings as their hunger demanded."

Thanks to the wonder of Web searching, I found another, even earlier, first-person recollection of burgoo. Samuel Corbley grew up on an Indiana farm and witnessed an event where the cook was from Kentucky, lending credibility to the recipe:

> I think it was the spring of [18]43 that my father's neighbors proposed to kill all the squirrels [that were destroying the corn crop] around his farm and he would furnish the bread for a burgoo. A day was appointed and corn bread enough for a small army baked by my mother and the neighbor women. Three larger iron sugar kettles filled with water were hung up near a spring. Beverly Ballard, a Kentuckian, was appointed chief cook. The neighbors with rifles approached the farm from every direction and there was a continuous fusillade until 10 o'clock when, by agreement, the hunters met and threw down not less than two hundred squirrels. As they were skinned and washed they were handed over to the cook for boiling. There followed a feast. Soup was served in tin cups; squirrels were taken out whole with pointed sticks and corn pone was served with soup made hot with home-raised pepper.

Most interesting in this description is that "burgoo" is the name of the event, not just the food served, much the same as "barbecue." That is the frosting on the cake, to mix courses. A barbecue served pit- or gridiron-roasted meats with bread, and a burgoo was something very different. Both were and are mighty fine eating.

But wait, there's a second helping. The folks in Springfield decided to have their own Fourth of July celebration after all. On Monday the 5th, Lincoln, the guest of honor at a dinner held at 2:30 p.m. at the St. Nicholas hotel, "gave a toast to the assembled fire companies 'May they extinguish all the bad flames, but keep the flame of patriotism ever burning brightly in the hearts of the ladies.'"

SLOW-COOKED BARBECUE

• • • • • • •

You don't need a prepared barbecue sauce with meats cooked using this method. The molasses infuses the meat with a wonderful sweetness tempered by the black pepper and a hint of salt. This recipe uses smaller chicken thighs so the slow cooking is accomplished in an hour or two, depending on the size of the thighs, while keeping the flavor of a mid-1800s barbecue.

> **5** **pounds bone-in chicken thighs**
> **1** **teaspoon salt, divided**
> **1/2** **teaspoon freshly ground black pepper**
> **1/3** **cup light molasses**
> **1** **cup warm water**

Wash chicken thighs and pat dry, removing the skin if desired. Mix ½ teaspoon of the salt and the pepper. Sprinkle lightly over the chicken, then brush both sides with a light coating of molasses. Place in a single layer in large baking dish. Cover and refrigerate for at least an hour and up to overnight.

Preheat the oven to 300°F. Line a baking sheet with foil for easy cleanup. Place a wire cake rack on the baking sheet. Gently wipe the chicken pieces with a damp cloth to remove most of the molasses. Set the pieces on the rack.

Mix the remaining ½ teaspoon salt with 1 cup warm water. Baste the chicken with this salted water and roast, basting and turning about every 20 minutes until chicken is deliciously browned and the meat is well done. (You may cook these thighs on a grill over a low fire.) Baste, turn, and watch carefully as molasses has a tendency to burn. Overall cooking time will vary depending on the thickness of the pieces of meat. For the bone-in chicken thighs, allow about 1 hour.

Makes 6 to 8 servings

RE-CREATED FROM PERIOD SOURCES.

PEACH-AND-HONEY

· · · · · · ·

The "peach-and-honey" served at Thomas and Nancy Lincoln's wedding celebration may well have been an alcoholic beverage similar to this one from Miss Corson's Practical American Cookery and Household Management: *"A good winter drink is made by mixing together one tablespoonful of honey and a wineglassful of peach-brandy." This "serving suggestion" follows the recipe for making the brandy from 10 pounds of good peaches and 2 ½ gallons of 95 percent alcohol.*

ADAPTED FROM "PEACH AND HONEY," JULIET CORSON, *MISS CORSON'S PRACTICAL AMERICAN COOKERY AND HOUSEHOLD MANAGEMENT*, 1885.

SHORT BISCUITS

· · · · · · ·

This recipe resembles classic southern beaten biscuits, which are somewhat flat and like a thick, chewy cracker. Before baking soda and powders made their way into kitchens, beating the dough with a rolling pin or mallet as the dough was folded and turned incorporated air and lightness. Old books suggest "100 strokes"; others said it could take as long as a half hour before the dough "squeaks" with bubbles. This style of biscuit has been so popular through the years that inventors developed a wide range of laborsaving devices to help "break" the biscuits.

The butter in this recipe helps keep the biscuits tender. The type of dough made from cutting the cold butter into the flour is traditionally called "short." That's where the word "shortening" has its origin.

>   **2** **cups unbleached all-purpose flour,
>   plus extra for dusting**
>
> **1/2** **teaspoon salt**
>
>   **4** **tablespoons (1/2 stick) cold salted butter**
>
> **1/2** **cup very cold water**

Preheat the oven to 400°F. Lightly grease a baking sheet. Combine the flour and salt in a mixing bowl. Cut the butter into the dry ingredients with a pastry cutter or 2 knives until the mixture looks like uncooked oatmeal. Stir in the cold water to make a dough that is moist, but not sticky. You may need to add a bit more water or flour. Knead a few times until you have a cohesive ball of dough. Now beat the dickens out of it. The old beaten biscuit recipes say to beat "until it blisters or squeaks." Instead, I whirled the ball of dough in my food processor with the smooth-edged dough blade for about 4 minutes. It formed a smooth and almost glossy ball of dough that rolled out on a floured surface beautifully.

Roll the smooth dough out on a floured work surface to ½-inch thickness. Cut biscuits with a 1-inch cutter, flouring the cutter between biscuits. Transfer the biscuits to the prepared baking sheet. Prick top of each biscuit with a fork. Bake until light brown, about 12 to 15 minutes.

Makes 1 dozen biscuits

RE-CREATED FROM PERIOD SOURCES.

BARBECUE "FIXIN'S": Mrs. Bryan did offer some serving suggestions with her recipe for barbecued shoat. When we lived in Alabama for a while, we came to call such dishes "fixin's." *The Kentucky Housewife* described serving barbecue: "When it is well done serve it with a garnish ... squeeze over it a little lemon juice and accompany it with melted butter and wine, bread sauce, raw salad, slaugh or cucumbers and stewed fruit."

BREAD SAUCE

• • • • • • •

This wine-soaked bread packs a flavor wallop, cutting through the richness of dark barbecued meats of the time—turkey, beef, and mutton. A small serving is just enough.

> **2 cups fresh breadcrumbs, grated from a stale homemade-style loaf**
>
> **¹/₂ cup dried Zante currants**
>
> **³/₄ cup white wine**

Combine all ingredients in a small saucepan and simmer over very low heat until the wine has been completely absorbed by the bread and currants. Serve warm with barbecued pork.

Makes 6 to 8 servings

ADAPTED FROM "BREAD SAUCE," MRS. LETTICE BRYAN, *THE KENTUCKY HOUSEWIFE*, 1839.

CUCUMBER SALAD

• • • • • • •

A modicum of vinegar and lemon juice and a smattering of cayenne and ginger transform normally mild-mannered cucumbers into a snappy salad. Easy to make, this relish lasts for several days in the refrigerator. It is tasty alongside any meat, adds zest to vegetables, and can be mixed with mayonnaise for a sandwich spread or tartar sauce.

- 2 **large or 4 medium cucumbers**
- 1 **teaspoon salt**
- 10 **green onions, peeled and thinly sliced into rings**
- 3/4 **cup white or cider vinegar**
- **Juice of 1/2 lemon (2 to 3 tablespoons)**
- 1/8 **teaspoon ground cayenne pepper**
- 1/8 **teaspoon ground ginger**

Pare the cucumbers, cut in half, and remove the seeds. Chop into about a 1/2-inch dice. Place in a nonreactive bowl and mix with the salt. Let stand for at least 1 hour. You may keep the cucumbers salted down for about 4 hours at the most. Drain off the accumulated juices and rinse well under cold water. Add the sliced green onions to the cucumbers.

In a small saucepan, mix the vinegar, lemon juice, cayenne, and ginger. Heat to boiling and pour over the vegetables. Let stand for at least 3 hours before serving; overnight is better. Store in a covered container in the refrigerator for up to 4 days.

Makes 6 to 8 servings as a relish

ADAPTED FROM "CUCUMBER SALAD," *PRAIRIE FARMER*, JULY 1859.

8

"SALT FOR ICE CREAM"
SPRINGFIELD SCENES FROM DIARIES AND GROCERY LEDGERS

I have a distant and vague memory of the first time I visited Abraham Lincoln's home in Springfield, Illinois. I was nine years old and remember looking up and seeing a tall black hat hanging on a peg by the front door. The hallway seemed dark and narrow. Stairs to the second floor took up more room than the front-hall steps in my grandparents' house. Nanny and Pa's house was smaller. Their narrow stairs went up an outside wall with a window, and there was only one set of rooms on each floor. The Lincolns had parlors on either side of the central hall and several bedrooms upstairs.

Visiting the Lincolns' house, squished among grown-ups and crowded up to the protective barrier, I peered into rooms set up with old-fashioned furniture, books, and toys for the boys in the upstairs bedroom. I don't remember the kitchen. All in all it was a dissatisfying visit. The year before, our parents had taken us to Mount Vernon. Now, there was a house fit for a president of the United States. The rooms in George Washington's home were high ceilinged and grand. The lawn down to the river was fun to run across. The garden of hedges smelled different than any I'd been near. Lincoln's house smelled dry and stuffy, but at least it didn't burn my eyes the way the smoky and damp cabin rooms in New Salem Village had. We'd stopped at that state historic site on the same trip.

In the time since, I've read accounts of the events and lives in the Lincoln home written by neighbors, friends, and political guests. One comment runs through many of them: the Lincoln boys were never shushed and hardly disciplined. Both Abraham and Mary were indulgent parents. Abraham enjoyed spending time with his sons. Neighbor James Gourley told how Lincoln would walk out along the railway with his children, way out into the country talking and "explaining things." Another friend, Joseph Gillespie, reflected that Lincoln's children "literally ran over him and he was powerless to withstand their importunities." Gillespie said, "He was the most indulgent parent I ever knew."

I wanted to shake the "historic house cobwebs" out of my mind and find the ingredients to create a real sense of life in the Lincoln home. And I was pleased to find some of those ingredients the Lincolns bought during their years in Springfield listed on ledger pages from a couple of local stores. Abraham and Mary Lincoln purchased the house seventeen years before they left for the White House. They actually lived in the home for just fifteen years, as they rented it out while Lincoln served his one term in Congress.

I hadn't known too much about Mary Lincoln until I started this research. I had a vague awareness of the common characterizations in books, magazines, and movies that focused on Mary's shortcomings, easily suggesting the Lincolns' marriage was troubled. Now, after reading scores of first-person narratives from friends and relatives, I've come away with a more complete, complex understanding of Mary and of her life with Abraham. As Mary Lincoln's authoritative biographer Ruth Painter Randall concluded, in the home at Eighth and Jackson "there was love ... fun and playfulness, there was the joy of children."

Mary and Abraham knew each other extraordinarily well. Once, when she took him to task for being hours late for supper, he teased her back. Everyone had waited to eat. The chickens were overcooked; the rest of the dishes were cold. He said he was just "two minutes" late. She promptly corrected him, "two hours," and the family settled in to eat with good humor. That Mary's exuberant opinions and criticisms sometimes spilled into public view gave some Springfield folks cause to cluck their tongues in dismay at a nontraditional behavior and to write about it later.

In everything he did, Lincoln was "regularly irregular; that is he had no stated time for eating, not fixed time for going to bed, none for getting up." As frustrating as that would be, his long absences—riding the court circuit for weeks at a time or traveling to give political speeches—were harder on Mary. She became, essentially, a single mother, with little household help and no means of immediate contact with her traveling husband, whom she loved deeply, until he walked back in the door. She "often said [to neighbor James Gourley] if her husband had stayed at home as he ought to, that she would have loved him better."

During the 1950s, the Lincoln house volunteers displayed freshly baked bread on the kitchen's cast-iron stove. Visitors treated to that lived-in aroma must have built a layer of possibility onto the experience of walking on the same floors that Lincoln trod, looking out into his backyard, and sensing the wholeness of family life. I hoped to re-create some sense of their lives in my kitchen.

I began with the published recollections hoping to find mentions and even descriptions of food that I could use to build a vivid picture to connect with the specific purchases detailed in the ledgers. I sat with two sets of books open on my desk and my computer's desktop—remembrances of the Lincolns and period cookbooks. Later I took to my kitchen and began to cook.

I sorted through stories and recipes trying to match foods to events. Alas, for all the entertaining the Lincolns did during the winter session of the Illinois legislature and the rest of the year, few of their guests described exactly what they served. In recollections published years later, Donn Piant wrote that Mrs. Lincoln offered pie to her guests, but he didn't say what kind. In a speech twenty years after the Lincolns left Springfield, their friend Isaac Arnold said that Mrs. Lincoln's "table was famed for the excellence of many rare Kentucky dishes and in season it was loaded with venison, wild turkeys, prairie chickens, quail and other game, then abundant." In the 1890s Noah Brooks reported to journalist Ida Tarbell that Mrs. Lincoln served corned beef and cabbage during a supper he shared with the family in 1857.

Caroline Owsley Brown described Springfield society in general and calling among friends and neighbors on New Year's Day. Everyone was expected "to eat oysters, chicken-salad, drink coffee, put down a saucer of ice cream and cake and nibble a few bon-bons." Oranges, raisins, almonds, and white grapes also graced the table along with the fancy macaroon pyramids held together with spun sugar made by

Mr. Watson, the local confectioner, who had traveled to St. Louis to learn the trick of making them.

As to contemporaneous descriptions, Orville Hickman Browning, a lawyer from Quincy, spent the legislative seasons in Springfield and visited the town on other matters during the years. His diaries have some of the few contemporary descriptions of events. However, his entries are irritatingly short on details:

Monday Jan 19 1852 Delivered a lecture at 3rd Presbyterian Church for the benefit of the poor. After went to Mr. Lincoln's to supper. Thermometers ranged 19 to 23 below zero.

Thurs. July 22 1852 The warmest days of season. Mrs. B and self spent evening at Lincolns.

Feb. 5 1857 Thurs At night attended large & pleasant party at L[incoln].

Thurs. Feb 4, 1858 Called at Lincoln's.

Wed, Feb, 2 1859 At large party at L[incoln]'s. cloudy, foggy. Muddy, dismal day.

Thurs, June 9, 1859 Went to party at night at L[incoln].

Wed, Feb 1, 1860 After tea went to L[incoln] for an hour or two.

Thurs. Aug. 9, 1860 In forenoon called at L[incoln] and spent an hour with him, Mrs. Lincoln and Mrs. Judd.

Another diary from this period gives some sense of the social life Mary Lincoln had among her neighborhood and church friends. On January 1, 1851, Mrs. William Black began her diary with an entry "Took tea at Mrs. Lincoln's." Her third child, Samuel Dale, was born five days later. On February 11, she "spent the evening at Mrs. Lincoln['s]." She called on Mary with her daughter and the baby on February 26 and March 5, when she "spent the afternoon," as she did again on March 10. Little Samuel died on March 24, 1851, a little more than a year after the Lincolns' four-year-old son Eddy had died. Mrs. Black spent much of the next month in mourning and at prayer. On May 3, "Mrs. Lincoln insisted on our coming over in the evening—we did so and found Dr. Smith [the Presbyterian minister] there he prayed with us before leaving." Two days later Mrs. Black once again spent an afternoon with Mary after she "sent a second message for me" to come. Mary must have been feeling low or ill with Abraham out of town on the court circuit in Urbana and Danville, as the next day Mrs. Black wrote, "called on Mrs. Lincoln—found her in better spirits."

After the 1860 presidential nomination and then the election, the Lincolns received political and journalist guests from around the country who wrote their impressions of the Springfield home. Carl Schurz of the *New York Evening Post* described what he called the "modest frame house" with Lincoln standing at the rear of the front parlor: "tall and ungainly in his black suit of apparently new, but ill-fitting clothes, his long tawny neck emerging gauntly from his turn-down collar, his melancholy eyes sunken deep in his haggard face." The reporter had kind words about Mrs. Lincoln: "Whatever awkwardness may be ascribed to her husband there is none of it in her. She converses with freedom and grace, and is thoroughly *au fait* in all the little amenities of society." Frequent mentions were made of her distinguished family, sophisticated education, ladylike courtesy, ability to speak French fluently, their son's enrollment in Harvard, and her membership in the Presbyterian Church.

Many years later, Phillip Wheelock Ayers captured evocative scenes when he asked his mother (then Miss Wheelock) to tell him about her time living as a neighbor: "Mr. Lincoln would help freely in the kitchen. On coming from his office he would take off his coat, put on a large blue apron, and do whatever was needed. At such times the family used sometimes to eat in the kitchen. Happening in, my mother was once invited to share a kitchen luncheon and vividly remembers Mr. Lincoln's large figure against the kitchen wall. To him the matter of food was always one of comparative indifference.... In the numerous social gatherings at Mr. Lincoln's house, Mrs. Lincoln was a very great help to her husband. A lady of refined tastes with a large social experience, and with considerable political insight she carried the social end of the campaign admirably. She used frequently to ask my mother to assist in passing the refreshments, a service gladly rendered."

Lincoln's law partner, William Herndon, told how sometimes Abraham would bring what we might consider a carryout breakfast into the office. He would "have in his hands a piece of cheese, or bologna sausage, and a few crackers, bought by the way." Period recipes for bologna sausage are different from the common, bland childhood lunchmeat we buy today. Looking at the recipes in a number of period cookbooks and considering the large number of Germans living in Springfield, it makes sense to me that Lincoln's "bologna" was more like the richly seasoned and dryer-textured "Lebanon bologna."

All the words written about Lincoln, and these descriptions were the closest I could come to food in the Lincolns' daily lives? Although we know Mary Lincoln owned a copy of Miss Leslie's *Directions for Cookery in Its Various Branches*, 1845 edition, we don't have her copy with its grease- and batter-spattered pages. Mary did not leave a collection of handwritten recipes tied up with a ribbon. There isn't a diary with highlights of the guests, discussions, and foods served. None of the women who helped in her kitchen shared comprehensive menus.

The charge accounts the Lincolns kept at local stores provide an important clue to the foods they prepared and served. Mary bought a set of cups and saucers and two preserve dishes in January 1845 from Irwin's store. The family also purchased "gun powder tea" and some sugar. From Bunn's store in 1849, the Lincolns bought a half dozen tumblers, candles, sugar, and at the end of September, a gallon of vinegar. We have the extraordinary good luck to have the account books of C. M. Smith's dry goods store listing the purchases the Lincoln family made in 1859. (Smith was married to Mary's sister Ann.) Records of a few other Springfield stores have Lincoln purchases, too, but Smith's is a year's worth of records that can be matched with events in the family's life.

That's the good news: these records give a day-by-day accounting of the things the Lincoln family purchased. The not-so-good news: this store is just one of many stores in town where the Lincolns shopped. We know Abraham wrote checks to settle accounts with several dry goods stores, and the family probably paid cash at other merchants. Certainly the newspaper ads of the day are filled with stores selling their goods "at the lowest price for cash."

With such incomplete information we must take care when making assumptions. Without knowing all of the Lincolns' purchases, we can only draw a limited picture. This is the story those purchases tell: the groceries available in Springfield were some of the fanciest available in the country, and by 1859 Mary Lincoln was an experienced and sophisticated cook—or she had one in her employment. She bought cream of tartar and baking soda in the proper proportion to make tender cakes and biscuits at a time when most cookbook recipes primarily leavened with saleratus or the interaction of soda and sour milk. Twice in January the family bought "Cooper Isinglass" and "red gelatin." These items are certainly the ingredients for some kind of fancy molded dessert such as Charlotte Russe or blancmange. Corneau & Diller's store advertised "red, pink and white gelatine" in 1856 Springfield newspapers at a time when articles in national ladies magazines still suggested adding spinach to make desserts green, using cochineal dissolved in a little brandy to color them red and saffron for bright yellow.

Sugar and syrups are among the most common and regular Lincoln family purchases from the Smith store. In the winter months, the family purchased a gallon of syrup every ten to twelve days. I'm pretty sure this is a plain syrup, a by-product of sugar processing, what the British call golden syrup and similar to table syrup enjoyed in the South today. Just the perfect thing to pour over pancakes or biscuits. Although a gallon sounds like a lot, I did some quick calculations. For the six people living in the house (Abraham, Mary, the three boys, and a live-in household helper), it works out to a quarter of a cup a day. Kids I know could easily pour that much on their flapjacks.

The Lincolns bought regular amounts of sugar, too, about eleven pounds every two weeks. Again, some quick culinary calculations bring this amount into perspective. Eleven pounds of sugar measure out to twenty-two cups, or less than two cups a day. Most recipes for cookies, muffins, or cakes call for at least a cup. A cup of sugar also measures out to sixteen tablespoons. Three adults who put a teaspoon of sugar in a cup of morning coffee would consume a cup of sugar in the two weeks. Two teaspoons per cup or two cups per person would double the amount. So each person in the Lincoln household was consuming about a quarter of a cup of sugar a day. That still sounds like a lot, but I looked at the current national data from the U.S. Department of Agriculture. In 2008 the average per capita sweetener consumption in the United States was 136 pounds, or about three-quarters of a cup a day—three times the amount the Lincolns used.

The Lincolns broke this regular pattern in July 1859, when they bought thirty-three pounds of sugar between July 23 and 25, prime fruit season in Illinois. Strawberries were probably finished, but raspberries, peaches, and plums would have been in full season, as were the summer-bearing apple trees the Lincolns had in their yard. Combine the sugar purchase with the half gallon of vinegar the week before, and it seems obvious that someone in the household is putting up fruit preserves, jams, jelly, or pickles, as they probably did in 1849 when they bought a gallon of vinegar from Bunn's store.

One purchase can even be linked to a specific event. They bought "salt for ice cream" on June 9, the same evening Quincy lawyer Orville Browning made a diary entry, "Went to a party at Lincoln's at night."

Homemade ice cream was popular. Reviewing a new "patent family ice cream maker" for its readers, *Godey's Lady's Book* noted that ice-cream making was especially important to ladies "residing outside the cities." By the mid-1850s hand-crank ice-cream machines were readily available, and recipes appeared in cookbooks and magazines, so homemakers could easily convert simple ingredients into family treats or entertaining delights. As the review explained: "H. B. Masser's Patent Family Ice-Cream Freezer ... is a most excellent and useful labor-saving invention enabling a mere novice to make ice-cream equal to the best.... It is said to take less than one-half the usual quantity of ice and salt, and a child can perform the operation."

Other Lincoln family purchases are more broadly suggestive of social life in Springfield, where the Ladies' Aid church functions played an important role. Ask any midwestern woman about her community, and you'll hear all about the various fund-raising and social efforts involving food. From 1950s potlucks and cakewalks to twenty-first-century women's club charity sales of nuts for holiday baking, women and food are the engine of social progress.

Life in Springfield in the 1850s was the same. Caroline Owsley Brown recalled those days in an article about Springfield before the Civil War. "I have heard it said the foundation walls of old St. Paul's ... were built on cakes baked by Mrs. Ninian Edwards, Mrs. William Pope, Mrs. John S. Bradford and Mrs. Antrim Campbell and other good church women. Mrs. Edwards was especially noted as a cook and the fame of her chicken salad spread far and wide.... A church supper with Mrs. Edwards's chicken salad, Mrs. Pope's beaten biscuit, and Mrs. Campbell's pound cake was an event to call all society together.... Presbyterians, Methodists, Baptists, ... all flocked to eat in the service of a good cause."

In the first week of October 1859, Lincoln was out of town all week attending both political events and circuit courts. When Mary bought ten pounds of sugar, three-and-one-half pounds of pulverized sugar, and the same amount of crushed sugar along with nutmeg, lemon extract, and a dozen eggs, cakes for a First Presbyterian social seems the logical conclusion. Similarly, the thirty-two pounds of "Java coffee" Smith's dray delivered on March 28 could have been for another church function. The price was just over sixteen cents a pound, about half the price the Lincolns usually paid for their regular three- or five-pound purchases. Was this a bulk discount, or reflecting a charitable discount by Mr. Smith?

The family purchased other baking ingredients—cinnamon, nutmeg, almond extract—as well as ordinary groceries, such as coffee, tea, potatoes, and turnips, from Smith's store in 1859. And that's about all we know, hints, but no real information.

My period cookbooks had the opposite problem: too many possibilities. The ones I have stacked at the side of my desk are filled with hundreds of recipes. A few keystrokes and mouse clicks, and a Google Books search makes it so temptingly easy to find specific recipes and ingredients from even more period cookbooks and magazines. Time to make a decision. Even though the Springfield stores did have a wide variety of foods available, I held my choices against the words of Harriet Hanks, the daughter of Dennis Hanks, Lincoln's cousin. She lived with the family during their first years in the Springfield house and said of Mary that she was "very economical. So much so that by some she might have been pronounced stingy."

I selected four recipes: a children's treat, an easily prepared family dinner, a simple dish for a late-night supper, and sausage we know Lincoln served to political guests. As you can see from these descriptions, some of the dishes can be linked directly to life in the house, while others are simply logical choices. As I made nutmeg doughnuts, mutton harico, beef cakes, and December sausages, the aromas filled my kitchen and later, still lingering, wafted up the stairs embracing me as I sat at my desk. When we ate these dishes, their appearance, textures, and flavors added to the details of the recipes themselves and built layers onto my understanding of the period when the Lincoln family lived in Springfield in a home that was, by all accounts, filled with life.

NUTMEG DOUGHNUTS

I had to begin with the children. They filled the home and the Lincolns' lives. Mrs. Lincoln was said to have had cookies or doughnuts on hand for her sons' playmates.

When I saw the name of this 1856 recipe for a nutmeg-flavored doughnut leavened with cream of tartar and baking soda, I knew it was just the thing. Store records show the family bought quantities of nutmegs on more than one occasion. Mary Lincoln could have made "Extempore Doughnuts" at the drop of a mixing spoon. They mix up and cook much faster than cookies, and hungry children would have gobbled them up by the hands full.

Of course, the recipe was short on directions. The only important clue was to "cut them like Yankee nuts." Other doughnut recipes of the time do describe cutting the dough into diamonds "with a jagging iron" or a knife. No one knows exactly when the doughnut became a ring rather than a diamond. In the middle of the nineteenth century, the only treat shaped that way is a cookie, a jumble (as I discussed in Chapter 5, page 86), made by joining the ends of a strip of dough into a circle. The clue in the name "doughnuts" suggests a small treat with a nut-like shape made out of dough.

These doughnuts were "extempore" all right. It took me no more than fifteen minutes to make up the dough and fry them in a bit of fat, much faster than the era's typical yeast-raised doughnuts. The spicy nutmeg smell wafting on the sweetness of crispy fried dough called hungry children in for these inch-square treats. Worked on my husband, too.

I can picture the Lincoln boys careening through the backyard, dashing from the barn shared by the horse, Old Bob, the cow the family kept for milk, and countless cats. The boys roamed around the neighborhood with friends all about the same ages as Robert born in 1843, Willie in 1850, and Tad in 1853—John and Frank Roll; Isaac Diller; Henry Remann; Johnny Kaine; Fred, Jess, and Lincoln Dubois; Charlie Melvin; and the Sprigg, Wallace, and Wheelock children, too. I can just imagine some of the children ducking through the bottom sash of the floor-length, double-hung dining room window to shortcut their friends, who came in through either of the two kitchen doors. Fido, the family's yellow mixed-breed dog, was doubtless chasing them about and begging for crumbs.

When the Lincolns left for the White House, Fido was adopted by John Roll, the son of Lincoln's carpenter and friend, who lived just down Eighth Street. The instructions for the dog's life in his new home shed light on the everyday events in the Lincoln household. Fido was indulged as another "child" in the family. He was never tied up alone in the backyard; was let inside whenever he scratched at the door; and was never scolded for wet, muddy, or dusty paws. At mealtime Fido was allowed to wander around the table, just as he had in the Lincoln dining room, so everyone could give him bits of food from their plates.

MUTTON HARICO

We've all been there—Dinner Crunch Time. Demands of work schedules, children's activities, social responsibilities, and entertainment opportunities collide with the need to get the family fed. As I looked in my copy of Miss Leslie's book for a family dinner recipe to test, it occurred to me that life in the Lincoln household was probably not that different from the chaos that happened in our home kitchen when our children were growing up.

For the Lincoln family at Eighth and Jackson, Robert studied at a local preparatory school and the younger boys were in school as well. Though some evenings were spent quietly with Abraham stretched out on the floor, in his habitual manner, reading aloud, the Lincolns had plenty of obligations and opportunities. A number of sources tell how Mrs. Lincoln entertained friends from the neighborhood and her church circle in the afternoons. The Lincolns invited friends over in the evenings, too. Along with Mrs. Black's diary entries, a surviving invitation handwritten by Mary suggests a pattern of easy entertaining: "My dear Mrs. Brayman If your health will admit of venturing out, in such damp weather, we would be much pleased to have you, Mr. B- & the young ladies come round, this evening about seven & pass a social evening also any friend you may have with you, Yours truly."

State capital Springfield was filled with possibilities for entertainment and education. Newspapers and Orville Browning's diary tell of lectures by famous people—Ralph Waldo Emerson was in town for two nights in 1853—as well as presentations by local ministers and other experts. Lincoln repeated his lecture on "Discoveries and Inventions" he had presented in Jacksonville, Illinois, ten days earlier to a hometown audience in the Concert Hall on February 21, 1859. Visiting luminaries performed on the Springfield stage. Browning attended a concert "by Halberg pianist—Vieuxtemps violinist & Perring & Madam D'Augri vocalists." He found the music "too artistic for my taste." There are notices of church socials, fund-raisers, and political meetings. And the circus came to town several times. The 1856 ad for Sands, Nathans & Co.'s American Circus filled a full column in the Springfield paper. They promised acrobats and gymnasts and six "wonderful performing elephants," "Mazeppa the wild horse of Tarary," and five clowns, all for "fifty cents admission, children under nine, half price."

The pressures of the Lincolns' active household must have called for a set of "go-to" meals. Although the ingredients at hand and cooking equipment may have been different between my modern kitchen and the Lincolns', the underlying get-the-meal-on-the-table strategy was the same: a main dish the cook could prepare quickly and that would essentially cook itself until the family was ready to eat, whenever they got around to it.

The two dishes we know were served at the Lincolns' dinner table— chicken fricassee and corned beef—don't fit the bill. The 1850s fricassee is a delicious dish of chicken that is simmered in a thickened cream sauce, seasoned with nutmeg, salt, and pepper. Even though it doesn't take too long to cook, fricassee cream sauce does require close supervision. Period corned beef recipes call for the meat to be soaked in water, rinsed, and soaked again before cooking slowly for hours without added seasonings. Not a lot of preparation, but a long time cooking.

Miss Eliza Leslie came to my rescue, and probably that of many a mid-nineteenth-century homemaker, with her recipe for "Mutton Harico." Here was the 1840s version of—if not fast food—food that could be prepared efficiently in the middle of a busy home. Her directions speak to the situation: brown the cheap and thinly cut mutton chops and put them in a pot with a bit of water and some seasonings to simmer on the back of the stove or cook in a pot hanging over a low open-hearth fire. Half an hour, or even an hour later, all the cook has to do is quickly dice up four vegetables so they will cook fast, toss them in, and simmer for another half hour or until the family is ready to eat. That's it, dinner cooking practically by itself, in a flexible time frame. This dish fits perfectly with the vision I have of the Lincolns in the kitchen.

I'm imagining a time when Mary didn't have a live-in household helper, a relative or hired Irish, Portuguese, or Illinois farm girl staying in the Lincoln home to help with chores and cooking. Mariah Vance, a free woman of color, sometimes came by to help with the laundry and cooking, but on this day Mary would be at home alone with her own family. Only the Lincolns would occupy the kitchen.

Picture Abraham walking in after a day at his law office. He would have put on the blue apron and, between them, Abraham and Mary would get the mutton harico on the stove. First, Lincoln might have taken up the "porcelain steak maul" sold at McCabe's store as "just the thing to make old and tough steaks young and tender." While the meat was cooking, Abraham would have gone to the neighboring open-commons grazing area to fetch home their cow for evening milking and then stabled the animal for the night. This may be the day that when he got there, as Henry C. Whitney related to William Herndon, Lincoln didn't recognize his animal. He explained his solution to this neighbor: "She was a new cow and I didn't know her thoroughly but I did know her calf. I could not pick out my cow from the other cows & so I waited a little while & my calf went to a cow and sucked her & in that way I knew my own cow."

After milking the cow, Abraham would have brought the gallon or so of milk in to serve with dinner, or put it by in the pantry room across the open porch from the kitchen. Meanwhile, Mary would have gone down to the basement root cellar to fetch up onions, carrots, and turnips. We know they liked turnips as they bought a peck in December 1859 for eight cents. She then would have put the diced vegetables into the pot and perhaps asked one of the boys to set the dining room table while she tidied the front parlor for evening guests. She might even have mixed up batter for corn cakes, a dish Harriet Hanks reported Lincoln said that he "could eat as fast as two women could make them."

When it was time to eat, the family sat in the dining room and ate while sharing events of the day. They would finish the meal with a quick cleanup—dishes washed in water from the backyard pump heated on the stove while the family was eating.

As to the kitchen luncheon Miss Wheelock described sharing, that would have been a simple meal as well. In the era, "luncheon" was a fancy word for a kind of anything goes using-up of the previous evening's leftovers. As described in an 1856 *Godey's Lady's Book* article: "The dishes generally served for luncheon are remains of cold meat neatly trimmed and garnished; cold game, hashed or plain. Hashes of all descriptions; curries; minced meats; cold pies, savory, fruit or plain; plainly cooked cutlets, steaks and chops, omelettes, bacon, eggs, devil[ed dishes] and grilled pones, potatoes, sweetmeats, butter, cheese, salad pickles. In fact, almost anything does for lunch, whether fish, flesh, fowl, pastry, vegetables or fruit."

BEEF CAKES

This next dish is one I envision Lincoln making for himself after a long day's ride back home. We know that when Abraham Lincoln was in Springfield, working on cases out of his law office near the corner of Fifth and Washington, he would often do the grocery marketing first thing in the morning. Springfield resident Page Eaton described how on winter mornings Lincoln "could be seen wending his way to market with a basket on his arm and a boy at his side." He would stop at the butcher or baker and then take the groceries, and the boy, home before heading into the office at nine o'clock.

However, Lincoln spent days and even weeks away from his cheerful, hectic home at Eighth and Jackson as he rode around the state attending political events or working the circuit court. He stayed in inns and boardinghouses, traveling sometimes on trains, riverboats, stages, or in his own buggy, and sometimes just riding Old Bob. Neighbor John B. Weber described Lincoln late one night perhaps as he returned home from defending clients in distant towns: "I heard an ax ring out at Lincoln's. Saw Mr. Lincoln in his Shirt Sleeves Cutting wood—I suppose to cook his supper with."

There were taverns, hotels, and restaurants in Springfield where he might have stopped off to eat—the city directories for the three years at the end of the decade list at least twenty-one restaurants and saloons—but I imagine Lincoln would have eaten at home as often as possible. A simple supper such as beef cakes, made from food in the pantry storeroom, would have been just the ticket. He would have settled Old Bob safely in the barn and walked through the yard, taking off his coat and picking up the ax.

Chopping up a bit of kindling and wood for a small fire was the first step. Then a look in the freestanding kitchen cupboard, although it might have been locked with the key safely kept by Mary to prevent young boys from eating up all the breads, jams, or even pies stored there. There was also the pantry, a room across the open porch from the kitchen lined with shelves holding the pounds of raw ingredients in sacks, firkins, and barrels. Baskets of carrots, turnips, parsnips, and other sturdy vegetables would keep well in the root cellar under the house. The Lincolns may even have had a container for ice. Local merchant H. C. Myers & Co. grandly announced its availability for sale:

"Ice! Ice! Our friends will please hear that we have filled three ice houses for this season and hope to receive their orders."

Small stoneware crocks could have held potted meats and cheeses. Eggs and leftovers could be kept either in the kitchen or in the pantry.

Cooking up a quick supper would have been second nature for Lincoln beginning with his youthful experiences after his mother died. Back then he easily could have helped his sister prepare their meals, or fended for himself. We know that during his time on the Mississippi heading to New Orleans and in the army he cooked for himself and for his companions. I can see him cooking for friends in Springfield, too. When Lincoln first came to town he shared above-the-store rooms with merchant

Joshua Speed. The two became fast friends. With storytelling Lincoln in residence, Speed's store became a "popular evening gathering place for the young men of the town." Lincoln may have simply made popcorn or even cooked more substantial meals in the hearth from time to time for what must have been a rollicking group.

And, even though Lincoln may have seemed more occupied with the conversation than with the victuals, when he was served food at boarding tables or in the middle of family gatherings, there is evidence that he did care about what he ate. Fellow lawyer Charles S. Zane related an evening in a circuit town inn. There was a "large basket of apples in the sitting room and we were invited to help ourselves. Mr. Lincoln was a great eater of apples. He said to me once that a man should eat and drink only that which is conducive to his own health. 'Apples,' he said, 'agree with me.'"

Many is the time we've come home from a trip, grabbed a few eggs, and made an omelet. Lincoln could have done the same and whipped up what Miss Leslie calls an "Omelette Natural." But fancy takes me to a couple of recipes for simple dishes made with leftover meats, like the beef cakes, that are as delicious and satisfying as they are easy to make. Perhaps he ate a solitary meal mulling over his travels and the cases he had tried. Perhaps the chopping awakened Robert, and he could have come down from his bedroom at the back of the house. Mary could have heard the backyard or kitchen noises and come down as well. The two of them then joined Lincoln, sitting about in the kitchen, listening to him tell tales of his adventures in the courtroom or on the road as he ate his simple supper of meat and bread.

DECEMBER SAUSAGES

Now here is a dish we know was served in the Lincoln home, and we even have a narrative of the meal thanks to New York newspaper editor and political activist Thurlow Weed. In farm country, hogs are frequently slaughtered in late fall. Pieces of meat and bits of fat too small to be pickled or smoked are put to good use as fresh sausage.

As the rich and spicy smells of freshly made sausage filled my kitchen, I could fully understand Thurlow Weed's comment: "If I have an especial fondness for any particular luxury, it manifests itself in a remarkable way when properly-made December sausages are placed before me." In addition to his appreciation for sausage, Weed, the editor of the Albany, New York, *Evening Journal*, valued the way food could help illuminate a story. I was delighted to make sausage from the period and read his story.

Weed paid his second visit to Lincoln in December 1860. The two had first met in New England during the 1848 presidential campaign when Lincoln called upon Weed and they then called upon Millard Fillmore, Whig candidate for vice president. In the 1860 campaign Weed had actively supported Lincoln's chief competitor, William Seward, for the presidential nomination. After Lincoln's success at the Republican Convention held at the Chicago Wigwam in May, Weed called upon Lincoln in Springfield on his way home to New York. Weed left ready to "go to work with a will" for Lincoln's election as he wrote, "the interview had inspired me with confidence in his capacity and integrity."

Lincoln asked Weed to return in December after winning the election, to help him plan his cabinet. Ultimately, it would take until the eve of the March 4, 1861, inauguration to complete the task, but the December meetings in Lincoln's home were a good start. Among others, Lincoln sought the counsel of Leonard Swett and Judge David Davis, colleagues from his circuit-riding days who had been active in his political campaigns since his election to the U.S. House of Representatives in 1846. For two days, the men began meeting at breakfast and continued through the evening, eating at the residence as Lincoln considered the local hotel foods not suitable.

Weed described the meeting in his autobiography:

Mr. Lincoln remarked, smiling, that he supposed I had had some experience in cabinet-making; that he had a job on hand, and as he had never learned the trade, he was disposed to avail himself of the suggestions of friends. Taking up his figure, I replied, "that though never a boss cabinet-maker, I had as a journeyman been occasionally consulted about State cabinets...."

Mr. Lincoln observed that "the making of a cabinet, now that he had it to do, was by no means as easy as he has supposed...."

In this way the conversation being alternately earnest and playful, two days passed very pleasantly.... I wish it were possible to give, in Mr. Lincoln's amusing but quaint manner, the many stories, anecdotes, and witticisms with which he interlarded and enlivened what with almost any of his predecessors in the high office of President would have been a grave, dry consultation.

As you'll see, we know Mrs. Lincoln served sausage at their breakfasts. Menus from Miss Leslie's cookbook for hearty "Autumn and Winter Breakfasts" provide some suggestions for the other foods she may have served. They included white or sweet potatoes, mashed, baked, or broiled; biscuits; griddle cakes or toast; eggs in omelets or poached; and even "small hominy, boiled," what we call "grits."

We don't know much about the appetites of Swett and Davis, but evidently Weed was a man who enjoyed good food. Weed also recounted an anecdote of Lincoln's about food that dramatized the balancing act inherent in their goal of selecting a cabinet that would come to include Lincoln's rivals for the office, men from all regions of the country, and even some, if not from the restlessly dissatisfied South, at least from the border states. Conscious of the risks inherent from hurt feelings and jealous responses, Lincoln recounted a story powerfully demonstrating the possible irreparable harm to reputation caused by insult or from ill feelings.

According to Weed:

While at breakfast, Judge Davis, noticing that, after having been bountifully served with sausage, Oliver Twist like, I wanted some more, said, "You seem fond of our Illinois sausages." To which I responded affirmatively, adding that I thought the article might be relied on where pork was cheaper than dogs. "That," said Mr. Lincoln, "reminds me of what occurred down at Joliet, where a popular grocer supplied all of the villagers with sausages. One Saturday evening when his grocery was filled with customers, for whom he and his boys were busily engaged in weighing sausages, a neighbor with whom he had had a violent quarrel that day, came into the grocery, made his way up to the counter, holding two enormous dead cats by the tail, which he deliberately threw on to the counter, saying, 'This makes seven to-day. I'll call around Monday, and get my money for them.'"

Others did take note of and publish more of Lincoln's stories. The two that follow, like Thurlow Weed's recollection, also center on foods. In the first story Lincoln used the anecdote of an Illinois prairie-chicken hunter's unusual methods to demonstrate the idea that every man has his own particular ways of doing things. And even if these ways seem strange, the idea is to do whatever you can to accomplish your goals. Lincoln recounted this story:

That reminds me of a fellow out in Illinois who had better luck than any one in the neighborhood. He had a rusty old gun no other man dared handle; he never seemed to exert himself, being listless and indifferent when out after game, but he always brought home all the chickens he could carry, while some of the others, with their finely trained dogs and latest improved fowling-pieces came home alone.

"How is it, Jake?" inquired one sportsman, who, although a good shot, and knew something about hunting, was often unfortunate, "that you never come home without a lot of birds?"

Jake grinned, half closed his eyes, and replied; "Oh, I don't know that there's anything queer about it. I jes' go and git 'em."

"Yes, I know you do; but how do you do it?"

"You'll tell."

"Honest, Jake, I won't say a word. Hope to drop dead this minute."

"Never say nothing, if I tell you?"

"Cross my heart three times."

This reassured Jake, who put his mouth close to the ear of his eager questioner, and said, in a whisper:

"All you got to do is jes' to hide in a fence corner an' make a noise like a turnip. That'll bring the chickens every time."

In the second tale, an apple, one food for which Lincoln expressed a particular fondness, played a key role in his story told to a petitioner at the height of the Civil War.

During a public reception, a farmer from one of the border counties in Virginia told the president that the Union soldiers, in passing his farm, had helped themselves not only to hay, but to his horse, and he hoped the president would urge the proper officer to consider his claim immediately. Putting the man's request into the larger war perspective, Lincoln said:

This reminds me of an old acquaintance. "Jack" Chase a lumberman on the Illinois [River], a steady sober man, and the best raftsman on the river. It was quite a trick to take the logs on the rapids; but he was skillful with a raft and always kept her straight in the channel. Finally a steamboat was put on and "Jack" was made captain of her. He always used to take the wheel, going through the rapids. One day when the boat was plunging and wallowing along the boiling current, and "Jack's" utmost vigilance was being exercised to keep her in the narrow channel, a boy pulled his coat-tail and hailed him with:

"Say, Mister Captain! I wish you would just stop your boat a minute—I've lost my apple overboard!"

STRAWBERRY ICE CREAM

· · · · · · ·

It's hard to find a more refreshing treat than period fruit ice creams. Made from half fruit and juice and half milk and cream, the dessert is like a beautiful blending of Italian ice and rich ice cream. The icy fruit melts quickly on your tongue while the creamy half lingers flavorfully. But don't analyze it too much. Just spoon out a dish and enjoy.

4 cups sliced strawberries
1/2 cup sugar, or more to taste
2 cups cream
1 cup milk

Mix the berries and sugar and let stand, stirring from time to time, until the sugar dissolves. Then mash the berries and measure. You should have 3 cups. Stir in the cream and milk. Freeze according to the directions on your ice-cream maker. If you don't have an ice-cream freezer, pour the mixture into a shallow metal bowl and put it in your freezer. Beat occasionally with an electric mixer once the ice cream begins to freeze.

Makes about 1 ½ quarts

ADAPTED FROM PERIOD SOURCES.

CHICKEN SALAD

· · · · · · ·

Up until the 1950s, unless you lived on a farm, chicken was reserved for special occasions. In Springfield a century earlier, much of the fowl enjoyed by the Lincolns and their neighbors was wild game, brought in by local hunters and sold in the stores or served in restaurants. Chicken salad would have been a rare treat. The usual homemade dressing can be considered a culinary cousin to the not-yet-widely-available mayonnaise. The sharply flavored mixture uses a hard-boiled egg yolk and mustard as the binders. Equal amounts of chicken and lettuce or celery make a particularly light, yet satisfying dish.

- **1 hard-boiled egg yolk (dice the white for garnish)**
- **1 teaspoon Dijon mustard**
- **1 tablespoon olive oil**
- **1/4 cup white vinegar**
- **2 cups diced cooked chicken**
- **1 cup finely diced celery**
- **1/2 teaspoon salt, more or less to taste**
- **1/2 teaspoon freshly ground black pepper, more or less to taste**
- **1 cup shredded firm lettuce, such as romaine**

Make the dressing by mashing together egg yolk, mustard, and olive oil until smooth in a small bowl. Gradually stir in vinegar with a fork or whisk until the dressing is smoothly blended. Then toss the dressing with chicken and celery. Taste and add salt and pepper as desired. Chill salad. Toss with the shredded lettuce right before serving. Garnish with diced egg white.

Makes 4 cups of chicken salad, for eight 1/2-cup servings

ADAPTED FROM PERIOD SOURCES.

NUTMEG DOUGHNUTS

•••••••

Occasionally called "Yankee nuts," nineteenth-century doughnuts were frequently small and diamond shaped. Cream of tartar gives these easy-to-make treats a lightness, while the hint of nutmeg brings just enough spice. It is the kind of treat Tad and Willie Lincoln could have enjoyed by the handful.

> **2** **cups unbleached all-purpose flour, plus extra for rolling**
> **1/2** **cup sugar**
> **1** **teaspoon cream of tartar**
> **1/2** **teaspoon baking soda**
> **1/4** **teaspoon freshly grated or ground nutmeg**
> **2** **tablespoons cold butter**
> **1/2** **cup milk**
> **Shortening, vegetable oil, or lard for frying**

Combine the flour, sugar, cream of tartar, baking soda, and nutmeg. Cut the cold butter into the dry ingredients until it disappears. Quickly stir in milk and mix with fork. Once the dough begins to form, knead it with your hands into a smooth dough. You may need up to a table-spoon additional milk, added 1 teaspoon at a time.

Roll out the dough to ½-inch thickness on a lightly floured surface. Cut into rectangles or diamonds, about 1 x 2 inches, with a jagging iron or sharp knife. A jagging iron is a rotary cutting tool with a zigzag cutting edge.

TO FRY: If you have a deep-fat fryer follow its directions. Or carefully heat about 2 inches of fat in a deep frying pan with sides at least 3 inches tall. Heat the fat to 365°F. Carefully place a few doughnuts at a time in the hot fat. Fry until golden, turning them over as they rise to the top and the bottoms brown. Drain on paper towels.

Makes about 3 dozen small doughnuts

ADAPTED FROM "EXTEMPORE DOUGHNUTS," ELIZABETH NICHOLSON, *WHAT I KNOW, OR, HINTS ON THE DAILY DUTIES OF A HOUSEKEEPER*, 1855.

MUTTON HARICO

• • • • • • •

This recipe appears in several mid-nineteenth-century cookbooks. Left to simmer on the back of a wood-burning stove, it was a meal that practically cooked itself. In today's kitchens, the slow cooker can fill in once the meat is browned. It is also a dish that improves when the flavors have a chance to mellow, so make enough for two meals.

- **1** teaspoon dried marjoram
- **1** teaspoon dried thyme leaves
- **¼** teaspoon ground cloves
- **¼** teaspoon ground mace
- **½** teaspoon salt, more or less to taste
- **½** teaspoon freshly ground black pepper
- **4** lamb steaks, about 1 ½ pounds total (you can substitute pork chops or beef)
- **2** tablespoons butter or olive oil
  Boiling water to cover the meat, about 1 to 2 cups
- **1** cup carrots (cut into ½-inch dice)
- **1** cup turnips (cut into ½-inch dice)
- **1** medium onion, sliced
- **1** cup thinly sliced celery

Mix herbs, spices, salt, and pepper together and rub into the meat. Heat 2 tablespoons of the butter or oil in a large, heavy frying pan with a lid. Brown the lamb on both sides and cover with boiling water. Cover, lower the heat, and simmer for about a half hour. Add carrots, turnips, onion, and celery, then cover again and continue simmering until tender, about another half hour. Harico can stay barely simmering on the stove, flavors melding, for as long as an hour. Serve the meat surrounded by the vegetables. Mashed potatoes would be a good side dish or, for a particularly hectic dinnertime, just have bread and butter.

Makes 4 servings

ADAPTED FROM "MUTTON HARICO," MISS ELIZA LESLIE,
DIRECTIONS FOR COOKERY IN ITS VARIOUS BRANCHES, 1845.

BEEF CAKES

• • • • • • •

A variation on the classic shepherd's pie, the potato-topped beef cakes can be made quickly from leftovers. You could just take the meat and place it between slices of bread, top with pickles and onions, and that would be fine. But with just a little more effort with the knife and frying pan, you have a tasty, fulsome meal, ready in less than 15 minutes. Although it may seem like a lot to mix equal portions of bread and meat, once cooked, a hungry eater really couldn't tell the patty is not entirely beef.

1	cup minced roast beef
1	cup fresh breadcrumbs, grated from stale homemade-style bread
1	tablespoon grated onion
1	tablespoon minced parsley
1	tablespoon pickle relish or pickle juice, optional
2	tablespoons minced raw bacon, optional
1/4	teaspoon salt, more or less to taste
1/4	teaspoon freshly ground black pepper, more or less to taste
2 to 4	tablespoons melted beef drippings or butter
2	tablespoons butter, for frying cakes
1	cup leftover mashed potatoes, at room temperature

In a mixing bowl, blend together beef, breadcrumbs, onion, parsley, pickle relish, bacon, salt, and pepper. Add enough melted beef drippings or butter to moisten and hold the mixture together. Form into 4 cakes. Heat 2 tablespoons butter in a medium frying pan over medium heat and brown the cakes on one side. Carefully turn and top with mashed potatoes. Lower heat, cover the pan, and cook until browned on other side and the potatoes are warmed through, about 5 to 10 minutes.

Makes 4 meat cakes, to serve 4

ADAPTED FROM "BEEF CAKES," MISS ELIZA LESLIE,
MISS LESLIE'S DIRECTIONS FOR COOKERY IN ITS VARIOUS BRANCHES, 1845.

DECEMBER SAUSAGES

• • • • • • •

Late fall and early winter were typically the time when farmers' hogs that had been roaming free in the woods, or city dwellers' animals that had had the run of the town streets, were herded to the butchery. Some of the meat was smoked, some was pickled in barrels with salt brine, and a bit of it was eaten fresh. This uncured "December sausage" is highly spiced with just black pepper and dry sage. Cook the patties slowly and enjoy the delicious aroma. Prepare them within a day of making the meat, or freeze. The original recipe called for a 50:50 ratio of fat to lean ground pork. It also called for 2 tablespoons of salt. The adapted quantities provide much of the flavor of the original but are a bit healthier.

3 **tablespoons ground sage**
1 **tablespoon freshly ground black pepper**
1 **tablespoon salt**
2 ½ **pounds ground pork (75 percent lean/25 percent fat)**

Combine the seasonings and mix thoroughly into the pork. Form into small patties and cook slowly in a skillet, or on a barbecue grill, until browned on both sides and cooked to an internal temperature of 160°F, as measured by an instant-read meat thermometer. As they cook, the sausages will release a lot of fat, so if you are cooking on a grill, take care that the dripping fat does not catch fire. You could also stuff this mixture into casings and make link sausage if you prefer.

TIP FOR SUCCESS: One easy way to mix the spices into the meat is to cover your work surface with foil or plastic wrap. Pat the ground pork out into a rectangle about ½ inch thick. Sprinkle the mixed seasonings evenly over the pork. Slice off 1-inch strips and mix with your hands until the spices are evenly distributed. When all the sections have been mixed, combine them into a single large mixture.

Makes about 2 dozen small patties, to serve 6 to 8

ADAPTED FROM "SAUSAGE," *PRAIRIE FARMER*, DECEMBER 1859.

CORNED BEEF AND CABBAGE

• • • • • • •

Corning was primarily a meat-preservation technique. Leading Lincoln-era cookbook authors Sarah Rutledge, Mary Randolph, Eliza Leslie, and others present directions for keeping beef by rubbing it well with salt and putting it in a cool place. Some of the recipes call for the addition of saltpeter or molasses. When it was time to cook the meat, the goal was to remove as much of the saltiness as possible by slowly simmering it in a lot of water.

1 3- to 4-pound corned beef round or brisket
1 medium head green cabbage

Remove the beef from the package and rinse well. Do not use the seasoning packet if one is enclosed. Put the beef in a large, heavy stewpot and cover with at least 6 inches of cold water. Cook over medium heat until the liquid just comes to a boil, then lower the heat and simmer, skimming off any foam that rises to the top. Cook until the meat is fork tender, about 30 to 45 minutes per pound. About a half hour before the beef is finished, cut the cabbage into 8 wedges. Arrange the wedges around the top of the simmering beef, cover with a lid, and continue simmering until the cabbage is tender, about 15 to 20 minutes. To serve, let the beef stand in a platter, covered to keep warm, for about 10 minutes. Then slice across the grain into very thin pieces.

Makes 3 to 4 servings per pound of meat

RE-CREATED FROM PERIOD SOURCES.

WHITE FRICASSEE OF CHICKEN

• • • • • • •

Period cookbooks offered recipes for two kinds of chicken fricassee. For the "brown" fricassee version, the cook fries the chicken first and then adds the cream sauce. I think this "white" version, where the chicken is seasoned and simmered in cream or milk, is more like the comforting home cooking Mary knew would tempt Abraham's appetite. Some recipes call for adding a strip of lemon peel or mushrooms to the simmering sauce. This delicious recipe, adapted from the cookbook Mary Lincoln owned, is simply chicken, cream, and a few seasonings.

- 1 whole chicken, 3–4 pounds
- 1/8 teaspoon salt
- 1/2 teaspoon freshly ground black pepper
- 1/2 teaspoon freshly grated nutmeg
- 1/4 teaspoon ground mace
- 2 teaspoons fresh marjoram or 1/2 teaspoon dry leaves
- 1 1/2 cups cream, half-and-half, or milk
- 3 tablespoons butter
- 3 tablespoons flour
- 1/4 cup thinly sliced ham, optional

Remove the skin from the chicken and discard. Cut the chicken into 8 pieces roughly the same size. Cut each leg joint to separate into thigh and drumstick pieces. Working with the knife close to the ribcage on the first side, cut breast and wing in 1 piece from the ribcage. Slice the breast into 2 pieces, leaving some breast meat attached to the wing end so the portions are of roughly equal size. Repeat with the other side.

Combine the seasonings and sprinkle on the meat. This is a flavorful mix; you may want to use only half, reserving the rest for another time, or to incorporate into the sauce. Place the chicken pieces in a large frying pan with a lid. Pour the cream, milk, or mixture of both over the chicken, lifting the pieces to make sure it flows under the chicken as well.

Cook over medium heat until the liquid begins to bubble, then lower the heat and cover. Simmer until the chicken is fork tender, about 30 minutes. Remove the chicken to a platter and keep warm. Mash the butter and flour together with a fork and add, bit by bit, to the pan liquids. Continue to cook, stirring frequently, until this sauce thickens. Return the chicken to the sauce. Place thinly sliced ham around the edges of the platter, if desired.

Serve with biscuits. The biscuits on page 68 are particularly delicious.

TIP FOR SUCCESS: I find using all cream makes for an overly rich sauce. I usually mix a cup of cream with skim milk, but any combination will work.

Makes 6 to 8 servings

ADAPTED FROM "FRICASSEED CHICKENS," MISS ELIZA LESLIE,
DIRECTIONS FOR COOKERY IN ITS VARIOUS BRANCHES, 1845.

9

PICCALILLI
OF FRUITS AND VEGETABLES

Piccalilli is a mixture of all kinds of pickles ... small cucumbers, button onions, small bunches of cauliflowers, carrots cut in fanciful shape, radishes, bean-pods, Cayenne-pods, ginger, olives, grapes, limes, strips of horse-radish, etc., etc.... It is an excellent accompaniment to many highly-seasoned dishes; if well put up, it will keep for years.

—MRS. BLISS OF BOSTON
THE PRACTICAL COOK BOOK, 1850

As I read through biography and historical narratives, I noted incidental descriptions of Abraham Lincoln's encounters with fruits or vegetables. Indiana neighbors remembered the fruits growing wild near Griggstown along with the vegetable crops that would have been raised on the Lincoln farm.

Reports from Springfield, Illinois, are less complete than those from Lincoln's youth. Springfield store records show the Lincolns purchased turnips. Alas, the White House information is just as sparse. There aren't any cook's notes or menus, but visitors did report that Lincoln enjoyed spinach, cabbage, and baked beans.

Lincoln did recognize the economic importance of vegetables as he used a farmer's crop of vegetables and fruit in an argument he developed on the impact of tariffs shortly before he took his seat in Congress in December 1847. He named "radishes, cabbages, Irish and sweet potatoes, cucumbers, water-melons and musk-melons, plumbs [*sic*], pears, peaches, apples and the like; all these are good things" which could be traded with a neighbor producing iron tools.

Then there is the statement of his friend and law partner, William Herndon. In describing Lincoln's eating habits Herndon wrote, "He loved best the vegetable world generally ... and especially did he love apples." Not only did Abraham Lincoln eat his vegetables, he loved them "best." There's a sentence to warm the heart of any mother trying to encourage her children to eat healthfully. "Eat your veggies and you can be president, not only president, but perhaps the best one the country ever had."

As my father would have said, these incidental descriptions "didn't amount to a hill of beans." There isn't enough to build a narrative chapter, but I do think these side dishes provide interesting clues. They, and the research that rounds them out, present insights into culinary and gardening practices in the middle of the nineteenth century and add a bit of relish to the Lincoln story.

We'll start with the fruits. Early midwestern settlers delighted in discovering locally growing fruits: wild plums, pawpaws, strawberries, and other berries. Newcomers to an area often planted fruit trees. Thomas Lincoln planted peach trees in Kentucky and peach and apple trees in Indiana. The practice continued as communities grew. Springfield newspapers and agricultural journals were filled with nursery advertisements listing dozens of apple, peach, and other fruit trees and bushes. Abraham and Mary had a pair of apple trees growing in their yard. Apparently it was some kind of late-summer or early-fall apple, maybe a Jonathan, a popular variety from the 1850s we still enjoy today.

Springfield's winter climate limits the availability of homegrown fruits, but all was not lost for those who wanted fresh fruit in the fall, winter, and early spring. The November 1856 Springfield newspapers bragged of fresh and exotic produce as they offered customers tastes from far away and out of season. Meyers's grocery declared: "Just received by express, 200 pineapples, fresh and in splendid order. Two barrels sweet oranges from New York." Mr. John Snelling's advertisement provided the full transportation details of his fresh citrus: "Just arrived from Havana via New York lemons and oranges."

A short report in the St. Louis *Valley Farmer*, quoting the *New York Times*, explained why Meyers emphasized the quality of his fruit. "Pineapples furnish the palate with perpetual illusion. You lay hold of one, and its delicious flavor promises great pleasure to the palate, but it seems to fail of meeting the demand exactly, and though you stuff with the woody fibrous body of the [pine]apple till your judgment forbids any more, you still experience a craving for it. They are not worth what they cost to common folk."

Whereas Mr. Meyers asserted that his pineapples were fit to eat, period cookbooks offered ways for unfortunate shoppers to transform the "illusionary" ones into jams and jelly. I have to confess that I've used nineteenth-century recipes from time to time to make pineapple preserves with modern pineapples that were less than perfect.

Preserving foods was an important part of nineteenth-century homemaking. Every period cookbook had a chapter or two or three covering the basics of jams, jellies, pickles, including the end-of-season garden relish piccalilli, and "store sauces," ketchups and other bottled concoctions that cooked down pecks of vegetables into pints of sauce ready to add savory and sharp flavors to winter meals.

Francis & Barrell's store advertised that they had "new pattern preserving glass jars" for sale on September 10, 1858, just in time for the ladies of Springfield to put up fruit for winter and prepare their entries for the state fair. In a remarkable achievement, or endorsement of the jar's effectiveness, Mrs. Simeon Francis, the merchant's wife, took away first place for her peaches, currants, gooseberries, strawberries, apples, crab apples, pears, and red raspberry jelly.

Homemakers were not the only ones to preserve seasonal goodness. By the middle of the nineteenth century, commercial canneries were "putting up" jellies, jams, fruits, and even some vegetables, in glass jars sealed with corks or in cans with soldered-on lids for sale across the country and around the world. As early as 1847, tomatoes were commercially canned in Pennsylvania.

In June of 1858, Lavely's Springfield market advertised some of those canned tomatoes along with currant jelly and "peaches and fresh strawberries in cans." Back in January 1858, Wilson & Curry's market had offered "Tomato sauce—something new" and "Apple butter—a choice article."

Uncanned fresh fruits arrived in Springfield, too, shipped in on the railroad before local crops ripened. Stores offered peaches, pears, quinces, strawberries, blackberries, cherries, and damsons (plums). On

July 5, 1856, Francis & Barrell store shouted: "TOMATOES just received from the South. Lovers of these delicious and esculent foods will find a large supply."

Fruits may have been available "fresh in cans" throughout the year, but vegetables, with the exception of tomatoes, were largely home- and locally grown. The Lincolns had ready access to the freshest locally grown fruits and vegetables. The Market Square at Ninth and Market Streets, just two blocks from their home, was filled from spring through fall with fresh farm produce.

As to the Lincolns' own backyard garden efforts, recollections differ. Certainly, Lincoln knew how to grow vegetables; he was raised on a hardworking farm. Back in Indiana settlement days, maintaining a substantial vegetable garden would have been essential. Now, in the mid-1850s, for the Lincolns and many Springfield residents, gardening was more of a hobby. Magazines of the day promoted gardening not so much as an essential source of foods but as a useful enterprise for city dwellers. "No professional man, nor any other one confined to in-door employment, who has the command of a rod of ground, ought to be without the exercise and the exertion required for keeping in good order a small garden.... A garden, in fact, is essential to the health, comfort, and well-being of the mechanic and day-laborer; and it may also be said to be essential to the comfort and enjoyment of individuals of every class."

I know something of gardening in the Midwest. I grew up in Indiana, went to college in Iowa, and then moved, over the course of thirty years, to Indiana, Illinois, Iowa, and Minnesota, with Virginia, New Jersey, and Alabama in between. So, although I'm familiar with the culture of the South, the Deep South, and the East Coast, I've always been a midwesterner.

There is a midwestern worldview, one that in Lincoln's time was categorized as "western," because, of course, Illinois and the Mississippi River were the western edge of the United States, California notwithstanding. Then, as now, crops and food were an important part of the midwestern psyche. We can't escape their influence. We're surrounded by millions of acres of bounty-filled fields. And most of us, given half a chance, will grow some kind of vegetable garden, even if it's only a cherry tomato plant in a pot on the back deck.

Back in Lincoln's backyard, neighbor James Gourley told Herndon, "He once—for a year or so—had a garden and worked in it." But Lincoln's niece, Harriet Hanks Chapman, said that he "never knew him to make a garden, but no one loved flowers more." Mary Lincoln's sister Frances Todd Wallace noted that Mary wasn't much of a gardener either, reporting, "She never made a garden, at least not more than once or twice." Whether or not the Lincoln family raised their own vegetables, the now-huge persimmon tree still standing in the neighbor's yard to the north of the Lincolns' home must have witnessed gardens growing all around the neighborhood with plenty of produce to share.

Businessman and newspaper editor Simeon Francis provided a valuable window into Springfield's gardening culture. In addition to Francis and Burrell's store, Francis operated a nursery selling a variety of fruit trees and other landscaping trees and shrubs. He sold flower and garden seeds, too. His March 1859 ad in *Illinois Farmer* offers a mostly alphabetical listing of popular vegetables. Beginning with beans and ending with tomatoes, the list (see next page) provides insights into popular crops for Springfield farmers and backyard gardeners.

Just look at it—seven different kinds of snap beans, seven kinds of cabbage, and five of pole beans. To satisfy early fresh vegetable hunger, there are four kinds of cucumbers and radishes, and three varieties of lettuce. And then there are the two kinds of rhubarb. One of the earliest crops up in the spring, rhubarb is one part vegetable—you eat the stalks; one part fruit—you cook those stalks with sugar like a dessert; and one part tonic—my grandmother used to say it was "just the thing to clean your blood." The *Tennessee Farmer* was more precise: "No head of a family who regards the health of his offspring should be without some dozen plants in his garden as in them he will have a sure and certain curative for [digestive diseases]."

To keep the tables filled with delicious vegetables during the winter, there are the root crops perfect to put down in the root cellar next to the bushels of potatoes. Carrots, turnips, parsnips, beets, and onions all keep well sheltered under a blanket of straw.

Nineteenth-century gardening and cookbooks suggest letting the flavors of these varieties shine on their own. The recipes and preparation instructions in book after book are mostly simple: boil and top with a bit

VEGETABLE SEEDS
Offered for Sale in Springfield—March 1859

BEANS FOR SNAP: Valentine, early Newington, thousand-to-one, early Mohawk, early China white, cranberry bush, Royal white bush

POLE BEANS: London horticultural cranberry, Siva, Lima, Red cranberry, Indian chief

CABBAGE: Early Wakefield, early York, early sugar loaf, premium flat Dutch, large American drumhead, drumhead, Kohl Rabi

CAULIFLOWER: Early London

CORN: Early red cob dwarf, mammoth sweet, Smith's early white

BEETS: Early blood turnip, long blood, red mangle, English sugar beet, white sugar

CUCUMBERS: Short green early, long London, long turkey, gherkins

CELERY: Solid white, crystal white, solid red

CRESS: Curled double, broad leaf

CARROTS: Common yellow, early born, blood red, Belgium yellow

EGG PLANT: Early long purple

KALE

LETTUCE: Ice cube, green drumhead, early white

MELONS: Cantaloupe, pine apple, nutmeg, green citron, large yellow cantaloupe

WATER MELON: Mountain sprout, Long Island, Ice cream, black Spanish, citron melon, Nasturtium

OKRA: Short and long green

ONIONS: Large red, early red, Danver's yellow, yellow silver skin, white Portugal

PEPPERS: Large bull, large squash, Spanish, cherry, small cayenne

PEAS: Early Comstock dwarf, Bishop's long pod, champion of England, dwarf Prussian, Prince Albert

PUMPKINS: Large yellow field

PARSNIP: Long sweet

PARSLEY: Double curled, Myatt's garnishing

RHUBARB: Mitchell's early, Hyatt's Victoria

SPINACH

SQUASHES (WINTER): winter crookneck, Hubbard's winter

SQUASHES (SUMMER): Karly crookneck bush, early yellow bush

TURNIP

TOMATOES: Large red, red cherry, yellow

RADISHES: Early red turnip, early long, red short top, long black radish

SALSIFY: White

of butter. But there are a few intriguing ideas. I discovered a simple way to season Brussels sprouts with vinegar, butter, and nutmeg. Eggplant is fried, and its taste explained as "nearer to that of a very nice fried oyster than, perhaps, any other plant. Lettuce is described as an agreeable salad, but also as a "useful ingredient in soups." Homemakers cooked cucumbers, too. As for tomatoes, although in her 1860 cookbook Mrs. Putnam does offer a recipe for "tomatoes raw," dressing the slices with pepper, salt, and vinegar, it appears most tomatoes were cooked rather than sliced. There are recipes for baked tomatoes, tomatoes sliced on tarts, stewed for soups and sauces, and preserved for winter use like ketchup. The edition of Miss Eliza Leslie's cookbook owned by Mary Lincoln notes, "Tomatoes require long cooking, otherwise they will have a raw taste, that to most persons is unpleasant."

Though the recipes for cooking all kinds of vegetables may be simple, the varieties of the vegetables themselves were not. The market for native American-grown seeds was slow to develop. Through the middle of the nineteenth century, seed sellers trumpeted their stock of imported seeds. According to an 1840 Rochester Seed Company advertisement, "The present stock of imported seeds is very extensive; they were selected with great care among the best growers in England and Scotland.... The stock of American seeds is also very large." Even in the 1850s, some advertisers still described their stock as coming from England or France.

But many seedmen were developing and promoting plants that would thrive in the American climate. Scores of new seed varieties listed in the U.S. Patent Office report demonstrated American innovation. We can easily enjoy one of these varieties today. The winter Hubbard squash comes to market every fall. In an advertisement in the April 1860 issue of *American Agriculturalist*, J. H. Gregory staked his claim to speak to the nature of the squash: "Having given the Hubbard squash its name and having been the first to introduce it to the public notice." He promoted its virtues in his own advertisement for its seed. "It is the sweetest, richest, driest of all winter squashes."

The 1854 *Farmer's Dictionary* gives some clues to the value of some of these American-cultured vegetables and fruits: "Cauliflower—an improved cabbage, the flowers of which form a mass of great delicacy. Early white, late white and purple." "Melons—the best varieties are Skillman's netted, green-fleshed citron, green-fleshed nutmeg ... and pineapple." And the "Tomato—much used as a vegetable, preserve and pickle. Seed sown in a hot bed in March and plants set out in May."

And, as Simeon Francis's ad suggested, beans were an important food of amazing variety. I'm used to growing green "snap" beans where the bean we eat is just the pod with the small, immature seed inside. I've grown lima beans, too, where we ate just the bean seeds and not the pod. We've picked them fresh, or let them dry so that I could cook them baked-bean style in the winter. Many of the beans grown in Springfield gardens did double duty, some enjoyed as fresh green "snap" beans, some left to mature for use as dried beans, as these nineteenth-century descriptions of some of Francis's varieties demonstrate:

> *Early Mohawk* pods are pale green, long and flat. *Early China* excellent variety for both snaps and shelled beans, green and dry. Seeds white with bright red eye and round oval shape *Early Valentine* snaps only having round fleshy pods which remain a long time brittle and tender. *Thousand-to-One* late round-podded variety. *Royal White* pods long and rather flat, excellent green and equal to any in a dry state. *Horticultural Cranberry* used both in the pod and shelled, pods striped with red, medium-sized oval bean light red and cream color speckled. *Indian Chief* best of all poles beans for cooking in the pods which are tender and delicious when the beans are fully grown. *Newington Early* and prolific long slender pods.

Some of these heritage varieties, once nearly crowded from culture, are available now from organizations and companies that specialize in seed saving and nurturing. I've found several of these historical Springfield varieties by simply doing a Web search for the name of the plant.

I tried growing a few varieties this past drought-stricken, travel-filled summer. Melons, beets, and Hubbard squash failed, but I managed to harvest a few tasty yellow crookneck squash after a clever gardening neighbor told me how to thwart the squash borers by burying the vine every few inches. Freshly pulled white Belgian carrots filled the kitchen with a rich, sweet, and earthy aroma before they were cooked. While the squash and carrots were more flavorful than modern varieties, pole beans were an education in heritage eating. Simeon Francis's descriptions of bean production were bountifully proved even in my somewhat neglected garden. The McCaslin and Kentucky Wonder beans filled the pods much earlier and faster than the skinny almost non-seedy green snap beans I'm used to. I cooked the bumpy pods, and we enjoyed a meaty texture and rich taste in the same mouthful with the green bean flavors. Served with a bit of butter and a dash of vinegar, they were wonderful.

At the end of the summer, I left beans to dry on the vine so we could try these varieties in winter soups. An early killing freeze sent me out to the garden to pluck the pods before they froze on the vine. Some were close enough to finish drying on the counter. Most had just passed beyond the snap bean phase. I popped the beans out of their leathery pods and tossed the pods away. Then I cooked the beans like lima beans. Most tasty. From one planting of beans, I ended up with three kinds of meals. I will definitely plant these again.

Some of the heritage seed companies offer historic beans ready for cooking, so you don't have to wait to grow your own. As a testament to this shortcut, I have a lovely five-pound bag of cranberry beans sitting in my pantry. The baked beans made from them following Miss Leslie's method are simply delicious, although I will admit to adding the traditional "Boston baked bean" spoon of molasses. As the lightly peppered beans, salt pork, and water to generously cover sat all afternoon in the oven simmering in my mother's old bean pot, the kitchen filled with their earthy smell.

We do have an image of President Lincoln eating baked beans. Dr. Henry M. Pierce and his nephew called at the White House. They were shown into a room and discovered President Lincoln "eating a plate of Boston baked beans" for breakfast. This was not an uncommon breakfast during the era. Many period cookbooks suggest hearty breakfast fare in their sample menus and include baked beans among them. Mrs. Bliss wrote in her cookbook, "Baked beans having stood a day or two, are very good warmed over. In some parts of New England they are considered indispensable at a Sunday breakfast."

Like beans, cabbage is another key crop with many uses. Of course it is good fresh and it keeps nicely in the root cellar well into the winter. Transformed by the German traditional, salt-cured recipe for sauerkraut, it keeps even longer. The Lincolns' German neighbors may well have shared some of this homemade kraut to round out one of the family's favorite dishes, corned beef.

Even if the Lincolns didn't raise a vegetable garden, they did have apples. And something had to be done with them. Famously frugal Mary Lincoln would have seen to it that they were not wasted. There are a lot of uses for sweet early apples like Jonathans. They make fine pies and sauce. But two trees could produce a lot of apples. When excess fruit is the challenge, recipes that convert the most fruit into the smallest amount for easy storage work well.

It seems to me that a traditional apple butter would be the perfect way to preserve the Lincoln apples. Still, I can't see Mary Lincoln actually doing the "putting up." With three young boys about the house, all the sewing and mending she did, not to mention entertaining, she had enough to keep her busy. Making apple butter takes several hours of watchful stirring. It makes much more sense to let live-in or daytime help take charge of preserving. Or maybe Mary would have split the harvest with Mariah Vance, the free woman of color who worked on and off in the Lincoln household for years. Vance could have made the apple butter at home and brought back the Lincolns' share.

Most period apple butter recipes cook the apples in cider. Miss Leslie offers an apple butter recipe "without cider," an essential for the Lincolns' crop, as cider would not be plentiful when these first-of-the-season apples were ripe. Her recipe is huge, calling for eight bushels of apples and gallons of water and molasses. With all of those apples, of course, the apple butter would take a good while to cook. Miss Leslie specified eighteen hours! This kind of recipe also requires a huge cast-iron kettle cooking away on a backyard fire—and close attention, stirring the apples as they cook down and thicken. I decided to make a much smaller batch and let my slow cooker do the scorch-free simmering. I did a few quick calculations, basing them on a forty-two-pound weight for a bushel of apples and reducing the other ingredients in proportion. Two pounds of apples cook down to a couple pints of very nice apple butter, and it only took six hours!

PICCALILLI

• • • • • •

*This recipe takes advantage of pre-pickled vegetables as the basis for
the layering of the exotic "Indian" flavors. The earliest recipes in the
1830s called for cooking the raw vegetables in the seasoned brine, drying them, and then covering them with cold vinegar. By the 1850s,
cooks discovered that the delightful mixture of "white and green pickles" could be made by steeping already pickled vegetables in the new
flavored solution.*

    2 (16-ounce) jars pickled mixed vegetables
    1 teaspoon salt
    1 tablespoon dry mustard
    1/2 tablespoon ground ginger
    3/4 teaspoon freshly ground black pepper
    3/4 teaspoon ground allspice
    1/2 teaspoon ground turmeric
    2 cups white wine vinegar

Drain the mixed vegetables, put into a nonreactive, heatproof container, such as a stainless steel pot, and set aside. Wash the pickled
vegetable jars in hot water and set aside. Combine the dry seasonings
in a small saucepan. Gradually add the vinegar, stirring to dissolve the
spices. Bring to a boil over medium heat and boil for 1 minute. Pour
the vinegar mixture over the vegetables. Stir from time to time as they
cool. Put vegetables back in their jars, add the spiced vinegar to cover,
and store in the refrigerator for the flavors to mellow, about 2 days.
Piccalilli will keep in the refrigerator for up to 2 weeks.

Makes 2 pints

ADAPTED FROM PERIOD SOURCES.

PINEAPPLE PRESERVES

• • • • • • •

Fresh and canned pineapples were sold in the Midwest by the 1850s. Homemakers who wanted to have these hospitality-famed fruits available year-round could use this simple technique for preserving the fruit in a jam-like spread. These preserves are easy to make. Just make sure you keep the heat moderate and stir frequently. The only other caution: make sure you use a pot that is four times larger than the volume of juices. They bubble up quickly as they get to the gelling point.

A medium pineapple weighs about 3 ½ pounds; a trimmed pineapple weighs about 1 ½ pounds. A cup of white sugar weighs a half pound.

**1   pineapple, peeled, cored, and sliced
    with any "eyes" removed
    Sugar equal in weight to the trimmed pineapple**

In a food processor or bowl to capture the juices, chop pineapple into ¼-inch pieces. Combine the sugar and pineapple and let stand for a half hour, stirring to dissolve the sugar. Pour the juices into a large, heavy nonreactive saucepan. Simmer until the juices have reached the gelling point, about 10 minutes. To test, spoon some hot juice onto a chilled saucer. Return the saucer to the fridge for a minute. Then look at the jelly; if it wrinkles when you push it from the side and seems tender firm, it's time to add the chopped pineapple to the cooking liquid.

Add the pineapple to the saucepan and simmer, stirring frequently, until fruit is cooked and the juices are thickened, about another 10 minutes. Preserves may be stored in the refrigerator for up to a month or in the freezer for up to 6 months. See pages 160-61 for home-canning directions.

TIP FOR SUCCESS: If you don't have a kitchen scale to weigh the pineapple to determine the amount of sugar, don't despair. Most grocery stores sell peeled and cored pineapples in the produce department. Weigh it on the self-serve scales and you'll be in business.

Makes two 2-pint jars of preserved pineapple

ADAPTED FROM PERIOD SOURCES.

CUCUMBER CATSUP

• • • • • • •

During the nineteenth century, homemakers made ketchup out of just about anything they could find in the garden or at the grocer's. Everything from lemons to walnuts to mushrooms joined cucumbers, and finally tomatoes, as produce they chopped, simmered, and strained. This cucumber catsup is a tasty accompaniment for chicken, fish, or pork dishes.

3 **large cucumbers (about 2 pounds), peeled, seeded, and grated**

1 **small onion, peeled and minced**

1 **tablespoon salt**

2 ½ **teaspoons freshly ground black pepper**

1 ½ **cups white vinegar**

Mix the cucumbers and onions with salt. Put the vegetables into a cheesecloth-lined colander and let stand for 1 hour. Pour out drained juices and gently squeeze the vegetable mixture until dry. If you want to reduce the salt content, you may rinse off the vegetable mixture before you squeeze it dry.

Mix the salted vegetables, pepper, and vinegar in a heavy 3- to 4-quart pot. Cook gently until the mixture is hot and has turned somewhat yellow, about 5 to 10 minutes. Process with an immersion blender. (Or cool and then carefully process in a food processor or regular blender until smooth.) Return the puree to the pot and simmer until thick, about 20 minutes, stirring to prevent sticking as it reduces and thickens. Pour into clean, sterilized jars and seal. Keeps for a month in the refrigerator. Recipe may be doubled and the catsup may be canned, following the directions on pages 160-61, or frozen.

Makes about 2 cups

ADAPTED FROM "CUCUMBER CATSUP," *PRAIRIE FARMER*, AUGUST 1854.

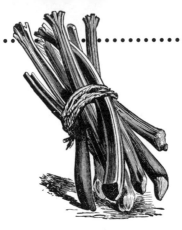

RHUBARB SPRING TONIC

• • • • • • •

Most of the rhubarb recipes in period sources are essentially the same as our modern rhubarb sauces and pies. However, this tonic deliciously sums up some of the thinking about the refreshing essence of rhubarb, the best thing to get your system back up and humming after sluggish winter doldrums.

> **4 cups sliced rhubarb**
> **6 cups water**
> **¹/₄ to ¹/₂ cup sugar, depending on taste**
> **Peel from 1 lemon, sliced thin**

Combine the rhubarb, water, and sugar in a large, heavy saucepan. Cook over medium heat, stirring from time to time until the rhubarb breaks down, about 10 minutes. Cool.

Line a colander with several layers of damp cheesecloth and place it over a large bowl. Strain the liquid from the rhubarb solids, discarding them. Pour the rhubarb tonic into a jar or pitcher, add the lemon peel, and serve chilled in small glasses.

Makes about twelve 4-ounce servings

ADAPTED FROM "SPRING FRUIT SHERBET," MRS. N. K. M. LEE,
THE COOK'S OWN BOOK, AND HOUSEKEEPER'S REGISTER, 1842.

TOMATO KETCHUP

• • • • • • •

Cloves, two kinds of pepper, and cider vinegar combine to make a significantly spicy ketchup that stands up to the robust flavors of barbecue and grass-fed or free-range meats. I've given a range for the spices. Start off with the lesser amount, cook a bit, and taste. You may add more if you like.

- **4 cups peeled and seeded fresh tomatoes, or one 28-ounce can of crushed no-salt-added tomatoes**
- **1 tablespoon salt**
- **1 to 3 teaspoons ground cloves**
- **1 to 2 teaspoons freshly ground black pepper**
- **1 to 2 teaspoons freshly grated or ground nutmeg**
- **¼ teaspoon cayenne pepper**
- **1 cup white or cider vinegar**

Chop the tomatoes into chunks and mix them with the salt. Set aside in a cool place (or refrigerate) overnight. Drain off the accumulated juices and reserve for another purpose. Rinse the tomatoes if you want to remove the excess salt.

Process the tomatoes in a food processor or blender. If you are using canned tomatoes, start here. Put the tomatoes in a 3- to 4-quart heavy nonreactive pot. Stir in spices and vinegar. Cook until thick over medium heat, stirring frequently so the mixture doesn't scald. Ketchup will keep in the refrigerator for up to a month. It may be frozen, or you may can the ketchup following the directions on pages 160–61.

Makes three or four 8-ounce jars

ADAPTED FROM "TOMATO KETCHUP,"
PRAIRIE FARMER, AUGUST 1858.

PUTTING UP PRESERVES AND PICKLING: Back in Mary Lincoln's day the local dry goods merchants advertised "new pattern preserving glass jars," and the state fair awarded prizes for all manner of home-preserved fruits and jellies.

Traditionally, those ladies stored their pickles in heavy stoneware crocks and sealed their jelly jars by the somewhat hopeful method of soaking a sturdy cloth in brandy, putting it over the top of the jar, and securing it with a strong piece of string. Sometimes they advanced to using a pig's bladder.

Modern canning jars are a lot easier to seal securely, and they still come in pretty pressed-glass patterns. Home canning of preserves, pickles, jams, and jellies is fairly simple. It does involve boiling water, hot jars, and some common sense. These steps will work for the pre-serve and ketchup recipes in this book.

You will need jars specifically designated for home canning and their related two-part lids. You will find them in most grocery stores. You also need a very large, deep pot with a lid. Hardware and cookware stores sell specialized "canner kettles" with racks that hold the jars up off the bottom of the pot. They are not very expensive and do a good job. Clean kitchen towels, a pair of kitchen tongs, and a ladle or 2-cup glass measuring cup round out the equipment.

As your preserves or ketchups are cooking, wash the jars and then sterilize them either in the dishwasher or by boiling them, open side up, in the canning kettle for 10 minutes. Keep them warm in the dish-washer or kettle. Wash the lids and put them in a saucepan of just boiled water. Set the screwbands aside.

When your preserves finish cooking, it's time to can. Lift out a jar, drain out the water if necessary, and carefully pour the hot preserves into the hot jar using a ladle or the measuring cup. Do not fill the jar all the way to the top. Leave a ½ inch of head space between the preserves and the jar's rim. Wipe the edge of the jar so that it is perfectly clean. Using the tongs, pull a warm lid out of the water and set on the rim. Take a screw-band and screw it on until it is fairly tight, but not all the way.

The next step is putting the filled jars back in the canner kettle. Do not fill more jars than will fit into the kettle. If you are using a regular pot, put a folded kitchen towel in the pot so that the jars are not in direct contact with the bottom of the pot. Also, when you put the filled jars in the pot, make sure to leave space between them so that the jars do not touch each other during processing.

Now it is time to process. There should be enough water in the canner kettle to cover the tops of the jars by at least 1 inch. Return the water to a full boil and start keeping time. All the recipes in this book should be processed for 15 minutes for half-pint or pint jars. If you live at high altitudes, the timing will be longer. See the resources below for more information.

After the processing time is finished, turn off the burner and carefully lift the jars out of the canning kettle and place on a heatproof surface away from any drafts. A sudden chill could cause the jars to break.

If all has gone well, you will soon hear the cheery sounds of the jars sealing down. These "plinks" let you know your jars are safe to store in a dark cupboard or to give as gifts. As another test, you can press on top of the lids once the jars have cooled. If the jar is safely sealed, the lid will feel just like the lid on a tin can—sturdy and immovable. If some of the jars didn't seal, not a problem. Just put them in the refrigerator. They will still keep for several weeks.

There is an excellent online resource for home canning: the National Center for Home Food Preservation based at the University of Georgia, http://nchfp.uga.edu/index.html. There are other sources as well, including those by the manufacturers of canning jars.

TOMATO TART

· · · · · ·

Even though this tart might look like a pizza, the taste is very different.
With a simple crisp piecrust base, the spiral of tomato slices mellow
under the slightly sweet and spicy sugar and cinnamon topping. As the
tart bakes, the topping transforms the surface of the tomatoes almost
into tomato jam, with the still-fresh slices below. An elegant appetizer
or snack from four easy ingredients.

½	**of the Double-Crust Pie Dough recipe (see page 51)**
6 to 8	**fresh plum tomatoes, thinly sliced**
2	**tablespoons brown sugar**
1	**tablespoon ground cinnamon**

Preheat the oven to 425°F. Roll the pie dough out to a 10-inch circle
and place on a lightly greased cookie sheet. Fold the outside inch of
crust inward to form a slightly raised edge. Place sliced tomatoes on
the crust, overlapping slightly in concentric circles. Mix the brown
sugar and cinnamon and dust over the top of the tomatoes. Bake until
the crust is lightly browned around the edges and the tomatoes are
tender and lightly glazed, about 15 to 20 minutes.

Makes 1 tart, to serve 4 to 8 as an appetizer

ADAPTED FROM "TOMATO TART," *PRAIRIE FARMER*, JULY 1860.

BAKED BEANS

• • • • • •

Prolific cookbook author Miss Leslie called this "a homely dish, but it is by many persons much liked." Attesting to its satisfying sustenance, she calls the dish "Pork and Beans" and categorized it with meats as a main dish, not as a vegetable. The beans are simply delicious. The key is the long and slow simmering with the salt pork before baking to concentrate the flavors.

1	**pound dry navy or white kidney beans**
1/4	**pound salt pork**
1/2 to 1	**teaspoon freshly ground black pepper**
3	**tablespoons molasses (if making Boston baked beans)**

The night before you want to serve this dish, wash the beans and remove any stray inedible bits. Put the beans in a large pot and add warm water to cover the beans by at least 4 inches. Let stand overnight.

In the morning drain the liquid from the beans. Then add the salt pork, pepper, and enough cold water, again, to cover by 4 inches. Bring to a boil over medium heat then lower the heat and simmer until the beans are tender, about 1 to 2 hours. Preheat the oven to 325°F. Reserving the cooking liquid, spoon the beans into a bean pot or 3-quart casserole dish. Bury the salt pork in the middle. Add enough of the cooking liquid to cover the beans by about ½ inch. If you want Boston baked beans stir the 3 tablespoons of molasses into the pot. Cover the pot and bake until the beans are completely tender and the sauce is thickened, about 3 to 4 hours. Check about halfway through and add more of the reserved cooking liquid, if necessary, to keep the beans from becoming too dry.

Makes about eight ½-cup servings

ADAPTED FROM "PORK AND BEANS," MISS ELIZA LESLIE,
DIRECTIONS FOR COOKERY IN ITS VARIOUS BRANCHES, 1845.

MOCK-MOCK TURTLE SOUP

· · · · · · ·

Turtle soup was a rarity, but mock turtle soup recipes, where a calf's head took the place of the turtle, appeared in many of the era's cookbooks. A recipe for bean soup in the October 1855 issue of American Farmer *takes the mocking one step further, using black beans instead of the calf's head. "It is so like turtle soup that very many, who may eat of it, would smack their lips under the pleasing conceit that they had really partaken of the genuine article." This is a thin soup, typically served as a first course.*

> **2 cups small black beans**
> **1 gallon water**
> **2 sprigs fresh thyme**
> **3 hard-boiled eggs, sliced**
> **1 lemon, sliced**
> **2 tablespoons salted butter**
> **Salt and freshly ground black pepper, to taste**
> **1 to 2 cups white or red wine, if desired**

Wash and pick over the beans to remove any debris or stones. Soak the beans overnight or do a quick soak, following package directions. In a large stockpot, combine the presoaked beans and the water. Cook, simmering slowly, until the beans are very soft. This could take as long as 2 hours. Use an immersion blender to puree the beans. Or dip the beans out of the cooking liquid and press them through a food mill or process in a blender, using some of the reserved water if necessary. Return the beans to the soup pot and water. Add the thyme and simmer, stirring until smooth. Add the remaining ingredients and heat through.

Makes about 3 quarts of thin soup

Some like this soup with forcemeat balls, made as follows.

FOR THE FORCEMEAT BALLS:

- **1 cup cooked beef, finely chopped**
- **1 hard-boiled egg, grated on the small holes of a box grater**
- **¼ teaspoon *each* dried thyme and savory**
- **¼ teaspoon minced fresh parsley**
- **⅛ teaspoon *each* ground mace and cloves**
- **1 tablespoon soft butter**
- **1 tablespoon flour, plus extra for rolling**

Combine all the ingredients and knead into a cohesive mixture with your hands. Form into balls, slightly less than 1 inch in diameter. Roll the balls in flour and add to the simmering soup 5 to 10 minutes before serving. Forcemeat balls sink to the bottom at first and rise to the top when done.

Makes about 1 dozen forcemeat balls, one for each 1-cup serving of soup

ADAPTED FROM "MOCK TURTLE BEAN SOUP,"
AMERICAN FARMER, OCTOBER 1855.

APPLE BUTTER

· · · · · · ·

Old-fashioned fruit butters go well alongside meats or smeared on bread. One advantage of fruit butters is that the cook can use less-than-perfect fruits. The bubbling butter must be watched carefully as it nears the end of cooking or it will stick and scorch.

2 **pounds sweet cooking apples such as Jonathan or McIntosh**

1 **cup apple cider or water**

1/2 **cup light molasses**

1/4 **teaspoon ground cinnamon**

1/4 **teaspoon ground cloves**

1/4 **teaspoon freshly grated or ground nutmeg**

1/4 **teaspoon ground allspice**

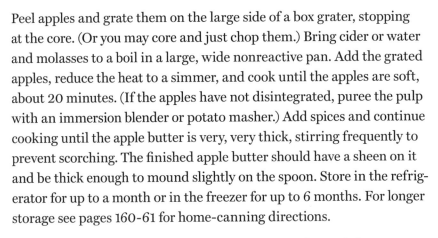

Peel apples and grate them on the large side of a box grater, stopping at the core. (Or you may core and just chop them.) Bring cider or water and molasses to a boil in a large, wide nonreactive pan. Add the grated apples, reduce the heat to a simmer, and cook until the apples are soft, about 20 minutes. (If the apples have not disintegrated, puree the pulp with an immersion blender or potato masher.) Add spices and continue cooking until the apple butter is very, very thick, stirring frequently to prevent scorching. The finished apple butter should have a sheen on it and be thick enough to mound slightly on the spoon. Store in the refrigerator for up to a month or in the freezer for up to 6 months. For longer storage see pages 160-61 for home-canning directions.

TIPS FOR SUCCESS: Perhaps the easiest way to make apple butter is in a slow cooker. Cooking times will vary depending on how your slow cooker is set up. The size of your slow cooker is important, too. The apple mixture should be at least 2 inches deep so that it will simmer properly. If you have just a thin layer, the mixture has a tendency to scorch. The quantities used in this recipe worked very well in my 2-quart cooker. I tripled the amounts for my 5-quart cooker.

Makes three or four 8-ounce jars of apple butter

ADAPTED FROM PERIOD SOURCES.

TALKING TURKEY
CLUES TO LIFE IN THE SPRINGFIELD HOME

T hanksgiving and Abraham Lincoln are inextricably linked. Although communities around the nation celebrated fall "Thanksgivings" during much of the nineteenth century, Lincoln's 1863 proclamation advanced the celebration to a true national holiday. He called upon his "fellow citizens in every part of the United States and also those who were at sea and those who are sojourning in foreign lands to set aside the fourth Thursday in November as a day of Thanksgiving." He concluded his proclamation with the hopes that the nation would soon be restored to the "full measure of peace, harmony, tranquility, and Union."

Although Mary Lincoln didn't leave behind recipes or diary entries of her own, it turns out the Lincolns did leave some tantalizing, tangible touchstones: her stove, her cookbook, and some garbage.

A few days before Thanksgiving, my trip to a local gourmet store opened an experimental window. As I stood amid the shelves of fancy cookware, racks of amazing gadgets, and displays of wonderfully practical tools, my eyes were distracted by the notice of "Red Bourbon heritage turkeys" listed on the chalkboard of local agricultural shares. I always buy a fresh turkey, but here was the chance to cook something from the nineteenth century. Granted, this breed of turkey was first sold about twenty years after Lincoln's day, but it was the closest I've yet come to a farm-raised bird of the era. There was one 8.2-pound turkey left and I took it without hesitation even though it cost a great deal more than the ten cents a pound Mary Lincoln once paid. I decided it was worth the investment to support local agriculture and to do research. I hoped we'd have some good eating, too.

Now it was time to dig in. Archaeologist Floyd Mansberger, historical architect Fran Krupka, and others have done a number of excavations and analyses of artifacts found at the Lincolns' Springfield homesite. Mansberger's 1985 excavations around the house produced a number of artifacts: broken plates—blue transfer, undecorated white, blue shell edged, and ironstone; nails and tacks; and some fragments from glass tumblers and medicine bottles. Most interesting to Mansberger's investigation was the area under the back porch, an abandoned well covered over by the mid-1850s house renovation. In addition to typical household goods, Mansberger's team found an eggshell, peach pits, and fifty-seven pieces of animal bones. These bones, added to two hundred other pieces of animal remains found in other excavations at the site, tell an interesting tale. The Lincolns ate beef sirloin, short loin round, and ribs. They also had a bit of mutton or lamb, a fair amount of pork, chicken, and turkey. The fifty-seven bones from the well included turkey bones and the remains of pigs feet. We know the Lincolns ate turkey in the early years of their residence in the home, and we know Mary purchased an eight-pound turkey on January 10, 1859, for eighty cents from C. M. Smith's store.

I figured I'd dive into Miss Eliza Leslie, the cookery book Mary Lincoln owned, to find era-appropriate directions for cooking the turkey I'd bought. How to cook this beautiful bird? I returned to my thinking about the way Mary Lincoln's cast-iron stove operated and the experiment I'd conducted back in October.

I'll have to admit I've never cooked on a wood-burning or cast-iron stove. My opinion of them had been colored by postfeminist writing in articles and books that speak of women spending "years slaving over a hot stove." The pictures of huge mid-nineteenth-century stoves didn't help. The Victorian version of today's 8-burner, stainless steel Viking Ranges, these nineteenth-century paragons had hot-water reservoirs, food-warming closet, baking ovens, and special roasting oven where the meat will be done "as perfectly as by an open fire." Harriet Beecher Stowe and her sister Catharine sang the praises of such kitchen-filling stoves by saying "proper management ... will for 24 hours keep the stove running." All that changed when I began to study the Royal Oak #9 stove in the Lincolns' kitchen. The Lincolns purchased it on June 9, 1860, to replace an earlier model.

The Royal Oak #9 was an award-winning stove design and a wonder of efficiency. There were four "burners" on top, two of them directly over the relatively small firebox—about the size of two men's shoeboxes placed end to end. The others were set up for slower cooking on days when the stove was going to burn wood for some time; they were gently heated by the current of air as it moved toward the stovepipe and was vented out of the house. A sturdy shelf stuck out in front of the firebox, just right for keeping food warm or heating flatirons.

The oven was not a cube like those in today's ranges. It was shaped like a trapezoid, a rectangle with four unequal sides, to take maximum advantage of the heat from the angled wall of the firebox that formed the right wall of the oven. In Mary's oven, the left side, where the door hinged, was 14 ¼ inches tall. The narrowest part of the oven opening, at the top, was 9 ½ inches wide. The wider opening at the bottom was 13 ¾ inches. The right side was angled to connect the top and bottom. This arrangement created a deep space: 22 ½ inches from front to back. There was a shelf about halfway up where Mary could have slid food that was 11 inches wide and 6 or 7 inches tall, like a sirloin beef roast.

But there is more: a second small door at the bottom right of the oven space, about under the firebox, increased the oven's usefulness. This door was hinged on the right side, so the two doors opened like a book. So, when Mary opened this roughly 6-inch square "cookie sheet" door, she had access to the full floor of the oven, expanding the 13 ½ inches to 23 inches wide and 22 ½ inches deep, but only for something that is less than 6 inches tall.

The more I thought about how the heat from the firebox would "work" this oven, the more impressed I became with the award-winning possibilities. As heat rose, the temperature in the lower, full-oven floor would have been cooler than for anything placed on the 11-inch shelf at the top of the oven. My electric oven heats from the bottom, and I have to switch cookie sheets from the top and bottom racks midway through baking so my cookies bake evenly. It wouldn't surprise me to learn that there could even have been significant oven-temperature differences in the Royal Oak #9 to allow high-heat meat cooking along with mid-range bread baking at the same time.

My fingers began to twitch with the possibility of cooking on such a stove. Of course, the Lincolns' stove was off-limits, but that didn't stop me from thinking of other ways to test my basic firebox theory: the way the firebox, oven, and burners were organized contradicted the image that stoves were kept hot all day. I was willing to bet that a well-laid fire could come up to heat fast enough to cook a meal and then would be diminished nearly as quickly.

A gift from the spirits of culinary experimentation helped me turn our trusty Weber grill into a cast-iron stove, in a manner of speaking. Earlier in the summer I had noticed a couple of very heavy-gauge racks from a gas grill in the road outside our garage. Not wanting to run over them, I waited until traffic cleared and picked them up. I purchased two solid iron plates at a camping goods store, and with two metal garden stakes, I wired the whole contraption together, ending up with a "firebox" about fourteen by eight by eight inches with the grills top and bottom and solid metal sides. I built a small but hot fire, carefully balanced my smallest cast-iron skillet on top of the upper grill, and melted enough fat to fry up a batch of nutmeg doughnuts (the recipe is in Chapter 8, page 138), rolling and cutting the dough on a tray on our picnic table.

I used about a dozen good-size dry tree limbs cut into foot-long pieces and a bit of kindling. This fire was much more efficient than I thought possible. I was ready to cook in about ten minutes. The oak branches kept a good enough coal base to finish the five dozen doughnuts but cooled off after an hour or so. Another time I built a bigger fire and cooked a small beef roast in a pan over the "stove." I would not recommend that anyone else be foolish enough to try this. Balancing a frying pan of melted fat on the top grill over hot coals was nerve-wracking and very dangerous.

As good as the doughnuts and roast were, I wasn't ready to risk the Red Bourbon heritage turkey to my jerry-rigged cooker. The gourmet store had recommended immersing the bird in a saltwater solution to brine it for a juicy result. I hoped Miss Leslie would have a better idea than infusing this beautiful bird with salt water. She did. More important, her directions for roast turkey did more than explain how to cook a turkey dinner. They hit me in the pit of my stomach with recognition of a significant fact I'd been overlooking, one that is key to understanding the lives of Mary and Abraham Lincoln.

Miss Leslie wrote: "Stuff the craw of the turkey with the forcemeat.... Dredge it with flour, and roast it before a clear brisk fire, basting it with cold lard. Towards the last, set the turkey nearer to the fire, dredge it again very lightly with flour, and baste it with butter. It will require according to its size between two to three hours roasting."

The recipe seemed simple enough and it was, in fact, the one I followed when I baked the Red Bourbon in my oven. I did cover the bird with cheesecloth to help the basting liquids—butter, not lard, in my case—keep the meat moister. I made the forcemeat from fresh breadcrumbs grated from a sturdy loaf, combining the crumbs with cold butter instead of Miss Leslie's suet, and a mixture of marjoram, nutmeg, black pepper, and finely grated lemon peel. I bound it with an egg yolk, and stuffed just the craw. It was delicious, as was the turkey, moist with a rich, meaty flavor. There was less white meat in relation to dark. The dark meat was more toothsome. This was a bird that had spent its days wandering about the yard, and we were thankful for its contribution to our dinner. I rounded out the period dinner with cranberry sauce simply made from three ingredients and mellow, lightly peppery mushroom sauce, both from Miss Leslie's book and suitable, as she said, for serving with poultry.

But here was the real revelation from this cooking adventure, one that drove me to think even more deeply about the lives Mary, Abraham, and the boys lived in their Springfield cottage: Miss Leslie's direction to "roast it before a clear brisk fire." This is the edition of the cookbook that we know Mary Lincoln bought on December 10, 1846, along with Miss Leslie's *The House Book: A Manual of Domestic Economy.* Importantly, it offered directions for open-hearth cooking as well as for stoves. Miss Leslie was writing just as American cooks were making the transition from hearth to stove and just at the time Mary Lincoln needed all the help she could get because she was cooking on an open hearth, the kind of arrangement young Abraham grew up with in Indiana in the 1820s.

I knew the Lincolns had remodeled their home extensively. In at least two or three phases, beginning in 1848 and ending in 1856, they enclosed the fireplaces so heating stoves could be installed, moved the kitchen, added a pantry and parlor, and partitioned off a dining room—all on the first floor—and raised the roof for the full second story. At some point they purchased a cooking stove. But I had been so wrapped up in the image of the Lincoln house as I saw it during my childhood tour and as it is presented today that I had not considered the full depth of those changes and what it meant to life in the home.

When Mary Lincoln began setting up housekeeping in the first and only home she and Abraham would own, Robert was a crawling baby just under a year old. The first floor of the house was essentially three equal-size rooms, about fourteen by eighteen feet, arranged like an upside-down letter *T*. Across the west front of the home (the top of the *T*) were the parlor and sitting room separated by stairs. The kitchen with its open hearth for heating and cooking was centered behind this front wing and extended eighteen feet to the east. There were three bedrooms upstairs tucked under the sloping roof of the one-and-a-half-story house. The small house was a huge improvement over the single room Abraham and Mary had lived in at the Globe Tavern right after their marriage in November 1842. They moved out with the baby, Robert, in the spring of 1844 to a rental home for a few months and then into the cottage at Eighth and Jackson.

At first Mary did have help setting up housekeeping and managing life in the cottage from Harriet Hanks, the eighteen-year-old daughter of Abraham's cousin Dennis Hanks. Hanks married Lincoln's stepsister, so Harriet was both a niece and a cousin. She came from the family farm to live with the Lincolns, go to school, and help around the house. Apparently she arrived sometime in 1844 and stayed for about eighteen months. She was gone by the time the Lincolns' second son, Eddy, was born on March 10, 1846. Harriet would have been as familiar as Abraham was with open-hearth cooking. Whereas Mary simply passed though the kitchen during her childhood in the large Lexington, Kentucky, home, Abraham and Harriet would have been raised in one in the one-room cabins of their youth.

The popular images of Mary Lincoln show her as first lady, in fancy dresses fit for balls or formal receptions. Even the earliest-known picture taken in 1846 shows Mary as a young woman with delicate hands, hair in ringlets down her neck, and wearing a dress sewn with a complex pattern of stripes, small sleeve ruffles, and a lace collar. It is hard to merge this picture with the realities of her bending over the hearth, moving iron pots on cranes, stirring food in low-to-the-ground spider frying pans, or managing a roast in a tin reflector oven. But she must have. For at least the first three years that the Lincolns owned the house at Eighth and Jackson, from 1844 until they left for Lincoln's congressional term in October 1847, the only cooking facility was the open hearth in the large kitchen wing.

Mary must have prepared some of the meals, even in the best of times when she had help from Harriet Hanks; Catherine Gordon from Ireland, the eighteen-year-old listed in the 1850 census; the unnamed ten-to-twenty-year-old female in the 1855 census; or Mariah Vance, the free woman of color who lived in Springfield and sometimes came to help with washing and cooking. Mary Lincoln advanced from her first basic cooking steps to a woman who impressed men accustomed to eating the finest restaurant meals. She produced delicious meals made from sophisticated ingredients, and to me, that effort and evolution as a cook is a testament to her intelligence and the love she had for her husband and family.

As Springfield grew, Mary and other homemakers in town would have had help from grocers, confectioners, and bakers. Mrs. John Stuart recalled the early days when "not even a loaf of bread could be bought in the town." Later newspaper advertisements shout out the goods: dried fruits, raisins, figs, apples, oranges, cranberries, fancy confections of all kinds, candies, ice, wines and liquors, meats, canned oysters, dried mackerel, and cigars, along with cooking staples such as flour, corn-meal, hominy, molasses, sugars of all kinds, salts, butter, spices, and flavoring extracts.

Mary was far from alone as she struggled with life in her Springfield cottage. Her three sisters were married and living in town. The Lincolns lived about a block and a half from her sister Frances and husband Dr. Wallace. Younger sister, Ann, and her husband, merchant C. M. Smith, lived about four blocks away; the oldest Todd daughter, Elizabeth, wife of Ninian Edwards, lived just another two blocks farther west of the Smiths and six blocks from the Lincolns. The sisters, for the most part, chose not to reveal much about their relationships when William Herndon came gathering information after Lincoln's assassination. Again, my imagination and common sense make me consider that there was significant interaction among them. The Lincolns did have a charge account at C. M. Smith's store. Mary lived with Elizabeth for three years before she married Lincoln. The newlyweds immediately moved into the single room at Globe Tavern. Robert was born just nine months later. I have to think that as the time came close, Mary would have moved into one of her sisters' homes, perhaps that of Frances, whose husband was a physician, to have her first child. The recollection of their mother's death right after childbirth must have been in all of the sisters' minds. Abraham lost his only sister in childbirth, too. A younger brother, born when Lincoln was just three, lived only a few days. Although there isn't any evidence to support my thinking, I can't see any of these sensible people risking Mary's or the baby's life by having her give birth in a small residential hotel room.

Mary did write one clear image of the close interaction she had with her sisters. In June of 1860, Ann and C. M. Smith's ten-year-old son died of typhoid fever. Mary wrote that the family was inconsolable and for a week she "spent the greater portion" of her time with them. Certainly her sisters would have supported her in times of sickness, loss, or loneliness.

Any of her sisters could have brought meals from their kitchens into the Lincoln home or invited Mary and the children to eat with them on the many times when Abraham was riding the court circuit or pursuing political obligations. Or when the cottage was being remodeled. Anyone who has ever lived in a house during remodeling knows how disruptive it is. The work at the Lincolns' home began simply with some whitewashing and brickwork and expanded into cutting through walls and raising the roof, twice. Even if Mary and her help were operating out of a summer kitchen set up in the backyard washing shed, I can imagine Elizabeth might have brought by some of her famed chicken salad, or Frances might have come round the block to offer to share a meal in her home. Frances describes a close relationship between the sisters during the one interview she did give to Herndon. She spoke of the Lincolns' backyard as "being used as a woodpile," describing how Abraham liked to saw wood for exercise. When she "used to go over to my sister's to visit ... many times," Lincoln would read aloud from Shakespeare and other books and sometimes "would all at once burst out in a joke." She also said she planted flowers around their home "often." Sharing of food could easily have been part of their family interactions.

Excavations around the home and into account books suggest specifics of the cottage's transforming steps, beginning with the return from Lincoln's congressional term in Washington, D.C. Mary and the boys, Robert born in August 1843 and Eddy in March 1846, had divided their time between the single room in a boardinghouse where Lincoln lived in Washington and her father's and stepmother's home in Lexington during the 1847–49 term. They had rented out the Springfield home and it appears they did not move right back in when the tenant left. At some point between 1849 and 1852, the first phases of remodeling were completed. With each step, the cottage became more sophisticated, until in 1856 it was a home designed and decorated to suit the position of one of the state's leading attorneys and a candidate for the Senate or even the presidency.

Initially they hired John Roll, a local carpenter and longtime friend of Lincoln's, to whitewash the walls and ceiling, close up the fireplaces, and install new hearths for heating stoves. Roll was one of the local lads who helped build the raft for Lincoln's 1831 trip to New Orleans. Later, the Lincolns expanded the rear of the first floor. Carpenters, perhaps Roll, sawed through the tenons attaching the kitchen to the front part of the home and slid the entire large room five and a half feet to the south. They then enclosed a new fourteen-by-eighteen-foot room made from the old north porch and the kitchen and created a pantry room at the northeast corner and an open porch between the pantry and the new kitchen opening into the backyard, squaring off the house.

This new unheated kitchen pantry provided storage for barrels of flour and casks for sugar and cornmeal, cheese, hams, and potted meats, shelves for milk to settle and maybe even a small container to keep ice. Mary could have put up any number of essential "store sauces" and kept them there, too—pink sauce, mushroom ketchup, lemon ketchup, apple ketchup, pickles, just the thing to put on ordinary meat baked or cooked on a gridiron. Anyone who has kept house in the Midwest knows how handy an unheated garage is for storing extra foods at holiday time. This five-by-seven-foot pantry was an important addition. A picture of the open porch taken in May 1865 dimly shows pails and washtubs hanging on the back wall and the nearby water pump in the backyard, clearly showing the utility of this open space. The new first-floor room, I call it a "master suite," with nursery sat between the old front parlor to the west and the moved kitchen to the south. With its own fireplace/stove, it would have been much warmer in the winter than the upstairs bedrooms tucked under the sloping roof.

In three more remodeling changes through 1856, the bedrooms were expanded upstairs as the front of the house was raised to a full two stories, the back was raised, and the large kitchen was divided to create a formal dining room.

With all these changes, areas of the homesite and yard were covered over—sealed up like time capsules, containing odd bits of discarded household goods, dishes, nails, and bones. Floyd Mansberger's study comparing the animal bone remains among houses in the neighborhood indicates the Lincolns ate a greater proportion of chicken and turkeys than their neighbors the Shutts, Allens, or the unknown renters of the house known as the Cook house. They also ate a higher proportion of the better cuts of beef. But it is the pork remains that may be the most intriguing.

Bones from pigs feet made up 45 percent of the pork remains at the Lincoln home. Although most Americans don't eat pigs feet today, they were a useful product in nineteenth-century kitchens. Cookery books offered up recipes for pigs feet stewed or barbecued, pickled, or soused in herbs and wine then chilled under a layer of fat to be eaten cold, suggesting they would keep a long time. Certainly I can imagine Abraham coming in from his travels, going into the pantry, and fetching out a crock of pickled or soused pigs feet. It is a food associated with Kentucky and southern Indiana rural foodways.

Mansberger's research shows the Lincolns were not the only Springfield family to have this high proportion of pigs feet in their archaeological excavations. Period recipes offer some suggestions as to their use. Like calves feet, pigs feet have gelatin that is extracted by boiling for hours, straining, and then boiling for hours on the second day. It could be that Mary and the other middle-class homemakers would find this an alternative for making a fancy molded dessert. Books of the era call for flavoring the clear gelatin with wine, nutmeg, or other spices and pouring it into a mold to chill before serving. Or it could be the stabilizing base for a blancmange, Charlotte Russe, Bohemian cream, or other fancy dessert. But I'm skeptical. I can't see Mary, or any busy homemaker, even with help, spending the time and attention to boil the pigs-feet broth to the reduction necessary for a fancy gelatin dessert, when they could buy any of a number of gelatinizing products at the grocery. We know that Mary did buy "red gelatin" and "Cooper isinglass" in 1859. I think there is only one reason to spend the time cooking pigs feet, and the answer demonstrates the soul of the Lincolns' home.

On December 11, 1850, Eddy, the Lincolns' second child, fell ill. He had always been somewhat weak and sickly. Nearly four years old, he came down with what most now consider a form of tuberculosis. There is a beautiful photographic image, easily available online, which some claim to be Eddy. It shows a sweet-faced boy with straight dark hair wearing an informal shirt and leaning against a brocade chair. The Lincoln Springfield Home staff do not think that photograph is a picture of him. However, we do know that Eddy was a sweet child, who shared his father's love of cats, as Mary wrote to Lincoln in Washington from her family's home in Lexington about a stray cat that Robert, the older boy, brought home: "As soon as Eddy [then two years old] spied it—his tenderness, broke forth, he made them bring it water, fed it bread himself, with his own dear hands, he was a delighted creature over it." Now, Eddy weakened by the day. As congestion filled the little boy's lungs, Abraham and Mary nursed him in the first-floor bedroom right next to the kitchen.

The nineteenth-century cookery books are filled with recipes for invalids, calves-feet and pigs-feet jelly among them. This is a reason for Mary to spend hours making a strengthening, clarified jelly or soup. I can imagine the cooking pot suspended over the fire or maybe sitting on a new cook stove, boiling away the pigs-feet soup until the four gallons of water are reduced to one gallon of sustaining broth, perhaps flavored with a bit of lemon, sugar, or nutmeg to tempt the young boy's appetite. Even though the pigs-feet bones hidden away in the covered-over well were put there before Eddy's illness, I can still see this cooking practice continuing. Mary would carefully dip the broth out and strain it though a flannel suspended over a bowl, then set the broth aside in the pantry to jell, where it would keep for a few days. I can see the worried parents, warming the jelly gently before the fire, I can see them lifting up Eddy's head and spooning a bit of broth into his mouth, cajoling him to eat just a little, before they fluffed up his pillow, wiped his brow, and tucked in the covers. They nursed him for fifty-two days. Eddy died at six o'clock in the morning on February 1, 1850, a bit more than a month from his fourth birthday. The funeral was held in the Lincolns' home the next morning.

When the struggle was over, Mary collapsed and could scarcely be roused for days. It is said that Abraham urged her to eat, saying "We must go on living." Near the end of the month, Abraham wrote to his stepbrother: "We lost our little boy.... We miss him very much."

The Lincolns' third son, William Wallace, was born December 21, 1850.

FORCEMEAT FOR STUFFING TURKEY CRAW

· · · · · · ·

This is a very rich, highly seasoned dressing. The small suggested serving is just enough to complement the turkey, cranberry, and mushroom sauces.

- 3 **cups fresh breadcrumbs grated from a sturdy loaf**
- ½ **teaspoon dried marjoram leaves**
- ½ **teaspoon freshly grated nutmeg**
- ½ **teaspoon freshly ground black pepper**
- ½ **teaspoon finely grated lemon zest**
- 3 **tablespoons cold butter, cut into very small pieces**
- 2 **egg yolks, lightly beaten**

Toss the breadcrumbs with the dried seasonings. Mix in the chilled butter with a fork and then stir in the egg yolks. Lightly press the forcement into the turkey craw, pulling the skin around and under. Secure the skin with a skewer, or by folding the wings backward to hold the skin in place. Store uncooked forcemeat in the refrigerator. You may form the extra into balls and place on a lightly greased cookie sheet, or simply put into a greased casserole, and bake alongside the turkey for about 15 minutes (for the balls) to 25 minutes (for the casserole) until lightly browned.

Makes about twelve ¼-cup servings

ADAPTED FROM "TO ROAST A TURKEY," MISS ELIZA LESLIE,
DIRECTIONS FOR COOKERY IN ITS VARIOUS BRANCHES, 1845.

ROAST TURKEY

• • • • • • •

When buying your turkey, estimate 1 pound per person.

1 8- to 12-pound fresh turkey
4 to 8 tablespoons salted butter, melted
2 to 3 tablespoons flour

Preheat the oven to 325°F. Wash the turkey and remove any parts packed in the cavity or craw. Pat the turkey dry and stuff the craw with forcemeat as directed in the recipe on page 179. Put the turkey in a large roasting pan. Cut a folded piece of cheesecloth 2 or 3 layers thick and large enough to cover the breast and legs of the turkey. Rinse it in cold water and wring it out until nearly dry. Dip the cheesecloth in the melted butter, pressing out extra butter with a fork. Then drape the cheesecloth over the turkey, completely covering it. Put the turkey in the oven and roast, basting it every 15 to 20 minutes with remaining melted butter and then the accumulating pan juices.

Calculate baking time allowing 15 minutes per pound. About 45 minutes before you anticipate the turkey will be done, carefully remove the cheesecloth and set it aside. Baste the turkey. Dust the top of the turkey very lightly with flour by putting a couple of tablespoons of flour into a sieve, holding it over the turkey, and tapping the side of the sieve with your hand. Return the turkey to the oven to continue roasting. Near the end of cooking, insert an instant-read meat thermometer into the meatiest part of the thigh to check for doneness. It will read 165°F when the turkey is done. Remove the turkey from the oven, cover with a lid or tent with foil, and let rest for 15 or 20 minutes before carving.

TIPS FOR SUCCESS: Here's a list of equipment to make the roasting easier—cheesecloth; bulb baster or large basting spoon; small, fine-mesh sieve. The basting cheesecloth can be added to the turkey carcass bones when you make broth from the leftovers. The flavor and browned color will simmer right out. Strain the broth before serving.

Makes 8 to 12 servings, depending on size of bird

ADAPTED FROM "TO ROAST A TURKEY," MISS ELIZA LESLIE,
DIRECTIONS FOR COOKERY IN ITS VARIOUS BRANCHES, 1845.

CRANBERRY SAUCE

· · · · · ·

Cranberries grow wild through much of the upper Midwest. Spring-field newspapers advertised the tart berries' arrival as fall turned into winter. Housekeeping columns in newspapers and magazines all suggested serving cranberry sauce as part of the holiday table. This version is quickly made with the small amount of brown sugar adding a mild caramel-like flavor to the sharp relish.

> **1 12- to 16-ounce package fresh cranberries**
> **¼ cup water**
> **½ cup firmly packed brown sugar**

Wash and sort the cranberries, discarding any that are spoiled or not ripe. Combine with water in a heavy, medium saucepan. Cover and cook over low to medium heat until berries pop and the mixture becomes jam-like. Be sure to lift the cover and stir from time to time so the sauce does not stick and scorch. Add the brown sugar and stir until sugar melts into the jam. Remove from the heat and refrigerate until ready to serve.

Makes about 2 cups

ADAPTED FROM "CRANBERRY SAUCE," MISS ELIZA LESLIE,
DIRECTIONS FOR COOKERY IN ITS VARIOUS BRANCHES, 1845.

MUSHROOM SAUCE

• • • • • • •

I had never considered mushroom sauce as part of my Thanksgiving dinner, but one taste of this deliciously mellow sauce put it at the top of my traditional menu. Steeping the mushrooms in a bit of salt overnight yields a superb concentration of mushroom flavor.

16 **ounces fresh white button mushrooms**
¼ **teaspoon salt**
½ **cup light cream**
½ **cup nonfat milk**
½ **teaspoon freshly ground black pepper, or to taste**
2 **tablespoons soft butter**
2 **tablespoons flour**

The night before you make the sauce, slice about one-quarter of the mushrooms and sprinkle with salt to draw out their juices.

The next day, cut off and discard the stems of the remaining mushrooms and slice the caps into quarters. If there are small ones, you may keep them whole. Combine the mushrooms with the cream and milk in a medium saucepan. Stir in the salted mushrooms and the accumulated juices. Cook over very low heat until the mushrooms are tender and the sauce is a light beige color. Add the black pepper. Mash the butter with a fork and work the flour into it until it forms a paste. Stir this bit by bit into the mushroom mixture. Continue stirring as the sauce thickens. If sauce is too thick, add a bit more milk. Store leftover sauce in the refrigerator for 2 to 3 days. Good with other meats and vegetables.

Makes about 1 ½ cups

ADAPTED FROM "MUSHROOM SAUCE,"
MISS ELIZA LESLIE, *DIRECTIONS FOR COOKERY
IN ITS VARIOUS BRANCHES*, 1845

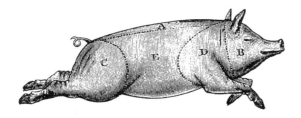

SOUSED OR BARBECUED PIGS "FEET"

• • • • • • •

"Soused" is slang for having consumed too much alcohol. In this case, simmering ribs in the highly seasoned wine sauce brings forth a wonderfully flavored meat. If you would like to give the ribs a traditional barbecue glazed look, a quick brush with honey and a few minutes under the broiler or on the grill will do the trick, but any additional sauce will overpower the meats. The leftover cooking liquid will nearly solidify when cold. In a Springfield back pantry, this aspic-like sauce would keep the meat shielded from drying air.

5 **pounds pork spareribs**

4 **cups white wine**

2 **cups water**

2 **bay leaves**

1/2 **teaspoon** *each* **ground cloves, mace, coriander, and ginger**

1 **teaspoon** *each* **dried marjoram and thyme**

Put the spareribs in a large pot with a lid. Combine the remaining ingredients and pour over the ribs. Simmer, covered, until tender. Or bake in a covered roasting pan in a preheated 300°F oven. A regular rack of ribs, cut into single rib sections, will be tender in about 45 minutes to an hour. Meatier "country style" ribs will take much longer, perhaps as long as 2 to 3 hours.

Makes 4 to 6 servings

ADAPTED FROM "PIGS FEET AND EARS, SOUSED," MISS ELIZA LESLIE, *DIRECTIONS FOR COOKERY IN ITS VARIOUS BRANCHES*, 1845.

11

AT THE CROSSROADS OF PROGRESS
IRISH STEW, GERMAN BEEF, AND OYSTERS

During the decade of the 1850s, Springfield, Illinois, grew to become a complex crossroads of transportation, commerce, politics, and influence.

Springfield benefited from the intersection of two newly constructed railway lines, completed by 1854. On these rail lines raw materials, farm produce, and finished goods traveled between surrounding country and cities to the east, south, and north. The Great Western of Illinois headed to Toledo and from there connected to the urban capitals of the East Coast. The Chicago, Alton, and St. Louis Railway allowed a vital commercial linkage between the Gulf of Mexico and Chicago. Goods traveled up the Mississippi River and were put on the train at St. Louis. From the north they came on rail from Chicago and the Great Lakes.

The town crowded with newcomers as people moved in to take advantage of the trade-created opportunities. Economic conditions improved as Springfield grew from a town into a city. The latest national newspapers and magazines brought current fashions and happenings into Springfield living rooms. These midwesterners could enjoy foods from Europe and the Caribbean, and even spices from the Far East.

Information arrived with the immediacy of clacking telegraph keys. Telegraph lines were strung in 1849, bringing Springfield nearly immediate access to events. Lincoln's friend David Davis described the impact on the community: "The wonder workings of the Telegraph are past comprehension. The wires are in communication from this place direct with

Phild [Philadelphia] & New York, and two or three hours after anything is done in those cities, it is known here."

The decade was critically important for Abraham Lincoln. He returned from his term in Congress in 1849 and began building his successful law practice. In just eleven years he would be heading back to Washington, D.C., to lead the nation through its most difficult challenges. Hundreds of authors have written thousands of pages explaining, defining, striving to capture the "real Lincoln." I decided to see where his words would lead me and what clues I could find to discover how the Indiana and Illinois Lincoln, seemingly removed from the power base of the nation, became the Mount Rushmore Lincoln.

I didn't find the answer, but I did come to an insight—a perspective I'd never realized. The more I read, the more convinced I became that the five years from 1854 to 1859 were pivotal for Lincoln, for the Union, and for the people of Springfield. And part of the story could be told through the food folks in Springfield ate, revealing a crossroads of cuisine feeding a complex society rooted in traditions, open to innovation, and influenced by non-midwestern opportunities.

In a nutshell, in 1854 the United States reached a political crossroads. Illinois senator Stephen A. Douglas sponsored a bill essentially overturning the Ordinance of 1787 and 1820 Missouri Compromise, which had limited slavery to Southern states. Douglas's bill established that new states entering the Union could, if their citizens wanted, become slaveholding states. The bill was passed by Congress as the Kansas-Nebraska Act and signed into law by President Franklin Pierce on May 30, 1854.

Lincoln and Douglas, arguably the men who were to become the nation's two most influential speakers on the topic, gave a series of speeches around Illinois that fall. Although the pretext was campaigning in the congressional election—Lincoln to reelect Congressman Richard Yates; Douglas to elect Thomas Harris—the real debate was the Kansas-Nebraska Act.

Lincoln gave at least nine major addresses between August 26 and November 1, 1854. Three of them were, in effect, joint appearances with Stephen Douglas. The audiences were very large, sometimes in the thousands. On October 16 in Peoria, Douglas spoke first for two or three hours. Lincoln followed, speaking for the same amount of time, and then Douglas had another hour to answer Lincoln's arguments. The topic was the role of slavery in the admission of new states to the Union. Douglas defended his position. Lincoln passionately argued against it. Newspaper reports noted the audience participation, cheering points they agreed with and shouting down those they did not.

I was struck by Lincoln's elaboration of his underlying principles. He explained his hatred for the spread of slavery. "I hate it because of the monstrous injustice of slavery itself," and also because it showed American leaders to be hypocrites: speaking of freedom while allowing slavery and, thus, "losing influence in the world." He continued that it put "really good men" into a war with the Declaration of Independence as they insisted, "there is no right principle of action but *self-interest*." The emphasis is Lincoln's.

One of Lincoln's supporting arguments jumped out at me. He demonstrated the real and positive economic impact of freedom as he characterized the settlement of the slave-free Midwest: "No states in the world have ever advanced as rapidly in population, wealth, the arts, and appliances of life and now have such promise of prospective greatness as the states that were born under the Ordinance of '87." Lincoln wrote that Douglas's Nebraska bill set the country "at once in a blaze" and into sectional conflict.

Four years later the men once again faced each other over the issue of slave and free states in the famous 1858 Lincoln-Douglas debates for Douglas's senate seat. As he accepted the Republican nomination, Lincoln addressed the extreme risks of Douglas's position. The most-remembered phrase from that speech is "A house divided against itself cannot stand," but there was much more. Again, Lincoln put Douglas's position into economic terms, suggesting it would set the stage for backward motion, a retreat from all of the progress the United States had made. Following Douglas's logic, Lincoln said, it was even possible that Illinois could become "a slave state" and that slave trade with Africa could be revived.

Lincoln lost the race but valued the successes of the campaign. He wrote to an associate: "It gave me a hearing on the great and durable question of the age, which I could not have had in [any] other way; and though I now slink out of view, and shall be forgotten, I believe I have made some marks which will tell for the cause of civil liberty long after I am gone."

Lincoln returned to his Springfield law practice, feeling the pressures of the loss of time and business. He wrote to his advisor and friend

Norman Judd of the cost of the campaign that, "I have been on expenses so long without earning any thing that I am absolutely without money now for even household purchases." But far from fading from view, he continued writing to political allies and public speaking.

Lincoln returned to the discussion of the economic advantages of free states as he closed his February 1859 lecture on "Discoveries and Inventions," saying that a "new country is most favorable—almost necessary—to the emancipation of thought, and the consequent advancement of civilization and the arts ... we, here in America, *think* we discover, invent, and improve, faster than any of them."

The railroad was a primary and progressive improvement and one that Lincoln had studied for years. In 1832 when he was campaigning to represent his New Salem neighbors in the Illinois legislature, Lincoln predicted "no other improvement ... can equal in utility the rail road. It is a never failing source of communication, between places of business remotely situated from each other." Now, in the 1850s, Lincoln recognized that this promise had proven true. The railroad "is growing larger and larger, building up new countries with a rapidity never before seen in the history of the world ... [promoting] young and rising communities" in the middle of the nation.

Now food traveled readily between sections of the country giving people more and more choices. Even though the political differences between North and South were increasingly tense, on Springfield tables Carolina rice could share a dinner plate with New England stewed codfish.

In Springfield the benefits of progress were now an obvious part of everyday life: Oysters! Pineapples!! Tomato sauce!! In cans!!!! As I read the foods heralded in the 1850s Springfield newspapers' grocery advertisements—oysters from the East Coast, pineapples and citrus from the tropics, and just-invented canned tomato sauce—I realized there could be no better realization of Abraham Lincoln's 1832 progressive vision than the food available to the people of Springfield. A huge variety of fresh and packaged food filled the stores, and the growing, diverse population had the money to buy it.

In 1853, Springfield businessman and newspaper editor Simeon Francis highlighted the change over the previous ten years: "In those times [1843] few of our farmers, indeed of our citizens, could indulge in such luxuries as coffee, sugar, tea, or a broadcloth coat." The price of farmland increased from between three dollars to eight dollars an acre and now sold for between fifteen to thirty dollars.

Farming and food were the engines of this economic progress. Far from being a sleepy backwater, Springfield was an active national trading hub. During 1856, for example, the two railway lines exported nearly a million bushels of wheat and corn grown on Springfield-area farms. Another half million bushels of wheat were ground into one hundred thousand 156-pound barrels of flour and sent along the rails. Eastward shipments of live cattle and hogs brought $1,500,000 to the city. Armstrong's woolen mill turned seventy-five thousand pounds of wool into blankets, flannels, and yarn. Another two hundred thousand pounds of raw wool, worth $100,000, were sent east for manufacturing.

Springfield's population grew from 2,600 in 1840 to 7,250 in 1855 as people from around the nation and across the ocean came to make their mark. Many early Illinois settlers had been from the upper South—Tennessee and Kentucky—others from Indiana and Ohio, and some from New England. Now European immigrants came directly to the center of Illinois, contributing their traditions into the cultural mix. These immigrants changed the nation and Springfield. Their foods were reflected in a variety of "American" cookbooks and magazines. Whether the Lincolns actually ate any "foreign foods" is another journey into speculation, but they had the opportunity, especially from three immigrant groups—Irish, Germans, and Portuguese.

Mary Lincoln and many of her neighbors employed as live-in help Irish girls, who arrived as part of the great migration following the Irish potato famine. Irish stew recipes began appearing in nearly every cookbook.

Springfield's substantial German population filled two churches: one Lutheran, one Methodist. The community had political clubs and a marching band. City directories displayed ads from grocers "Reisch & Helmle" and "Klaholt & Claus," along with three Bier Halles: "Leuterback & Sawer's," "Raps & Shoemaker's," and "Weideman & Schriefer's Lager Bier Halle." As to recipes for food to go with that beer, there was a German-American cookbook published in Philadelphia and printed in both languages, "a complete manual ... with particular references to the climate and production of the United States." The book has recipes for simple and sophisticated dishes including sauerkraut and beef with sour cream. For those who wanted Old Country flavors without the work and wait, Springfield residents only had to look to Lavely's grocery store for their supply of "crout." The store ran a large advertisement in January 1859.

Lincoln recognized the importance of the German population as a key voting block. He even purchased Springfield's German-language newspaper, the *Illinois Staats Anzeiger*. Control of the paper remained with the editor, Theodore Canisius, under the condition that the paper supported the Republican Party. Lincoln owned it from May 30, 1859, to December 6, 1860.

Springfield's First Presbyterian Church, the church the Lincolns attended, helped sponsor a large group of Portuguese who had fled religious persecution in their homeland. The families left Madeira and lived for a time in Trinidad before they were welcomed to Illinois. By 1855 some 350 Portuguese had settled in Springfield (about 4 percent of the population), working in a variety of trades. Mary Lincoln employed one Portuguese woman, Charlotte DeSouza, as a seamstress. Maybe DeSouza shared some of her favorite homeland foods with the Lincolns: chopped beef with eggs or a fancy egg custard encased in puff pastry. Regardless of my speculation about what the Lincolns may have enjoyed, Portuguese recipes were entering American life. Springfield homemakers may have happened on the recipe for the "Portuguese way to prepare mutton" as I did in Lucretia Irving's 1852 book *Irving's 1000 Receipts, or, Modern and Domestic Cookery*, a complex dish of chops stuffed with a forcemeat and dressed with the fancy "Sauce Robert."

Free people of color made Springfield their home, too. Mariah Vance worked for the Lincoln family on and off for several years in a variety of responsibilities, including cook. She was, evidently, a valued friend of the family. Years later Robert stopped to visit her when he passed through Danville, where she had moved. Another Springfield free person of color, a young man named William H. Johnson, born about 1835, accompanied Lincoln to the White House and functioned as his barber and valet.

Though there were occasional economic downturns in Springfield, the track was steadily ahead through the 1850s. Signs of success were all around. The clothing needs of the community were met by workers at Wiley's ready-made clothing factory. Craftsmen in the two hat stores made one-third of the hats they sold, and fifty shoemakers cobbled at the city's seven shoe dealers. Furniture builders made fine and everyday home furnishings. Laborers, who had earned about ten dollars a month working at Armstrong's woolen mill, Manning's carriage shop, flour mills, the pork-packing plant, and brickyard, now earned twenty dollars, while the prices of manufactured and imported goods declined.

Advertisements in Springfield's newspapers chronicled and sometimes even celebrated the community's economic advances in the kinds of foods—fresh, imported, and manufactured—people could purchase. In the early 1840s, grocers advertised mostly staples and a few fancy goods. In the fall of 1841, Barrett & Taylor offered 1,500 barrels of salt "sold low," for those who needed this essential ingredient for home curing or smoking meats. J. Bunn had two barrels of rice in stock along with Underwood's lemon syrup, pickles, ketchup, pepper sauce, and fresh lemons. John Buckhardt's store offered rice along with "New Orleans molasses" and barrels of both loaf and crushed sugar. Iles & Pasfield listed raisins, rice, allspice, cloves, nutmegs, mace, cinnamon, black and red pepper, vinegar, coffee, and tea, along with fish—mackerel, shad, herring, and cod. A. Lindsay and Bro. gave a more complete description of these fish in their July 11, 1842, ad. "Just received a choice lot of fish—consisting of Mackerel, Shad, Salmon, Herrings, pickled and smoked."

By the mid-1850s not only were prices lower, but more and more exotic goods were available at the dry goods, or grocery, merchants in Springfield. Fruits from the Caribbean included pineapples and oranges. Newly perfected canned tomato sauce put the useful "esculent" vegetable on Springfield homemakers' pantry shelves for year-round use. Cheese was popular. Favored kinds include some from the Western Reserve region of northeast Ohio and even a type of cheddar cheese shaped like a pineapple made in New York. Dried cod along with smoked and pickled fish were still advertised, perhaps reflecting the preferences of New Englanders and the Portuguese residents. But now, as the December 1856 newspapers exclaimed, the railroad could bring "the celebrated Baltimore oyster" to town. "Fresh Shell Oysters" were advertised by H. C. Meyers & Son and W. W. Watson & Son. W. Lavely offered "Fresh Cove Oysters."

We know the Lincolns had charge accounts at two of the twenty-three Springfield dry goods and grocery stores in business during 1859. Alas, we don't know their shopping habits at any of the butchers, bakers, or meat markets in town, but we do know they must have made purchases there.

However, we do have witnesses recording several times when Lincoln ate oysters. Lincoln scholar Wayne Temple suggests that if Lincoln had a favorite seafood, it "would have been oysters."

Oysters had been available in central Illinois earlier. Lincoln and the other Sangamon Long Nine, very tall legislators, served oysters and champagne at a party celebrating their success in passing the legislation to move the capital from Vandalia to Springfield in 1837. But this 1856 advertising intensity suggests a good supply for just about every Springfielder who cared to eat them. In January 1859, Hull's store even advertised "chafing dishes for cooking oysters." An illustration in the *American Home Cook Book* shows such a dish, fueled by an alcohol lamp "to keep steaks hot or to cook oysters, venison, mutton, etc. on the table." It looks like a modern, low chafing dish or one of those holders to disguise a utilitarian baking dish, with decoratively pierced "silver" sides surrounding some kind of cooking basin. Just the thing for a quick supper or an oyster party.

So we come to another common Lincoln food speculation: Did Springfield families hold parties that featured only oysters? Did the Lincolns host them? Certainly, there were such events as oyster parties. In 1855 a short story in *Harper's New Monthly Magazine* portrayed an oyster party held in New York: "Some ten or a dozen young men were seated round the long-table, some busily stewing oysters in silver chafing-dishes ... while more were sipping their Sauterne, and watching the operations of their companions with a sort of hungry interest.... The table looked like work. On the snowy cloth three or four silver chafing dishes glittered and one might hear in the pauses of conversation the bubbling of the savory stews within."

Alas, the household inventories and purchase records don't show that the Lincolns, or any of Mary's sisters, owned an oyster chafing dish. And even though archaeological excavations around the Lincoln Home National Historic Site have found oyster shells and shards of bivalve shells—possibly oysters—those shells are the only existing evidence. It will remain speculation whether the couple ever did feed their guests exclusively on the popular bivalve.

During the 1800s, a great many Americans enjoyed oysters. They were featured on the menus of swanky New York City hotels and were so plentiful they fed the masses inexpensively. Some oysters were pickled in water, vinegar, and spices and sealed in cans. Others traveled alive, in their shells, in barrels filled with seaweed and, sometimes, ice. Oysters can stay alive, holding their shells tightly sealed, for a number of days.

For longer life, several period cookbook authors suggested feeding oysters following this recipe: "Put them into water and wash them with a birch besom [small broom] until quite clean; then lay them bottom downwards into a pan, sprinkle with flour or oatmeal and salt and cover with water. Do the same every day and they will fatten. The water should be pretty salty."

Storekeepers Lavely and Meyers also mention "cans" in their ads for oysters. As early as 1825, New Yorker Ezra Daggett packed salmon, lobsters, and oysters in tin cans. But the process required the food to be cooked inside the closed cans for five hours so that it would be safely sealed. The Springfield merchants may well have been selling both canned and live oysters. Various ads state oysters "by the dozen or by the can," suggesting some merchants were dealing with live oysters. During the month of December, Watson proclaimed that his store was receiving oysters "daily." And H. C. Meyers & Son headlined "Prices Again Down!" on several occasions, perhaps in a hurry to get the live oysters out of the store and into customer's stomachs—stewed, scalloped, and maybe even on the half shell.

We do have a hint about how Lincoln liked to eat oysters. After a speech in Pontiac, Illinois, in January 1860, he declined an offered plate of raw oysters. "If I should eat a raw oyster with you it would be the first time I had ever eaten one. I like them cooked." A guest at a restaurant dinner in Springfield in 1856 reported Lincoln ate fried oysters. And, eight years later, fried oysters became part of an election victory celebration.

On November 8, 1864, President Lincoln anxiously awaited the returns for his reelection. He walked over to the Executive Office Building, next door to the White House. There were telegraph lines into Secretary of War Edwin Stanton's office. There Lincoln, his secretary John Hay, and friend and reporter Noah Brooks could monitor the votes as they came in from the states. It was a cold and rainy night. Clerks brought in the telegraphed reports showing Lincoln's vote totals growing higher than the Democratic candidate, Lincoln's former general George McClellan. At midnight, with the results certain, telegraph officer Major Thomas Eckert brought in supper. John Hay described the scene. "The President went awkwardly and hospitably to work shoveling out the fried oysters. He was most agreeable and genial all the evening."

After this submersion into oyster and Lincoln lore, I figured I'd best test a recipe. Like Lincoln, I wasn't ready to eat mine raw. But Miss Eliza Leslie's oyster stew did sound mighty good. As the simmering smells of lemon, mace, cream, and oysters filled my kitchen, I turned again to the question that started this chapter. What made Lincoln, well, Lincoln? Certainly the decade of the 1850s was pivotal: slavery in the Southern states, simmering through ten presidential administrations, came to a full boil of dissent as Kansas erupted into bloody riots in 1855 and '56 and John Brown raided the U.S. arsenal at Harper's Ferry in 1859. Lincoln's speeches and letters demonstrate a thoughtful, ideological, ambitious, and pragmatic man at the geographical and metaphorical crossroads of the nation.

And there was the palpable, unstoppable momentum of progress. Its sound was inescapable in Springfield. Our Ames, Iowa, backyard was about the same distance from the Union Pacific railroad line as the Lincolns' was from the Great Western line. The everyday sounds of the ninety trains passing through Ames added an underlying soundtrack mixed in with cars, air conditioners, the general hum of mechanized modern life, sounds you don't really realize are there. I could hear the trains as I worked in the yard and even inside the house on cold winter sound-carrying nights. Yet, the Union Pacific's diesel-electric engines are quiet compared to the chuff-chuffing and steam-whistle blowing of Lincoln's Great Western. During Lincoln's day there would have been a sustaining base rhythm of progress, too—mechanical sounds, perhaps felt more than heard—from the steam engines, drive belts, and machines of the various factories around town. At night there would have been only the trains and the ticking of the clock in the Lincolns' house. Progress calling, marking time.

Lincoln traveled by rail to some of the Lincoln-Douglas debate sites and was greeted by throngs of hundreds at the stations. He took trains around the state to court and to speak for Republican candidates. And he boarded the train at 11:15 a.m. on Wednesday, February 22, 1860, for New

York and Cooper Union. The trip took three days and Lincoln changed trains twice in the middle of the night. He made it to Philadelphia at 1:00 a.m. on Saturday and then into New York later that day.

Lincoln's Cooper Union presentation the night of February 27, 1860, is said to have been the speech that brought him to national prominence as a voice of reason against the continuing threat from the Southern, slavery-promoting political forces. It is a masterwork of perspective, argument, and persuasion. It was reprinted in newspapers across the nation. Again, Lincoln spoke of progress, saying that to adhere only to the past (as the opposition had framed the conflict) would "be to discard all the lights of the current experience—to reject all progress—all improvement." He ended with a call to action. "Let us have faith that right makes might, and in that faith, let us, to the end, dare to do our duty as we understand it."

In 1860, presidential candidates were nominated directly at political conventions, without primaries or caucuses. The April Democratic Party convention in Charleston, South Carolina, adjourned without a nominee. The Republicans were to meet in Chicago in the middle of May. In a candid letter to political ally Lyman Trumbull, dated April 29, Lincoln let it be known that he did see an opening for a run for the office. "I will be entirely frank. The taste *is* in my mouth a little."

Lincoln accepted the Republican nomination for president three weeks later on May 19, 1860. He ran against a Democratic party in disarray. Once again, Stephen Douglas was his main opponent; two splinter-faction tickets headed by John Breckenridge and John Bell divided the Southern states' votes.

When Abraham Lincoln was nearly eight years old, his father moved the family some sixty miles and across the Ohio River from Kentucky to Indiana—from a slave state to the opportunity of a free state. Sixty miles and the Ohio River had then effectively separated them from slavery. Not quite fifty years later, steamboats and railroads had overtaken long-distance travel by foot and horse. News and information sped across copper telegraph wires. And no state was isolated from the controversy of slavery.

The stage was set for Lincoln's presidency and the Civil War that was to follow.

IRISH STEW

· · · · · · ·

There are numerous Irish stew recipes in period sources. This is one of the best, not only of the period recipes, but also of any stew I've made. The ratio of a relatively small quantity of inexpensive mutton to the much larger amount of cheaper potato in this recipe and others reflects the challenging economic situation of many Irish immigrants.

1	**pound boneless breast of mutton or beef chuck**
1 ½	**cups water**
¼	**teaspoon salt**
½	**teaspoon freshly ground black pepper**
2	**pounds small, or B-size, red potatoes, cut into ¼-inch-thick slices**
1 or 2	**medium onions, peeled and thinly sliced**

Put the meat into a heavy stew pan with a lid. Add water. Simmer for 1 hour, or until the meat is tender. Spoon the meat from the broth and cut into small pieces. Sprinkle with salt and freshly ground black pepper to taste. Divide the meat into thirds. Divide the potatoes and onions into thirds as well. Put one-third of the potatoes in the bottom of the pot, cover and simmer with one-third of the meat and one-third of the onions. Repeat until all are back in the pot. Simmer until the potatoes are tender, about another half hour to an hour. Watch carefully, shaking the pot from time to time so the potatoes don't stick to the bottom and scorch.

TIP FOR SUCCESS: Having the right pot size is key to this delicious dish. A tall, narrow, heavy pot will allow you to have the nine layers of meat and potatoes so that the simmering broth will cook and flavor the potatoes evenly.

Makes 8 servings

ADAPTED FROM "IRISH STEW," AN AMERICAN LADY, *THE AMERICAN HOME COOK BOOK*, 1854.

GERMAN BEEF WITH SOUR CREAM

• • • • • • •

The kitchen fills with delicious aromas as this simply seasoned beef roasts to perfection while creating the basis for a sour cream sauce. Letting the roast rest while you finish up the gravy allows the juices to be retained in the meat as you slice it for serving. This hearty dish goes well with sauerkraut.

- 1   **2- to 3-pound beef round or rump roast**
- ³/₄ **cup sour cream**
- ¹/₂ **cup milk, approximately**
  - **Salt and freshly ground black pepper, to taste**

Remove the meat from the refrigerator and allow it to come to room temperature, about an hour.

Make a basting sauce by combining the sour cream with enough milk to thin to the consistency of whipping cream and put in the refrigerator. Depending on the size of your roast, you may need to mix up more.

Preheat the oven to 375°F. Sprinkle the meat with salt and pepper. Put fat side up in a roasting pan and roast for 30 minutes. Lower the oven temperature to 225°F. The meat should reach medium rare internal temperature of 135° to 140°F in 2 to 3 hours. After the first 10 minutes at this lower temperature, baste with the sour cream mixture. Continue basting every half hour. Stop basting about a half hour before you think the meat will be finished. Remove the meat to a plate and let it rest, covered with foil, for 15 minutes. Gently mix the juices and sour cream in the baking pan to make a sauce.

Makes 8 to 10 servings

ADAPTED FROM "TENDERLOIN WITH SOUR CREAM," WILLIAM VOLLMER, *THE UNITED STATES COOK BOOK: A COMPLETE MANUAL FOR LADIES, HOUSEKEEPERS, AND COOKS*, 1859.

SERVING SAUERKRAUT: Next to beer, sauerkraut may be the most famous German traditional menu item. Lincoln's neighbors and friends probably shared their homemade cabbage dish as a special treat. A German-American cookbook, *The United States Cook Book: A Complete Manual for Ladies, Housekeepers, and Cooks*, offers this way for serving sauerkraut:

> Sour Kraut is best, when boiled very slowly for six hours with some good roast meat-drippings and the requisite quantity of soup-stock. A few minutes before dishing, pour over it some good white wine and then send it to the table with an accompaniment to suit your taste. It must be very soft and nearly quite dry. If a couple of pounds of fresh pork are cooked with the sour kraut, it will give a nice flavor.

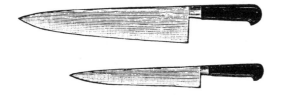

MINCED BEEF THE PORTUGUESE WAY

• • • • • • •

This version of steak and eggs makes the most out of leftover meat and bread. Quickly cooked, the ingredients are arranged in a fanciful manner and glazed with a sugar syrup. The communal serving platter welcomes guests to a hearty meal with a strong sense of international style.

> 1 ½ **pounds chopped cooked sirloin**
> 1 **tablespoon flour**
> 1 **cup prepared beef gravy**
> **Salt and freshly ground black pepper, to taste**
> ¼ **cup simple sugar syrup or melted apple jelly, to glaze**
> 3 **pieces of homemade-style bread, toasted, buttered, and cut into triangles**
> 6 **eggs, poached or hard-boiled**

Place the beef in a medium frying pan and warm it over low heat. Sprinkle with the flour and stir to blend. Stir in the gravy. Taste and add salt and black pepper if needed. Stir until thoroughly warmed, but do not let it boil. Stir in a tablespoon of the glaze or jelly.

To serve, take a large serving dish or pie plate and stand the bread triangles on edge so that the points meet in the center. Fill the areas in between with the meat mixture. Make a hollow in the center of each meat section for an egg. Sprinkle the eggs with a little pepper, salt, and a few drops of glaze. Glaze the combs of bread and serve.

Makes 6 generous servings

ADAPTED FROM PERIOD SOURCES.

OYSTER STEW

· · · · · · ·

In the nineteenth century, oysters were a popular, inexpensive, and well-traveled seafood. Barrels of live oysters traveled south and west from New York and Baltimore harbors. Canned oysters, too, filled store shelves in Springfield. Mace, the ground husk of a nutmeg, was a common seasoning at the time. Here it adds both a mellow and slightly sharp subtle flavor to the light stew.

TO STEW OYSTERS:

- **1 pint shucked oysters with liquid**
- **¼ teaspoon ground mace**
- **Peel from 1 lemon**
- **4 white peppercorns**
- **1 cup light cream**
- **2 tablespoons flour**
- **2 tablespoons butter, at room temperature**
- **"Snippets," small triangles of homemade-style bread, toasted and buttered, to serve**

Drain the oysters, reserving their liquor. Wash to remove any grit and filter the oyster liquor to remove grit as well. Place the oysters, liquor, mace, lemon peel, and peppercorns in a small saucepan. Stir in the cream and simmer very gently over low heat, until the edges of the oysters curl up indicating that they are cooked, about 5 minutes. Mix the flour and butter with a fork into a smooth paste. Remove the oysters from the cooking liquid and keep warm. Drop small bits of the flour mixture into the liquid then stir until smooth and thickened. Return the oysters to the liquid to warm through. Serve with "snippets."

Makes 4 servings as an appetizer.

ADAPTED FROM "OYSTERS, STEWED," MISS ELIZA LESLIE,
MISS LESLIE'S NEW RECEIPTS FOR COOKING, 1852.

12

INAUGURAL JOURNEY BANQUETS AND SETTLING INTO THE WHITE HOUSE

The Lincolns arrived in the City of Washington, as the downtown core of the District of Columbia was called, in the 1860s. They had left Springfield, Illinois, where they lived their daily routines surrounded by friends and family. They had traveled east buoyed on waves of adulation, but that changed as they entered the city filled with doubters and, at times, even enemies.

We lived in the Washington area for a while, moving there from the Midwest, as had the Lincolns. I was surprised at how southern the nation's capital felt in the mid-1970s. The rich aroma of boxwood hedges filled the air in the residential side streets of Washington, as well as in the gardens of George Washington's home, Mount Vernon, and the narrow, cobbled streets of Alexandria. There was a different rhythm to life and different foods, too. Some foods we know were common in the Lincolns' kitchen—grits and country ham—were unfamiliar to me and my midwestern way of cooking. It was our first experience living in the South away from family and familiar customs. As we tiptoed below the Mason-Dixon Line, southern style took some getting used to.

The Lincolns faced bigger changes when they arrived in the City of Washington. During the first year in the White House, Mary Lincoln invited Illinois friends and family to stay in the presidential home while she carefully reached out to old friends and new acquaintances to establish a secure world for their sons and to create moments of escape for increasingly besieged Abraham.

Julia Taft, whose younger brothers became constant playmates for Lincoln's sons Willie and Tad, wrote of the Southern influence even on Northern families living in Washington on the eve of the inauguration. "Before the war Washington was really a Southern city. We were accustomed to the convenience of having Negro servants and a good many Northern people like my parents hired such servants from their masters, though they would have been horrified at the idea of actually owning slaves."

I had thought that writing about the food during Lincoln's White House years would be a simple task. Certainly, now that the Lincolns were in Washington, there would be extensive reports of their every action, including the meals they ate. I was wrong. I did find people who presented key insights into life in the Lincoln White House, a few food descriptions, and an inaugural dinner mystery. I'll tell those stories in two chapters. This chapter focuses on 1861, the first year the Lincolns spent in the White House. The next chapter centers on their sanctuary at what is now called "President Lincoln's Cottage," a summer White House just three miles northeast of the White House.

We begin with the journey from Springfield. Abraham Lincoln had left Washington eleven years earlier when he completed his term in Congress. Now, the train carrying President-elect Lincoln, Mary, Robert, Willie, and Tad along with Lincoln's secretaries, John Nicolay and John Hay, and two people from Springfield (Ellen, a nanny, and William H. Johnson, the young man of color who served as Lincoln's barber and valet) traveled twelve days on a circuitous route from Springfield to Washington. Crowds thronged the route eager to see the new president and his family. Lincoln made speeches at nearly all of the seventy-five city and town stops along the way, no matter how brief. Even at small stations, he would appear and say a few words to the gathering. At many places he offered this standard comment: "I appear before you merely to greet you and say farewell. If I should make a speech at every town, I would not get to Washington until some time after the inauguration."

There was more time for entertaining and politics at the overnight stops in Indianapolis, Cincinnati, Columbus, Pittsburgh, Cleveland, Buffalo, Albany, New York City, and Harrisburg. In those cities Lincoln spoke to crowds numbering in the tens of thousands. Civic leaders and political allies tried to outdo each other, hosting receptions, levees, balls, and concerts. Former President Millard Fillmore headed the welcoming committee in Buffalo.

For all the meals in public and private on this journey eastward, the press reported only two menus. None of the travelers on the train or guests at these breakfasts, lunches, and dinners apparently noted them either. At a brief stop in Syracuse, lunch was brought on board. Waiters passed "various dishes including chicken, turkey, bread, and cake."

Finally, in New York City, a newspaper reports a full menu! And what a menu it was. The Lincoln party spent the nights of February 19 and 20 lodging at the famed Astor House, a six-story hotel on the west side of Broadway in the Wall Street area, between Vesey and Barclay Streets. Lincoln had stayed in the hotel just a year before as he prepared to give his address at the Cooper Union. Then, he walked from the station to the hotel and checked into a small, first-floor room. This time, the presidential party rode in eleven carriages from 30th Street Station to the hotel, where they stayed in a suite of rooms. Lincoln rode in an open carriage with a military aide, Colonel Edward Sumner, city alderman Charles Cornell, and Illinois friend Judge David Davis. The *Baltimore Sun* reported that there was no band or military company in this procession as there had been at some of the other overnight stops.

The New York agenda was full. Lincoln met with a constant stream of politicians, friends, and business leaders. Two competing hat manufacturers each presented him with a top hat. When asked their relative value, Lincoln tactfully replied, "They mutually surpassed each other." The Lincoln family did find time for sightseeing. President-elect Lincoln attended the opera at the Academy of Music. Mrs. Lincoln and the boys accepted P. T. Barnum's invitation to see the wonders at his museum.

The Astor House was the leading hotel of the day. Its 309 rooms surrounded a central courtyard covered by a cast-iron and glass roof. Many of its staff lived in the hotel, ready to provide top-level service. The presidential party dined in their suite both nights of their stay. The *New York Herald* published the details of the elegant "reception" dinner on the first night. The party of ten was seated at a round table with a nosegay of flowers at each place. The oval menu card was printed in black ink with a gold border, and "pink and other soft colors" formed the outer decorative edge. Although the menu reprinted in the newspaper lists the meal being served in five courses, the statement that "the buffet carried a handsome new silver service, never used before," and the number of entrée choices, suggest the meal was presented as a buffet or, perhaps, family style, with the Lincolns helping themselves to the rich foods.

As printed in the *Herald*, there was a first course of a light soup of julienned vegetables in broth, then a fish course of boiled salmon with anchovy sauce. Two cold dishes followed: tureen of goose liver and boned turkey with jelly. Next, the main course offered six choices: larded fillet of beef with green peas, larded sweetbreads with tomato sauce, fillet of chicken with truffle sauce, Shrewsbury oysters baked in their shells, roast canvasback duck, and roast stuffed quail. Sturdy vegetables rounded out the main course choices: potatoes—boiled or mashed—turnips in cream sauce, beets, lettuce, and celery. For dessert the Lincoln party could select fresh seasonal fruits, ice cream, champagne jelly, claret jelly—think wine Jell-O—or a variety of pastries: Charlotte Russe, cream cakes, cupcakes, ladies' fingers, and kisses—a meringue cookie.

The next evening Vice President-elect Hannibal Hamlin and his wife, Ellen, joined the Lincoln family group. The newspaper published this menu in French. The translated dishes included raw oysters in the shell, brunoise soup with poached egg—like the julienne soup the previous evening, only the vegetables are diced instead of thinly sliced—stuffed shad, stuffed quail, lamb chops with mushrooms and small potatoes fried in butter, chicken timbale—minced chicken molded with decorative pieces of beef tongue and black truffles—and partridge. The canvasback duck made a repeat appearance. Many of the same vegetables were served, too: boiled potatoes, potatoes au gratin, spinach with eggs, small peas French style, turnips in cream sauce, beets, celery, and lettuce. Champagne and Bordeaux jellies, Charlotte Russe, Swiss meringue, almond macaroons, and vanilla ice cream completed the meal.

But we have more than a menu from the Astor House. Thanks to the efforts of a *New York Times* reporter, we have a sense of the hotel's service standard and food quality. In 1859 the "Strong-Minded Reporter of the Times," as his articles were by-lined, embarked on a series of restaurant reviews from one end of New York to the other, from the swanky "Astor House restaurant to the smallest description of a dining saloon in the City." Of the Astor House he wrote: "The waiter who would permit himself to call out to another or in any way to disturb 'the harmony of the meeting,' would be—well, I should not like to state publicly what they really do with waiters at that establishment under such circumstances—but they do it immediately. The meats are all cooked in perfection and served in perfection, and the bread!—I am ready at any moment to go before a Justice of the Peace and affirm ... that it is the best bread in the Universe."

On February 21 the Lincolns left New York heading to Pennsylvania, stopping in the state capital, Harrisburg. On the 23rd, as the route continued southward, traveling through Philadelphia and Baltimore to Washington, the risk to President-elect Lincoln increased. There were rumors of a plot to assassinate Lincoln when he passed through Baltimore. To thwart the attack, Lincoln, friend Ward Lamon, and detective Alan Pinkerton with his female operative Kate Worne boarded a middle-of-the-night train from Philadelphia into Washington, arriving without incident at six in the morning. Mrs. Lincoln and the rest of the presidential party followed on the scheduled train, arriving at four in the afternoon. The Lincolns, their family, and small staff checked into the Willard Hotel, Washington's leading hotel, for the ten days until the inauguration and their move into the White House.

And now we come to the food puzzle during the first hours of the Lincoln administration, what I call the "Great Lincoln Inaugural Corned Beef and Cabbage Mystery." According to Willard Hotel oral history, Lincoln, after taking the oath of office, enjoyed an inaugural meal at the hotel consisting of mock turtle soup, corned beef and cabbage, parsley potatoes, and blackberry pie. Some print and Internet sources suggest that after the swearing-in ceremony and his inaugural address, Lincoln actually walked back to the Willard where he ate the corned beef meal, watched the inaugural parade, and then somehow got to the White House just a couple of blocks down Pennsylvania Avenue.

Much more reliable sources, including the benchmark *Day by Day*, an authoritative collection from primary sources, present a more realistic description of the full day's events. Outgoing President James Buchanan picked Abraham Lincoln up at the Willard shortly after noon. They rode to the Capitol in an open carriage. The family followed in another carriage along with the rest of the "procession." Sixteen-year-old Julia Taft watched from a window above Pennsylvania Avenue. "Troops lined the avenue and at every corner there was a mounted orderly. The usual applause was lacking as the President's carriage, surrounded by a close guard of cavalry, passed and an ugly murmur punctuated by some abusive remarks followed it down the avenue."

At about one o'clock from the East Portico, Lincoln began his inaugural address and, after speaking for about a half hour, he then took the oath of office. In his speech, Lincoln reached out to the Southern states considering secession: "We are not enemies, but friends." He closed with a call to unified patriotism. "The mystic chords of memory, stretching from every battle-field and patriot grave, to every living heart and hearthstone, all over this broad land, will yet swell the chorus of the Union, when again touched, as surely they will be, by the better angels of our nature."

After the ceremonies Lincoln got back into the carriage with now former President Buchanan and drove, again in a celebratory procession, "the parade," to the White House.

The Lincolns' first meal in the executive mansion was an "elegant dinner" arranged by Miss Harriet Lane, President Buchanan's niece and official hostess, as reported by Mary Lincoln's cousin Elizabeth Todd Grimsley, one of the relatives who traveled from Springfield for the inauguration. Mrs. Grimsley stayed with the Lincolns for six months and described the settling-in process. She wrote that at the end of the ceremonies former President Buchanan escorted President Lincoln to the vestibule of the Executive Mansion, "where, after courteous words of welcome, he left him."

Mrs. Grimsley explained that the White House was "in a perfect state of readiness for the incomers—A competent chef with efficient butler and waiters under the direction of Miss Lane had an elegant dinner prepared." Seventeen people sat down to dinner, including Mary's sister Elizabeth Edwards and her two daughters. Alas, Mrs. Grimsley neglected to provide the menu. The only food she mentioned on public or family tables during her whole six-month stay was Potomac shad. After eating it, everyone in the family took ill. Some suspected poisoning, but the reason she gave was simply overconsumption of a food "new to Western palates."

So, what about the corned beef and cabbage back at the Willard? On March 3, the evening before he was inaugurated, Lincoln hosted a dinner at the hotel for his incoming cabinet secretaries, William Seward, Salmon Chase, Gideon Wells, Montgomery Blair, Simon Cameron, Caleb Smith, and Edwards Bates. It seems to me there were two meals that could be considered "inaugural dinners": the elegant one served in the White House and this homey, welcoming meal Abraham Lincoln requested the day before for the men who would stand by him during the challenges to come.

Although we don't know the menu at the first White House dinner, Mrs. Grimsley's characterization does give us a clue. I would suggest that the "elegant" meal is similar to the ones served to the Lincoln party in New York, a Frenchified repast rich with choices and sauces. The Lincolns held their first official state dinner two weeks later. They hosted the members of the cabinet and a visiting reporter, William Russell of the *London Times*. He described the atmosphere and cuisine of the event but, again, not the menu. The state dinner "was not remarkable for ostentation. No liveried servants, no *Persie* splendor of ancient plate or *chefs d'oeuvre* of art glittered round the board. Vases of flowers decorated the table, combined with dishes in what may be called the 'Gallo-American' style, with wines which owed their parentage to France and their rearing and education to the United States, which abounds in stunning nurseries for such productions."

This style of food was not all that uncommon across America during the 1850s. Even in Minnesota at the western edge of the settled country, French-American dishes made their way onto tables, at least for special occasions. I've seen menus from those years in early St. Paul, Minnesota—when people had cows in their backyards and Native Americans walked the streets in tribal dress—menus with the same kinds of dishes that the chefs at the Astor House prepared for the Lincolns' stay. At a banquet for the Minnesota Historical Society on June 24, 1856, the chefs of the Winslow House Hotel prepared a rich and varied array including real turtle soup, oyster soup, boiled shad with "anchovia sauce," several roasted and boiled meat dishes, and a dozen entrées, all with Gallo-American flair: veal cutlets à la Florentine, calves feet à la tortune, fricandeau veal à la toulauce, and boiled beef à la Parisienne, to name a few. The twenty dessert selections included champagne jelly, Victoria and Albert pudding, and lemon ice cream.

Although there aren't any surviving Springfield restaurant menus from the era, display advertisements in the 1850s city directories certainly give the suggestion of similar fare. Springfield's fancy foods could have filled the bill. In 1857 Edmund Duchamel advertised his "French Restaurant" serving up "every delicacy in season ... in the most superior style and shortest notice." James Busher was serving "Persian Sherbet and root beer" from his brewery and malt house at the west end of Jefferson Street. In January 1858 editions of the Springfield newspaper, Edouard Doul of the St. Louis restaurant advertised that he had received, "from Paris (France) of his own importation the delicacies ... Pates du Fois gras (Strasborg) and Pates du Poulard." He offered them "cheap for cash."

We don't know if any of these fancy foods made their way onto the Lincolns' table. They "often entertained small numbers of friends at dinner and somewhat larger numbers at evening parties." Although that unnamed writer says these were held in a "simple way," that doesn't mean a few bits of fancy foods couldn't have been served. Young Mary Lincoln did, after all, attend a French boarding school in Lexington and grew up in a home where her family entertained leading politicians and businessmen. These are just hints at the sophisticated foods and beverages the Lincolns left behind in Illinois.

The Lincoln family left more than familiar foods and shops behind. They left behind family and friends and the certainty of their place in society. One of the first things Mary did as the family settled into the White House was to seek playmates for Willie and Tad, and the Taft boys fit the bill perfectly. Mrs. Lincoln and Mrs. Taft had met at a reception and on learning Bud was twelve and Holly eight, near enough in age to the Lincoln boys who were ten and almost eight, Mrs. Lincoln asked that they come to play. Older sister Julia described the first time they came to call at Mrs. Lincoln's request. "We went into the conservatory and there stood the boys by the water-lily tank watching the goldfish. Such nice, quiet, shy boys, I thought. In five minutes the four boys had disappeared and I saw them no more that day." The Taft boys returned home filthy dirty at dark and reported that they "had the best time and had been all over the White House. Mrs. Lincoln said we must come every day and bring Julia ... Mr. Lincoln jounced us on his lap and told us stories."

The boys did eat hard-boiled eggs, at least once. On Easter Monday, April 1, the Lincoln and Taft boys took part in the annual Easter Egg Roll on the White House lawn. The activity was new to Willie and Tad, and Julia reported they "enjoyed it immensely." Each of the four boys had a basket filled with the brightly colored eggs. "The players stand at the top of the hill and watch their eggs race to the bottom. The one which first arrives is the winner; the cracked or broken ones go to the victor who eats them or is expected to."

The children and their raucous activities were an important escape for President Lincoln. Mary Lincoln invited adult guests, too, for breakfast, tea, and dinner in an attempt to relieve the stresses of office. But Willie, Tad, Bud, and Holly had the run of the place. Once, Julia walked in on them wrestling Lincoln to the ground. Another time, Tad fired a toy cannon into the Cabinet Room while the cabinet was meeting, and there were countless other adventures involving dolls that needed pardoning and animals that needed rescuing. It was the boys' attic theatrical event, which all the staff and soldiers who had five cents could come and watch, that caused Lincoln to throw back his head and laugh heartily. Julia recounted that it was the "only time I ever saw Mr. Lincoln really laugh all over."

When Lincoln first took office, he was besieged at all hours by people who wanted to be appointed to office in the new Republican government. In 1861 the city was smaller than it is today and so was the White House. The Oval Office wasn't added until the twentieth century, when the wings on either side were expanded. Today the second floor of the White House is private. In 1861 there were public and private rooms on both the first and second floors. Even the president's office was upstairs. The White House was seemingly as open as the streets. Reporter Noah Brooks described the daily access: "Let us go to the Executive Mansion, there is nobody to bar our passage, and the multitude washed or unwashed always has free ingress and egress.... The right or west wing of the house is occupied by the President's family, the center by the state parlors and the east wing has below stairs the famous East Room and upstairs the offices of the President and his secretaries."

During this time, Lincoln was trying to manage conditions to avoid the looming war. He said of those days that he was "like a man so busy renting rooms at one end of his house that he has no time to put out a fire burning in the other." Concerned for her husband's health, Mary Lincoln instituted a daily carriage ride to "induce him to take the fresh air."

The crush of presidential social obligations was seemingly equal to the besiegements of office seekers and petitioners. The president was to hold a kind of open house, a levee, on Tuesday evenings and Saturday afternoons when Congress was in session. These events were essentially receiving lines. The Marine Band played and President and Mrs. Lincoln greeted all the guests, the president shaking each person's hand and Mrs. Lincoln simply speaking with them. After all guests had been greeted, the Lincolns would mingle a bit. There weren't any refreshments served. It was also expected "that during each winter he will entertain at dinner all the members of both Houses of Congress and the Diplomatic Corps so that official dinners have to be given by him as often as twice a week."

On March 12, 1861, President and Mrs. Lincoln held a party with "music and dancing," according to a letter sent by John Nicolay. On June 7, 1861, Mrs. Grimsley quoted the *Washington Star* report of the first formal dinner the Lincolns hosted for the diplomatic corps: "The dinner was served in a style to indicate Mrs. Lincoln's good taste and good judgment had exercised supervision."

Lincoln hoped with his inaugural address and policies that he could buy time to solve the problems with the rebelling states, but when he first entered his office on March 5, 1861, he received a letter from Major Robert Anderson at Fort Sumter in South Carolina, stating that the garrison would run out of supplies in a month or six weeks. Lincoln said later, "Of all the trials I have had since I came here, none begin to compare with those I had between the inauguration and the [April 13] fall of Fort Sumter."

After the South Carolina troops turned back a supply ship and fired on Fort Sumter, Southern states continued to secede from the Union. Topographically, Washington sits in a bowl, and when Lincoln took office, the militarily advantageous "high ground" surrounding it was in opposition control. Baltimore, just forty miles north of the capital city, had strong Southern sympathies. Richmond, Virginia, soon to become the capital of the Confederate States, was just a hundred miles south.

Washington became isolated. As Julia Taft described, "There was one Sunday [in April] when Washington realized that it was entirely cut off from the North. Wires were down and rails torn up and the city shivered in fear of a mob of Baltimore 'pug-uglies' that were reported on the way to burn and pillage."

The Lincoln and Taft boys built a fort on the roof of the White House with a small log serving as a cannon and a "few old condemned rifles." All four boys spent hours up on the roof during 1861 pretending that it was a fort or a man-of-war ship.

Real troops from Massachusetts fought their way through Baltimore and reached the city on April 19. They arrived "with bands playing and flags flying as they came up to the [White House]." Soon more troops arrived from New York and other states. By early summer "Washington had become a great camp with more regiments arriving daily. Everyone breathed easier and felt that the war was as good as won."

Two months later, on July 21, 1861, the first battle was fought at Bull Run. The Union forces were routed. The nation was at war and it would not be over quickly.

From all accounts, the Lincolns fell into a work- and war-driven routine with chaotic interruptions from the boys. In the morning, President Lincoln was up reading, writing, and working long before the rest of the household or even the city. Mrs. Lincoln would call him in to breakfast about eight o'clock, and by nine he would be back at his desk with doors opened to the throngs. Mrs. Grimsley reported that Mrs. Lincoln frequently "invited well-known friends to breakfast and then sent word to the President we had company [and] breakfast was waiting for him."

His breakfasts were simple: an egg and some toast or other bread. If he stopped for lunch around noon, he often had just a biscuit and a glass of milk in the winter, and fruit, grapes, or apples in the summer. His law partner William Herndon later recalled the way Lincoln ate an apple. "His manipulation of an apple when he ate it was unique. He disdained the use of a knife to cut or pare it. Instead he would grasp it around the equatorial part, holding it thus until his thumb and forefinger almost met, sink his teeth into it, and then unlike the average person, begin eating at the blossom end. When he was done he had eaten his way over and through rather than around and into it. Such, at least, was his explanation. I never saw an apple thus disposed of by any one else."

In one of her few surviving 1861 letters, Mary Lincoln wrote that she had received a box of delicious grapes from General George McClellan and that they "often received delightful fruit from New Jersey."

Mary Lincoln wrote in a letter to her friend Hannah Shearer that entertaining in the White House was "very different from home." In the White House, "[W]e only have to give our orders for the dinner and dress in proper season."

Certainly not every meal in the White House was served with fancy French sauces and fussily fixed vegetables. As I tested a few of the French-inspired entrées, I quickly discovered those dishes are the culinary equivalent of an 1860s ball gown—all ruffled and tucked, decorated with lace and braid, and assembled with a lot of work, specialized ingredients, and skills—elevating something that could be simple and lovely into an extraordinary experience. Many of the dishes highlighted on inaugural-journey menus were designed to be made in restaurant or hotel kitchens, where hundreds are fed at each sitting. (During the pre-inaugural crush, the Willard Hotel sometimes fed 1,500 people in a day.) These fancy dishes called for an array of sauces that required hours to make from cooked-down stocks, only to have a tablespoon put onto the dish as a finishing flourish. Delicious, yes, but not practical for a working household with any number of guests invited to stay at the drop of a hat. Stews, roasts, soups, and masses of simply cooked vegetables made much more sense for the Lincolns to serve in the White House.

We do have a hint of very ordinary dishes on the menu. As I wrote in Chapter 9, Dr. Henry M. Pierce and his nephew discovered President Lincoln eating leftover baked beans for breakfast. And the Taft boys stayed to dinner so often that their mother scolded them about it. I can't imagine these active, mischievous boys between the ages of eight and twelve dining on veal cutlets à la Florentine. Julia recounted, "My mother often told them not to 'make a nuisance of yourselves by always staying at meals.' When the President and Mrs. Lincoln had distinguished visitors at dinner, the boys would sometimes have their dinner in another room and declared that to be great fun." All four boys even attended a state dinner, sitting near the foot of the table.

Fortunately, Illinois friend Orville Hickman Browning visited several times and commented in his diary. Browning was appointed to the senate seat of Stephen Douglas after Douglas died from typhoid fever in June 1861. As was his style in his Springfield diary entries, Browning did not detail menus, but we get the sense that the guests for breakfast, tea, and dinner were often last-minute invitations. If you were in the White House at mealtime, you were invited to sit down. He wrote on Sunday, July 28, 1861: "Got back to the city at 10 O'clock and I went to Dr. Gurley's Church. President and his wife there, and upon their invitation I went home with them to dinner. I had a great deal of conversation with the present [president], being left alone for an hour or two before dinner. At 5 ½ P.M. Mrs. Lincoln brought me home in her carriage." His entry for Sunday, December 15, 1861, noted, "At Dr. Gurley's Church in the morning. At 5 P. M. went with Colman Sympson to call on the President—I remained to tea—Galloway of Ohio & Colfax of Indiana at tea also."

On May 11, the president held an impromptu levee for children. Carl Schurz, political ally and ambassador to Spain, ended up staying for tea. I ran across a charming 1860 book, *Breakfast, Dinner, and Tea*, that describes the expectations for tea. "In fashionable life tea does not deserve the name of meal since it is seldom more than tea or coffee served in the parlor accompanied by cakes. Tea and cakes, bread and butter various relishes and fruits either fresh or preserved."

White House staff members needed to eat, too. The 1860 federal census, taken several months before the Lincolns moved in, lists fifteen people living in the White House in addition to the members of President Buchanan's family. Some of the names were still there in March, including Richard Goodchild and Pierre Vermeren, for whom the Lincolns later wrote letters of recommendation. Additional White House staff would have been present at meal times although they may not have lived there. Mrs. Grimsley mentioned Edward the doorman and [Thomas] Stackpole, in addition to "maids and scullions," the chef, butler, and waiters. Julia Taft names Mr. Watts, the head of the conservatory, and a "bouquet maker" who worked under him providing floral arrangements for the White House and bouquets for gifts. In the Lincoln personal household, there are the two servants who had come with them from Springfield: Ellen, who helped as seamstress, maid, and nanny for the boys; and valet William H. Johnson. Mrs. Lincoln hired Alexander Williamson as a tutor to teach the Lincoln and Taft boys, as the city schools were closed. And of course, Lincoln's personal secretaries John Nicolay and John Hay were there for meals.

Mr. Williamson provided a small homey detail in a reminiscence published in 1869. He wrote of Lincoln scarcely having "time even for his meals. I have found him in the office squatting on the rug in front of the fire trying to heat his cup of coffee, which, owing to early visitors, had been allowed to cool."

The White House's lower-level kitchen was originally located in the center of the ground floor, which could be considered a partial basement. It had north-facing windows. Sometime in the middle of the nineteenth century, the kitchen was relocated to the northwest corner. This may have been one of Mary Lincoln's improvements to the living conditions of the White House. After the North Portico was constructed in 1830, the kitchen windows were blocked by this new entrance to the White House. Relocating the kitchen to a corner with windows made sense.

As to what the meals were cooked upon, Thomas Jefferson had a large cast-iron stove installed sometime during his administration—1801–10. The thoroughly modern stove was fueled by coal and had "stew holes, or water heaters, spits, and a crane." This stove fit into one of the two original large cooking hearths and survived the 1814 White House fire set by the British during the War of 1812. It was repaired by a blacksmith and reinstalled when the White House was rebuilt in 1817.

Was this the stove used for cooking President and Mrs. Lincoln's meals more than forty years later? There isn't any clear evidence one way or another. But, one of Mary Lincoln's chief complaints was the run-down condition of the President's Mansion. The furniture in the family rooms was so "deplorably shabby" that it "looked as if it had been brought in by the first President." I'm willing to bet the third president's stove was still being used in the household of the sixteenth.

With all of these people to feed, it stands to reason that the food would be along the lines of typical home-cooked meals. Ladies' magazines and cookbooks of the era describe the order of basic dinners and suggest some of the dishes. Begin with a soup or fish course, move on to roasted meat accompanied by appropriate vegetables, perhaps with some pickles or other "relishes" on the side, and then a dessert.

Who cooked all those meals? We have a few names but no certainty.

Mrs. Grimsley mentioned a "chef" on-site who cooked their first White House meal. It may have been that the chef, typically a male, was a caterer brought in to cook the more elaborate meals. William Crook, one of the policemen who served as a White House guard, wrote that this was the case in the later years of the administration. Four women are described as "cook" by various sources. Two of them are named: Cornelia Mitchell, a woman of color, and Alice Johnstone, whom Mrs. Lincoln asked if she knew how to prepare chicken fricassee with gravy and biscuits to tempt President Lincoln's appetite when the stresses of office kept him from eating.

As 1861 drew to a close, the war and politics intruded into Lincoln's social life and even his recreational carriage rides. Often he would stop at military encampments. Frequently he took Secretary of State William Seward along, much to Mary's frustration. In December a cold snap brought hopes of snow to Willie and Tad. They described the fun of sledding, skating, and "snow-balling" to Bud and Holly, who had never seen snow. But the days only brought a few flurries.

Lincoln had to deal with another much more serious flurry in the White House: the Trent Affair that threatened to bring England into war against the North. Two Southern emissaries sneaking to England to request diplomatic recognition for the Confederate States of America were forcibly taken off the British ship the *Trent* by the crew of a U.S. ship. England saw this action as a provocation.

Orville Browning was at tea in the White House when Secretary Seward burst into the room with "dispatches [from the British] saying the arrests had been a violation of International law." Diplomatic and political discussions continued until Christmas morning, when the cabinet met at 10:00 a.m. to agree to a solution. Letters from England conveyed that the British "did not want war with us and that if this trouble is settled they will not interfere in our domestic rebellion." The meeting continued until 2:00 p.m., as Secretary Seward argued for releasing the emissaries without an apology to the British government, laying the groundwork for averting the crisis.

Christmas Day was bright and warm. Browning reported he "could walk about without his overcoat." The only thing we know of the White House Christmas holiday celebration was a dinner held sometime after

6:00 p.m. attended by Browning and about fifteen others, including members of the administration; friends from Kentucky; Dr. Jayne, an old Springfield friend; the pastor of the church the Lincolns attended, Reverend Dr. Phineas Gurley, and his wife, Emma; along with Postmaster General Blair and his wife; and Assistant Secretary of the Navy Gustavus Fox and his wife.

As to Christmas customs, the Lincolns had not put up a Christmas tree in Springfield, although some of their German neighbors probably had brought the custom with them to Illinois. *Godey's Lady's* magazine printed illustrations of candlelit Christmas trees annually and they published a short story in 1860 that practically gave a step-by-step description of how to install a tree on Christmas Eve and keep it fresh for a few days. As to presents, in Springfield shops advertised small gifts for Christmas giving and were even open on the day itself for shopping. Following the holiday custom related in "'Twas the Night before Christmas" (1823), the Lincoln boys may have hung their stockings by the chimney to find them filled with gifts on Christmas morning. And maybe they left cookies or some Christmas shortbreads for the red-dressed gentleman.

As to the dinner, we could do no worse than take a look at the *Godey's* suggested menu: "Boiled turkey with oyster sauce, roast goose with apple sauce, roasted ham, chicken pie, stewed beets, cole slaw, turnips, salsify, winter squash, mince pie, plum pudding, lemon custard, cranberry pie."

The new year began with a sense of normalcy in the midst of war. Lincoln faced major decisions in 1862 regarding the conduct of the war and, specifically, the need to replace his Secretary of War Simon Cameron. Still, President and Mrs. Lincoln held the traditional New Year's open house reception. The doors opened at 11:00 a.m. The cabinet members and their families walked into the East Room first, followed by the diplomatic corps in gold-braided formal dress. The members of the Supreme Court and officers of the army and navy shook hands with the president before the doors were opened for the general public between noon and 2:00 p.m. Mrs. Frances Seward, wife of the secretary of state, wrote to her sister that "the carriages are rolling along the streets as they used to in old times."

BRUNOISE SOUP

•••••••

This soup is a delicious demonstration of a French cooking term.
A "brunoise" is a fine and precise dicing of vegetables into tiny, uni-
form cubes. The soup's light and elegant look made a sophisticated
starting course designed to impress the president-elect and his
French-speaking wife.

- **3 tablespoons salted butter**
- **2 medium carrots, peeled and cut into ¹/₄-inch dice**
- **2 medium turnips, peeled and cut into ¹/₄-inch dice**
- **1 medium onion, diced**
- **2 ribs celery, cut into ¹/₄-inch dice**
- **1 leek, well washed and diced**
- **3 quarts low-sodium chicken stock**
- **2 tablespoons sugar**
- **¹/₂ teaspoon salt**
- **1 cup green peas (fresh or frozen)**
- **1 cup green beans, cut on an angle into diamond shapes**
- **1 cup asparagus tips**
- **Small toast triangles, to serve**

Melt the butter in a large frying pan. Add the carrots, turnips, onion,
celery, and leek. Cook over medium heat, stirring frequently until the
vegetables begin to turn color and the onion becomes transparent.
Transfer the vegetables to a soup pot. Add all but 1 cup of the chicken
stock. Pour the 1 cup of stock into the frying pan and cook over
medium heat, scraping up the browned bits from the pan. Pour this
into the soup pot. Add the sugar, salt, peas, and beans. Simmer until
the vegetables are tender. Stir in the asparagus tips, cover, and let
stand for 5 minutes. Serve with small toast triangles.

Makes 12 servings as a first course

ADAPTED FROM PERIOD SOURCES.

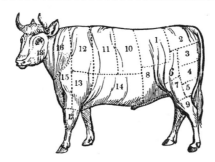

FILET OF BEEF À LA NAPOLITAINE

• • • • • • •

This delicious beef dish does take a lot of time and some attention, but it is possible to make this French-inspired period entrée successfully in a home kitchen. The recipe combines braising with baking and then making a sauce.

  1 **3-pound boneless beef roast such as eye of round, sirloin, or beef tenderloin**
  4 **slices lower-sodium bacon**
  2 **carrots, peeled and cut into 1-inch chunks**
  2 **ribs celery, cut into 1-inch chunks**
  1 **large onion, roughly chopped**
    Small bunch of fresh parsley
    Small bunch of fresh thyme
  2 **bay leaves**
 ½ **teaspoon ground mace**
  3 **cups white wine (one 750 ml bottle)**
  1 **1.5-ounce packet beef demi-glace (available at gourmet shops)**
  1 **large shallot, minced**
 ½ **cup prepared beef gravy**
 ¼ **cup red currant jelly**
 ½ **teaspoon grated horseradish (not cream style)**

Preheat the oven to 300°F. Place the bacon over the meat and tie in place with kitchen string. Put the meat, vegetables, herbs, and wine in a roasting pan just big enough to hold it with room to boil. (Or line a roasting pan with a double layer of heavy-duty aluminum foil long enough so that you can completely encase the meat, wine, and vegetables in it.) Cover the pan and roast until the meat is cooked to rare or medium (125° to 145°F) as measured by an instant-read meat thermometer. Allow about 30 minutes per pound. (If you use tenderloin, cooking time will be shorter.) Start checking after 45 minutes of braising.

The braising step is finished and it is time to move on to roasting and making the sauce. Remove the pan from the oven. Turn the oven up to 350°F. Lift the meat from the pan onto a plate. Pour the braising liquid into a large pot, using a strainer to capture the vegetables and herbs. Set them aside to be used for another meal. Put the beef back into the roasting pan. Brush the top of the beef and bacon with the demi-glace. Return it to the oven to "dry" and become lightly browned, about 10 minutes. Add the chopped shallot to the braising liquid and reduce it by cooking over medium heat until only about one-third of the amount is left, about ¾ cup. When the beef is browned, remove it from the oven and set aside. Cover it with a piece of foil to keep warm. To finish the sauce, stir in the gravy, jelly, and horseradish.

TIP FOR SUCCESS: The trick for this recipe is to make sure the braising liquid surrounds the meat. If you have a pan that will hold the meat and has just enough room for the vegetables and wine to cook without boiling over—great. I didn't. My pans were either too small—the liquids would overflow while cooking—or too large, and the braising liquid would spread out too much in the pan. I ended up using a double layer of foil to create a container inside a regular baking pan to hold the braising liquid up against the meat surface.

Makes 10 to 12 servings

ADAPTED FROM "FILET OF BEEF À LA NAPOLITAINE," CHARLES ELMÉ FRANCATELLI, *THE COOK'S GUIDE, AND HOUSEKEEPER'S & BUTLER'S ASSISTANT*, 1857.

PEAS À LA FRANÇAISE

● ● ● ● ● ● ●

This easy French-inspired dish is the essence of spring. Of course, the original recipe used fresh peas and new green onions pulled from the garden. You could use them as well; the initial cooking time will be longer and you may need to add a bit of water along with the butter so that they don't stick to the pan.

2 ½ pounds fresh peas, shelled, or 14 ounces frozen peas

2 tablespoons butter

1 bunch green onions, thinly sliced including about half of the green stem

2 tablespoons minced fresh parsley

½ cup water

1 tablespoon butter, at room temperature, plus more to thicken sauce

1 tablespoon flour

For fresh peas, cook in boiling salted water until just tender, about 2 to 10 minutes; drain. For frozen peas, thaw slightly. Over medium heat, melt the butter in a large saucepan. Add the peas, onions, and parsley. Stir from time to time, until the peas are warmed through and the onions begin to look soft. Add the water and stir to blend. While the water is coming up to a boil, mash the butter into the flour. Then drop bits of it into the simmering liquid. You may only need about half of this flour mixture. Stir until the mixture thickens slightly into a thin sauce.

Makes 4 to 6 servings

ADAPTED FROM "PEAS À LA FRANÇAISE," CHARLES ELMÉ FRANCATELLI, *THE COOK'S GUIDE, AND HOUSEKEEPER'S & BUTLER'S ASSISTANT,* 1857.

CRANBERRY PIE

• • • • • • •

This is a wonderful pie. Refreshing, tangy, and rich, a small slice is all you need.

- **2 cups fresh cranberries**
- **2 cups sugar**
- **1/4 cup unbleached all-purpose flour**
- **1 tablespoon water**
- **2 teaspoons pure vanilla extract**
- **Double-Crust Pie Dough (see page 51)**
- **Whipped cream or ice cream, to serve**

Chop the cranberries in a food processor until about 1/4-inch dice. Put into a saucepan and add the sugar and flour. Stir well, then add 1 tablespoon water. Begin cooking over low heat, stirring constantly until the sugar and flour are dissolved into the released cranberry juices. Continue cooking until the mixture is very thick, about 15 minutes. Cool and stir in the vanilla.

Preheat the oven to 425°F. Roll out one circle of pie dough and line an 8-inch pie plate. Roll the second circle of dough and cut into 3/4-inch strips to weave into a lattice. Pour cooled cranberry filling into the lined pie plate. Top with the second lattice crust. Bake for 15 minutes. Lower the heat to 350°F and continue baking until the juices bubble up and the crust is light brown, about another 30 minutes. Cut into thin pieces and serve with whipped cream or ice cream.

Makes one 8-inch pie, to serve 12

ADAPTED FROM PERIOD SOURCES.

CHRISTMAS SHORTBREAD COOKIES

• • • • • • •

Thanks to the melted butter in the ingredient list, this is one of the easiest shortbread cookies to make. The brandy lends a sophisticated flavor. You'll find yourself making these cookies frequently to enjoy and give as gifts.

BRANDY-SOAKED SHORTBREAD CRUMBS: If you end up with extra shortbreads, try soaking them in a bit more brandy. Give them a twirl in the food processor to create brandy-soaked shortbread crumbs, perfect for making a quick apple crisp or sprinkling on top of ice cream.

- 1/4 teaspoon *each* ground cinnamon, nutmeg, mace
- 1 1/2 cups unbleached all-purpose flour (up to 1/2 cup more may be needed)
- 1/2 cup sugar
- 4 tablespoons (1/2 stick) salted butter, melted
- 1/4 cup brandy
- 1/3 cup dried Zante currants, chopped

Preheat the oven to 350°F. Lightly grease a baking sheet. Make a mixed spice blend with the cinnamon, nutmeg, and mace and set aside. In a mixing bowl combine the flour and sugar. Measure out 1/4 teaspoon of the mixed spice and add to the flour and sugar. (Reserve the remaining spice blend for the next time you make the shortbread.) With a fork, stir in the melted butter and brandy. Add the currants. Knead with your hands until you have a smooth, non-sticky ball, adding more flour if needed. Divide the ball into four equal pieces. Pat each piece out into a circle about 5 inches in diameter and about 1/4 inch thick. Place on the prepared baking sheet. Score into the traditional 6 pie-shaped wedges by pressing a sharp knife through the circle of dough. Bake until the shortbreads are just starting to turn golden and are firm to the touch, about 25 to 35 minutes.

Makes 2 dozen shortbread wedges

ADAPTED FROM "SCOTCH SHORTBREAD,"
GODEY'S LADY'S BOOK, DECEMBER 1861.

13

SUMMER COTTAGE, SOLDIER'S BREAD

Washington was at its steamy, miasmal best as I sat in the back seat of the taxi taking me three miles from the Mall and toward the city's northern boundary to the "Lincoln Cottage." I was headed to President Lincoln's summer retreat on the grounds of what was known during his time as the Soldiers' Home, a hospital and residence for about 150 retired soldiers who didn't have the means to care for themselves. Many were veterans of the War of 1812. In addition to the dormitory building, there were three three-story homes on the grounds that provided housing for the senior administrators and chief physician. Abraham Lincoln's immediate predecessor, James Buchanan, was the first president to spend time in one of those houses and doubtless recommended it to the Lincolns. The Lincoln family spent the summers of 1862, '63, and '64 at the Soldiers' Home, arriving sometime in early to mid-June and leaving in late October or November each year.

In the summer of 1862, the Lincoln family, especially Mary Lincoln, needed "quiet" and a measure of privacy. In February the seeming war normalcy was shattered. On February 5 the couple hosted an extraordinary reception. Mary Lincoln decided to break with tradition and have a very large, formal, and invitation-only event with a midnight supper instead of the usual season-long series of open-door levees and small state dinners. This event would have the best of both, and it also enabled her to celebrate the just-completed restoration and redecoration of the White House public rooms. The event began at nine o'clock in the evening. The Marine Band played as the Washington elite gathered wearing their finest attire, and the Lincolns received their guests in the East Room. The doors to the dining room opened at midnight and five hundred guests feasted upon "mounds of turkey, duck, ham, terrapin and pheasant" served with excellent champagne and other wines until three o'clock in the morning.

The reception was a huge success, but it was overshadowed by the illness of the Lincolns' middle son, Willie. When he had become sick a week or so earlier, doctors thought he would recover. But his illness worsened. All during the party the Lincolns slipped upstairs to check on their fevered boy. Only days later Tad was also seriously ill with what scholars think was most probably typhoid fever. Willie died on February 20. Tad remained ill for weeks but slowly recovered.

The family moved out to the cottage in June. Mary wrote, "In the loss of our idolized boy, we naturally have suffered such intense grief, that a removal from the scene of our misery was found to be very necessary." She took comfort in the place. "We are truly delighted with this retreat, the drives & walks around here are delightful, & each day brings its visitors."

The National Trust for Historic Preservation has carefully restored the cottage where the Lincolns stayed. It opened as a historic site for the first time in 2008.

Holding my 1861 edition of *Bohn's Hand-Book of Washington* securely in my hand, I carefully opened the back cover, gently unfolded the attached map, and traced the taxi's journey up Georgia Avenue toward Rock Creek Church Road in Northwest Washington, D.C. In 1862 this was the Seventh Street Turnpike, the route Lincoln took morning and evening to and from the White House. Written before the war, *Bohn* describes "the drives leading to this retreat" as "among the most agreeable in the District."

The heat-trapping sprawl of Washington accompanied me on my ride. It wasn't until we turned off onto Upshur Street that I could sense the peaceful possibilities. Seven short blocks later, we passed through the Eagle Gate and quickly into another world. After spending four hours on these quiet grounds, I considered that this place might, in fact, be the best spot to experience the Washington of the 1860s. The Soldiers'

Home continues to provide service to today's veterans, although it is now known as the Armed Forces Retirement Home, but the open spaces, cooling breezes, and sweeping views of Lincoln's time are still there. As with the Lincoln Boyhood Home in Indiana, the cottage and surroundings are just enough removed from traffic to allow visitors to travel back in time. Sitting on the steps, or under one of the mature trees, I could almost completely shut out the modern world and reflect on the images and stories of Lincoln that soldiers and others wrote for us to consider.

Even at its tourist-swamped worst, the Washington, D.C., we visit is refreshing compared to the summer city during the Civil War years. The Washington Monument stood unfinished like a broken, ancient Roman ruin. The old and small Capitol dome was being replaced with the larger, soaring dome. The great Mall between the two was an empty lawn, save for the newly constructed redbrick Smithsonian Institution, which housed "the various curiosities and collections brought home by the Exploring Expeditions." Soldiers were camped everywhere.

Twenty hospitals were scattered about the city for the battle wounded, and reporter Noah Brooks likened the atmosphere throughout Washington to an "insidious enemy." "This ill-drained, badly governed, ill-kept, and dirty city built upon a marsh and bordered by a stinking canal which is but an open sewer, will certainly be the scene of a deadly pestilence during the coming summer ... [reeking] with garbage, offal and filth, heaps of which accumulate in back streets, lanes, door yards, and vacant lots." He described the canal as filled to the top with debris and "offal from the sewers." I thought about all the horses kicking up fetid, manure-contaminated dust with every stride and my eyes began to water.

The cottage was a good place for the president to escape the heat and disease-riddled air and to gain perspective among a small group of friends and callers. Yes, there were visitors—military, political, and social (both invited and surprise guests)—but Lincoln could sit out on the porch and play a game of checkers with Tad and then ask a soldier if "he would like a game."

It was the perfect place to be during the summer. The staff loaded up cartloads of household goods and moved out of the city in the middle of June 1862 for the first season. Secretary of War Edwin Stanton's family also occasionally occupied a cottage on the grounds. Lincoln and Stanton, who had replaced Secretary Cameron, sometimes breakfasted together before traveling down to town.

It is unclear how many White House or other household staff worked at the Soldiers' Home cottage. There would have been some household help, including a valet of some kind. Lincoln mentioned Thomas Stackpole, a watchman, and Mary Ann Cuthbert, the housekeeper, in letters he wrote. We do know the staff included a cook. An African American cook, "Aunt" Mary Williams, as the soldiers called her, worked for the Lincolns the first summer. Soldiers guarding Lincoln at the cottage wrote home about her. Sergeant Charles Derickson described how she once gave him leftovers from Lincoln's breakfast, calling him into the cottage and feeding him "off the very plate & fork & knife the President of the U.S. eats off!"

Another soldier's letter suggests Mary Williams cooked for the Lincolns in the White House. In June 1863 Private Willard Cutter wrote, "Aunt left in March, and there is a white cook in her place. She is a nice good looking woman." Cutter's unit guarded President Lincoln both at the cottage and the White House, so he was in a position to know when she left service.

Lincoln kept up his work schedule at the cottage, rising early for a light breakfast and riding either on his horse or by carriage down to the White House, returning in late afternoon. On his thirty-minute commute, Lincoln passed marching troops, caravans of wounded soldiers, hospitals, and the "contraband camps," where 4,200 runaway slaves lived under military protection. They were no longer slaves, as Emancipation was enacted in Washington, D.C., in April 1862, eight and a half months before Lincoln's nationwide Emancipation Proclamation took effect on January 1, 1863. They were, however, refugees with few resources. Lincoln may even have stopped on more than one occasion at one of the camps. In a postwar interview, one of the residents, Mary Dines, related that President and Mrs. Lincoln visited to hear a special musical performance of Negro spirituals. She also described how Lincoln stopped to "visit and talk" with the former slaves.

Nearly every morning and afternoon in the summer of 1863, Lincoln passed the home of poet Walt Whitman on the corner of Vermont and

L Streets. The two took to nodding at each other as Lincoln passed. Whitman described Lincoln's appearance on June 30, 1863, the day before the Battle of Gettysburg began. "He looks even more careworn than usual, his face with deep cut lines, seams, and his complexion gray through very dark skin—a curious looking man, very sad."

On his daily journey, once Lincoln crossed Boundary Street (today Florida Avenue), which separated the City of Washington from unincorporated Washington County, he was in agricultural land, home to the farmers who trucked their goods into the city markets. Bohn describes the Center Market of Washington before the war as overflowing with goods from the farms of both Maryland and Virginia: beef and mutton, along with a variety of fruits and vegetables. Foodstuffs from the waterways and forest made their way to market, too—oysters, shad, rockfish, and other varieties from the Potomac; and wild venison, turkey, and other fowl. Without a blockade, food continued to flow into the nation's capital. Markets and stores were well stocked, and a variety of foodstuffs filled tables from the White House to soldiers' bivouacs.

During the first months that the Lincolns were in residence, the Soldiers' Home grounds were unguarded, but by the end of the summer, General McClellan ordered Company K and Company D of the 150th Pennsylvania Volunteers to guard the president. They arrived on September 6, 1862. Mrs. Lincoln had also insisted upon a cavalry escort for the president to and from the White House.

On occasion Lincoln dismissed his escort, and instead of riding on horseback, used a driver for his carriage. Once he ordered the driver to take him, along with his secretary John Hay, to visit the Naval Observatory to look at the stars and moon through the newly installed telescope.

Noah Brooks reported on the president's summer routine. Writing in July 1863, he noted that "Mr. Lincoln comes in early in the morning and returns about sunset, unless he has a press of business—which is often—when he sleeps at the White House and his 'prog' [meals] sent up from Willard's [Hotel]."

For the rest of the year, we are fortunate to have two small descriptions that paint a clear picture of Lincoln's White House routine during the winter. Brooks offered a view of the end of a typical day in the White House during the year: "The President dines at six o'clock and often invites an intimate friend to take potluck with him but he and his estimable wife are averse to dinner-giving or party-making, only deviating from their own wishes in such matters for the purpose of gratifying people who expect it of them."

William Crook, one of Lincoln's guards assigned by the District police, related what happened next in a typical evening. After dinner, Lincoln would leave the second-floor library, wrap himself up in a gray wool shawl, put on his top hat, and head to the War Department next door to the White House to get the latest telegraphed news from the war front. Lincoln and his guard slipped out of the basement and walked across the garden, into the building, and up to Secretary Stanton's office on the second floor. After the telegraphs were read and the president and secretary of war met, Lincoln then walked back to the White House, and went to bed.

But in the summer there was the possibility of a brief escape from the war as Brooks and others reported on casual evening entertainments at the cottage. Here, Lincoln would be a gracious host at the dinner table and then stand before the fireplace, reciting poetry or telling stories. On other occasions he treated drop-in visitors to readings from Shakespeare's plays. Lincoln's head-of-table generosity was the center of one woman's recollection of a White House meal in 1864. Anna Byers-Jennings described Lincoln's home-style manner: "Of all the informal affairs I have ever attended, it certainly took the lead." She describes how she was seated at table at the right of the president. Mrs. Lincoln, Robert, and Tad were there along with two generals. When a dish was brought out to the table, President Lincoln "reached for it, handled the spoon like an ordinary farmer, saying to all in his reach: 'Will you have some of this?' dishing it into our plates liberally."

Lincoln was in residence at the Soldiers' Home cottage during the most critical months of his reelection campaign in the summer of 1864. The outcome was not certain. Not since Andrew Jackson in 1832 had a president been elected for a second term. The Democrats nominated General George McClellan on a "peace" ticket, reflecting popular dissatisfaction with the course of the war. At the cottage, Lincoln could meet with trusted advisors and the allies who would act as political surrogates influencing key constituencies.

Here, laughter could ring out from the cottage parlors. Hugh McCulloch, later to be Lincoln's treasury secretary, described an October 1864 evening when Lincoln and a few friends gathered at the cottage following General Philip Sheridan's victory in Winchester, Virginia, that effectively stopped the Confederate forces' invasion of the north. Lincoln and Assistant Postmaster General Alexander Randall entertained a gathering of close friends with a two-hour contest "as to which could tell the best story and provoke the heartiest laughter.... The verdict of the listeners was that, while the stories were equally good, Mr. Lincoln had displayed the most humor and skill."

Lincoln and Tad also interacted with the soldiers camped on the grounds surrounding the cottage and other buildings. Lincoln's association with these men was significant. He came into camp and laughed at their entertainments, including one with two soldiers under a blanket, pretending to be an elephant—one soldier being the hind end and the other, holding a board for the trunk, as the front. Audience members shouted out tricks for the "trained elephant" to perform. Lincoln sat and visited with these young soldiers, perhaps escaping in memory to the days in New Salem when he was a young man cavorting in wrestling matches and feats of strength with the boys from Clary's Grove or his own efforts at command and warfare during the Black Hawk campaign.

In the evenings, Lincoln wandered the grounds of the Soldiers' Home. He walked past the tents of both the cavalry and infantry companies and stopped, "passing a word with them." Members of the cavalry detail camped near the first national cemetery for soldiers just across the road from the Soldiers' Home. Dedicated after the loss at the First Battle of Bull Run in July 1861, the cemetery filled rapidly, and as the war continued it was the scene of several burials a day. By the summer of 1863 there had been more than eight thousand interments.

These soldiers not only protected the president, but they also provided companionship for Tad, now nine years old and the only child left at home. After Willie's death, distraught Mary Lincoln asked that the Taft boys no longer come to the White House for classes with the tutor or to play. Soon Bud and Holly Taft and their sister, Julia, were sent up north to school. The oldest Lincoln son, Robert, never lived at the White House; he began studies at Harvard before the war and visited on vacations. Secretary of War Stanton's children were sometime playmates, but Tad found good friends in the Pennsylvania "Bucktail" soldiers. They named him an honorary "third Lieutenant." Letters and memoirs from the members of Company K provide brief witness to the everyday events. Albert See, one of the soldiers, wrote that Tad showed up nearly every day "when the dinner bell rang" and would simply get in line and "draw his rations the same as the rest of us." Private Cutter recalled giving Tad some "bread and molasses."

In addition to the regular army ration of twenty-two ounces of bread, fresh beef (in place of salt meat), beans and rice or hominy, molasses, coffee, tea, salt, and pepper, soldiers could buy food from vendors who called on camp. As Cutter wrote to his brother, "Tell Grand Mother I have lots of Bread and Milk to eat. It is five cents a pint and the old woman is around most every day to sell cakes and pies, milk, apples, and a little of everything."

During the three summer seasons spent at the cottage, Lincoln came by the troop encampments for meals, too. He would sit and have a plate of beans and some coffee with the men. He also invited officers to come into the cottage to dine with him when Mrs. Lincoln was vacationing in New York or Vermont. Captains Derickson of Company K and Crotzer of Company D were dinner companions. Cavalry officer James Mix reported that he often ate breakfast with the president.

Mary Lincoln recognized the importance of the soldiers' service. Back in the city she often visited the hospitals and sent soldiers baskets of wine and fruit, "re-gifting" things that had been sent to the White House. Christmas of 1862 she was among a number of government wives who donated food from their homes and raised money to buy even more so that hospitalized soldiers would have a fulsome holiday meal. The women took plates and fed those who were bedridden. Mrs. Lincoln was one of the "waiters" at one hospital. Later when she heard that one of the cottage guard units was under orders to leave for combat, she gave the unit two bushels of apples.

The Pennsylvania guard continued their responsibilities when the Lincolns returned to the White House. Private Cutter's letters give a good sense of the bounty available in the city markets. "We were up around the city and had a mince pie that was first rate, you must not think that we have a hard time here and nothing to eat. We can get a pass to go in the city where the market is and get any thing we want there. There is more folks at the [M]arville market stand than there is in Meadville [Pennsylvania]. On fair days there is about 200 stands where they are and every other one is selling pies, cakes, and everything you can think of. I was up there the other day and bought butter and cheese."

The Lincoln family left the Soldiers' Home retreat for the last time in October 1864. The three summers there had been times of monumental events. Lincoln framed and wrote the Emancipation Proclamation during his first summer at the cottage, apparently beginning consideration of the policy in June, reading a first draft to the cabinet on July 22, and presenting the completed document to his cabinet on September 22, 1862. Major summer battles had taken a tremendous toll: Confederate victories at Second Bull Run, August 28–30, 1862, left 16,000 Union casualties; Antietam, September 17, 1862, 12,400 Union casualties; Chancellorsville, April 30–May 6, 1863, 14,000 Union casualties; Chickamauga, September 18–20, 1863, 16,170 Union casualties; and the great Union victory at Gettysburg, July 1–3, 1863, 23,000 Union dead and wounded.

At the Lincoln Cottage I could sit and reflect on where this journey brought me. I began with a simple understanding of the lives of Abraham and Mary Lincoln and a curiosity to see where an examination of the foods of the era might take me. Over all the miles between southern Indiana and this spot overlooking Washington, through the piles of recipes and plates of re-created foods, my admiration for the Lincolns had only increased as I was able, for a few moments, to come close to entering their world. I only wished I had a corn dodger to munch.

Today the tree-filled grounds are mostly still, except for the occasional voices of the veterans who live here and the visitors leaving the guided house tour. I sat in the small shelter a few yards from the house. Could it have been built on a spot where Company K set up camp and President Lincoln stopped by for some beans and coffee and maybe bread and molasses? I pictured him sitting among a company of men he commanded, committed to a course of national survival, and breaking bread with them.

And so I come to the last recipe mystery of this book. What was that bread? Noah Brooks gave me some clues in his report from the army bakery at the "upper end of G Street in Georgetown." He described the efforts of 280 men working twenty-four hours a day to make "sweet, wholesome and fresh" twenty-two-ounce loaves of bread for the army. The bread was formed like a large bun and baked fifteen to a sheet in ovens that could hold ten baking sheets at a time. Every day the men went through 210 barrels of "super" flour that cost Uncle Sam $8.87 per barrel. "Opposite each oven is the apparatus for raising and molding the dough and connected to it is the 'yeast manufactory.'" Brooks claimed the bread "compares favorable with the best private bakeries."

The key to the recipe is as much what Brooks doesn't mention as what he does. There is no list of firkins of butter or lard, gallons of milk, clutches of eggs, or barrels of sugar. Brooks was an accurate and descriptive reporter. If these ingredients had gone into the soldier's bread, he would have mentioned them. No, this was a simple flour-and-water bread leavened with a yeast sponge.

Reporter Brooks was specific about the "super" grade flour for this bread. Descriptions in agricultural journals of the day suggested that milling high-grade flour yielded fifty pounds of flour from a sixty-six-pound bushel. In milling terms, this would have been a 75 percent "extraction rate." Modern "white" flours are milled to 73 percent extraction. So the flour that the army bakers used was as white as the unbleached flour we use today. As to the yeast, Brooks described the "Germans" working in a separate building to prepare the yeast. Most of the period bread recipes began with a "sponge," a bubbly preliminary mixture of the yeast, water, and flour. The bubbles indicated that the yeast was working, so the baker would know that the bread would rise before mixing up ten quarts of flour and two quarts of water, the amount Mrs. Sarah J. Hale's 1857 cookbook suggested was enough for four loaves "for a small family." There were several ways to get the beginning yeast culture; brewer's yeast was one of the most common. But once they had that beginning culture, the men in the yeast manufactory would simply encourage it to multiply. This is not the same process as growing a sourdough culture. The prodigious rate at which they were turning out bread and Brooks's description of a "sweet" bread indicate that their starter was just a basic and quick-rising sponge. I make my sponge with standard dry rapid-rise yeast.

Now for some quick math to verify my one-rise recipe logic: The 280 army bakers used 210 barrels of flour a day. A little less than one pound of flour makes one loaf of soldier's bread. There are 156 pounds of flour in a barrel. That yields 32,760 loaves of bread. Divide the number of loaves by the number of loaves per pan (15), number of pans per oven (10), and the number of ovens (20) and you get 11 "batches" of bread. Divide the number of batches into the 24 hours a day they were baking and you get 2.2 hours to produce a loaf of bread. My jaw dropped when I finished the calculations—that was just about how long it took for me to mix and bake my test loaves.

Mixing the sponge into dough is a very hands-on and sticky process and kneading is critical to a loaf that rises well and has a good texture. The men who had the responsibility for that task in the army bakery were "neatly dressed and tidy men to whom tobacco in any form is a forbidden article so long as they are in the bakery."

Brooks ended his essay with the thought that "Uncle Sam's bakery is one of the sights of Washington, and many a soldier has reason to thank his lucky stars that its proximity has delivered him from the poor fare of 'hardtack' of doubtful age."

And as I come close to the last of Lincoln's recipes in this book, I am thankful for the time I've spent with these evocative foods. Brooks's vivid description gave me enough clues to devise the recipe. The bread is easy to make. Take your time, knead the dough well, and then chew on the sustaining textures of the past.

SOLDIER'S BREAD

• • • • • • •

This sturdy bread is just the kind of loaf soldiers would have tossed into their haversacks. The mild flavor stands up well to sharp cheeses and boiled meats, and it dunks well into all kinds of soups.

1	**envelope active dry yeast**
2 1/2	**cups warm water, divided**
1	**tablespoon sugar**
6 1/2 to 7 1/2	**cups unbleached bread flour, plus more for dusting**
1/2	**teaspoon salt**

Put the yeast in a mixing bowl; add ½ cup of the warm water and the sugar. Stir with a fork until blended and set aside until it begins to bubble. This is proofing the yeast to be sure it will make the bread rise. Mix in 1 cup of the flour and knead into a smooth dough. Put back into bowl and pour 2 cups of warm water around the ball of dough. Set aside for 15 to 20 minutes until the dough ball rises and is bubbly on the bottom.

Add 2 cups of the flour to the water and carefully begin to mix with your hand, breaking up the dough "sponge" and blending it with the flour. Continue adding more flour until you have a smooth and non-sticky ball of dough. Knead for several minutes on a lightly floured surface until it is very smooth. Divide the dough in half. Form each half into a tight round loaf. Place on a lightly greased baking sheet and put in a warm place to rise until doubled.

Preheat the oven to 350°F. Bake until browned on top and when you tap the bottom of a loaf it sounds hollow, about 45 minutes.

TIPS FOR SUCCESS: Yeast is a living thing. It needs the right warm temperature to make the bubbles that make the bread rise. A water temperature of 110°F is about right. An air temperature of about 125°F is about right for the sponge and loaves to rise. In my cold winter kitchen, I often boil a cup of water in the microwave and then put the bowl of dough in next to it. When the loaves are formed, I preheat the oven just to 95°F, turn it off, put the dough in, and leave the oven door cracked open a bit. If the oven is too hot, the yeast will die and the bread won't rise.

To knead your bread dough, push it down, turning and pushing again, until it is smooth. I divide the dough in half and knead each loaf for about five minutes

Makes two 8-inch round loaves

RECIPE DEVELOPED FROM NOAH BROOKS'S
INGREDIENT DESCRIPTIONS.

CAKES IN ABRAHAM LINCOLN'S NAME

The Lincolns were in residence at the White House on April 10, 1865, as the news spread throughout the city of General Robert E. Lee's April 8 surrender to General Ulysses S. Grant, bringing with it the end of the war. A great crowd walked through rain and mud from the Navy Yard to the White House lawn, picking up more and more people and even the Quartermaster's Band along the way. Nearly three thousand in number, they called for the president to come out. He spoke briefly and called upon the band to "play 'Dixie.' One of the best tunes I've ever heard." He concluded his appearance calling for three cheers for "General Grant and all under his command" and another three cheers for the navy.

The following evening Abraham Lincoln made his last public address. Speaking again from the upper windows of the White House, he called for reconciliation with the Southern states. "Let us all join in doing the acts necessary to restoring the proper practical relations between these states and the Union."

Three days later President and Mrs. Lincoln went to a performance of *Our American Cousin* at Ford's Theatre. In the middle of the play, John Wilkes Booth entered the presidential box and shot Abraham Lincoln in the back of the head. He was carried across the street into the home of Mr. William Petersen and laid in a small bedroom on the first floor. At 7:33 the morning of April 15, 1865, Abraham Lincoln's great heart stopped beating.

Walt Whitman wrote:

> When lilacs last in the door-yard bloom'd,
> And the great star droop'd in the western sky in the night,
> I mourn'd—and yet shall mourn with ever-returning spring.

At Lincoln's death, Secretary of War William Stanton said, "Now he belongs to the ages." The president, his accomplishments, and his ideas belonged so much to the country that people publicly mourned Lincoln's death almost as though he were a member of their immediate family. People wore black ribbons on their sleeves. Some even hung their homes with black crepe. There were mourning ribbons and badges, memorial portraits, articles and books celebrating his life. Nineteenth-century cookbooks brought forth a bakery case full of cakes paying homage to the martyred president. These cakes joined those named for Presidents Washington and Madison as well as other political figures on both sides of the Civil War.

Many of the published recipes for Lincoln cakes pass along the simple recipe that first appeared in *Godey's Lady's Book* in 1865: "2 eggs, 2 cups sugar, ½ cup butter, one of sweet milk, three of flour, 1 teaspoon cream of tartar, half teaspoon soda and one of lemon essence." Others are more like light fruitcakes.

After my Lincoln foodways talks, when the group is mingling and sampling the Lincoln cake, jumbles, apple butter, and other period foods, folks will frequently ask what happened after President Lincoln was assassinated. How did Mary survive yet another death? What happened to Tad and Robert? A complete response, as with the rest of Lincoln literature, fills many books and articles, but the short answer is this: Mary Lincoln remained in seclusion in the White House while the funeral train carrying her husband home to Springfield passed through seven states during nearly two weeks. The route, arranged by a committee of Illinois citizens, stopped in ten cities where the president-elect's train had stopped on its journey to Washington four years and two months earlier. Lincoln's coffin was taken in solemn procession from the train to lie in state in city halls or state capitols. Thousands of people walked past paying their respects. All along the route, scores of smaller cities and towns put up mourning arches over the tracks with banners celebrating the "martyred President." By mid-May, Mary was ready to move to Chicago with Robert and Tad. She left the White House on May 22, 1865.

Mary Lincoln lived seventeen more years, dying on July 16, 1882, in the Springfield home of her older sister Elizabeth Edwards. Mary survived the president's assassination and Tad's death six years later. For two multiyear periods she lived in Europe. Robert Lincoln became a successful attorney and strove to keep his mother in physical, mental, and financial health. He married and had three children. His only son, Abraham Lincoln II, died at age sixteen. The last surviving Lincoln descendant, a great-grandson, Robert Todd Lincoln Beckwith, died in 1985.

And so I've come to the end of this exploration that started with the recipe for Mary Lincoln's Almond Cake. My old oak table is now cleared of research books and manuscript pages. I've completed the notes on my last spattered recipe sheet. The kitchen is fragrant with yeasty smells from two round twenty-two-ounce loaves of soldier's bread cooling on my kitchen counter. Somehow the memories of my visits—recent, past, and in imagination—to the places Lincoln lived rise with their steam. This has been an extraordinary journey.

LINCOLN CAKE

• • • • • • •

*Nineteenth-century homemakers would have called this satisfying
cake "a good keeper." Its taste and texture are best when it has mel-
lowed a day or two in a covered container. A thin slice is all you need.*

3 1/2   **cups unbleached all-purpose flour, divided**

1   **teaspoon baking soda**

1 1/2   **teaspoons ground cinnamon**

1/2   **teaspoon freshly grated or ground nutmeg**

1/2   **teaspoon ground cloves**

1/2   **cups raisins**

1/2   **cup dried Zante currants**

1/2   **cup diced candied citron**

1   **cup chopped almonds**

1   **cup (2 sticks) salted butter**

1 1/2   **cups packed brown sugar**

3   **large eggs, lightly beaten**

1   **cup milk**

1/4   **cup brandy**

Preheat the oven to 325°F. Grease and flour a 10- to 12-inch angel food
cake pan. Mix 3 cups of the flour, the baking soda, and spices and set
aside. Mix the raisins, currants, citron, and almonds with the remaining 1/2 cup flour and set aside. Cream the butter and brown sugar. Add
the eggs and mix well. Add one-third of the flour-and-spice mixture,
then the milk, the second third of the flour, the brandy, and finally the
remaining flour mixture, stirring well after each addition. Stir in the
fruit-and-nut mixture. Pour the batter into the prepared pan, filling it

about three-quarters full. Bake until a skewer or thin knife inserted in the center comes out clean, about 1 hour and 15 minutes. Let the cake cool for 10 or 15 minutes before running a knife around the edge of the pan. Remove the outside section of the pan. When the cake has cooled completely, pop it off the center tube. Cut into thin slices and serve.

TIP FOR SUCCESS: The recipe makes 8 cups of cake batter. You can bake it in small or larger loaf pans, or even in cupcake tins, adjusting the baking time accordingly.

Makes 20 or more servings

ADAPTED FROM "LINCOLN CAKE," *AMERICAN COOKERY*
(THE BOSTON COOKING SCHOOL MAGAZINE),
FEBRUARY AND MARCH 1899.

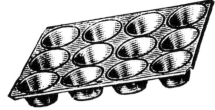

ACKNOWLEDGMENTS

This book began with a simple question: What do you think Abraham Lincoln enjoyed eating? I've pursued the answer in history, biography, cookbooks, and foodways, I've discovered wonderful recipes, benefited from scholarly support, and made new kitchen friends.

Anyone who writes about Abraham Lincoln's early life is indebted to William Herndon and the scores of "informants" he interviewed after President Lincoln's assassination. I begin my thanks there and to editors Douglas L. Wilson and Rodney O. Davis along with the University of Illinois Press for publishing Herndon's documents. Through their work I was able to read these Lincoln stories in their entirety, uncovering details often not included by other authors who quoted from them.

I am appreciative of the efforts of Google Books and the *New York Times* for their searchable resources that brought original documents from the nineteenth century to my desktop.

I am also indebted to the National Park Service Lincoln sites. It is still possible to walk the paths of Lincoln's childhood and married life. My deepest thanks go to those who work in Lincoln's spaces for providing information and for reviewing the manuscript as I developed it. Susan Haake, curator of the Lincoln Home National Historic Site in Springfield generously helped me understand Mary Lincoln's stove and so much more about the daily life in the home at Eighth and Jackson and the Springfield community. Thanks also to John Popolis, museum technician, Tim Townsend, historian, and Superintendent Dale Phillips. At the Lincoln Boyhood National Memorial in Lincoln City, Indiana, Michael Capps, chief of interpretation and especially Park Guide Taryn Hill helped me realize and express the details of that successful Lincoln farm.

At President Lincoln's Cottage, Washington, D.C., restored and now managed by the National Trust for Historic Preservation, Executive Director Erin Carlson Mast answered countless questions and shared copies from the diaries of the soldiers who camped around the president's cottage. Director Mast and Zachary Klitzman, executive assistant, kindly reviewed the manuscript chapters written about that time in the president's life. The staff at the White House Historical Association also provided insights as well as information and reviewed the Washington, D.C., chapters.

Staff members at the Abraham Lincoln Presidential Library and Patricia Barker at the Lincoln Library, the public library in Springfield, Illinois, provided important research resources.

I am indebted to many who have helped, encouraged, and supported my work over the several years of research, recipe testing and tasting, and writing. Early readers Robert Devens and Anne Kaplan helped me find the voice for this exploration of Lincoln's life. I thank Shannon Pennefeather, Hamp Smith, and Maureen Fischer, friends who read the work in progress, made comments and corrections, and asked clarifying questions.

I owe a special thank-you to Dr. Wayne C. Temple, whose clear comments and kind direction helped me make the last improvements to this biography. Any errors of fact or interpretation are mine.

At Smithsonian Books, insightful recipe editor Susan Struck and incomparable manuscript editor Lise Sajewski engaged in this project with a generous spirit of partnership. They were a joy to work with. Editor Christina Wiginton also helped make *Abraham Lincoln in the Kitchen* a better book. Thanks, too, to Director Carolyn Gleason and Marketing Director Matt Litts for their belief in the strength of this work and for supporting it so well. I am delighted with the attention, clarity, and creativity Mary Parsons brought to the design of the book's interior and its cover.

And always, my gratitude to John for his steadfast support, cheerful sampling of dishes made from old recipes, and especially for looking up during Thanksgiving dinner and wondering about what Lincoln might have enjoyed on his plate.

Rae Katherine Eighmey
Spring 2013

NOTES

I read both modern and classic biographies as I sought perspective and details of Abraham Lincoln's life and the lives of his family. As I selected material to quote or cite, I relied upon modern writers including Michael Burlingame (2008), David Herbert Donald (1995), Doris Kearns Goodwin (2005), and Louis A. Warren (1926 and 1991). I also cited from Lincoln biographers from the late nineteenth or early twentieth centuries, including Albert J. Beverage (1928), Francis Fisher Browne (1887 in 1995 reprint), William Herndon (1920), John Nicolay and John Hay (1890), and Ida Tarbell (1924 and 1928).

Earl Schenck Miers and C. Percy Powell's *Lincoln Day by Day: A Chronology 1809–1865* (1960 in 1991 reprint) was constantly open on my desk.

Wayne Temple took the title of his 2004 comprehensive listing of the foods Lincoln ate from one of Lincoln's letters. In the letter, the soon-to-be candidate said of seeking the Republican presidential nomination: "The taste *is* in my mouth a little." Temple's thorough and well-organized book often provided just the piece of information I needed to carry my story ahead.

Much of the material in this book is gleaned from the words of Abraham and Mary Lincoln. Roy P. Basler (1953) compiled Lincoln's complete works into eleven volumes. Those volumes and the collection of Mary Todd Lincoln's letters by Justin and Linda Levitt Turner (1972) were also constant desktop companions.

Finally, I own a tremendous debt to William Herndon and James Weik, who sought out Lincoln's companions and asked these informants insightful questions to describe the evocative details of daily life. The pages of my copy of the University of Illinois edition edited by Douglas Wilson, Rodney Davis, and Terri Wilson (1998) are littered with multicolored sticky notes.

INTRODUCTION

I found Phillip Ayers's remarkable story of Lincoln putting on the blue apron and cooking in Rufus Wilson (1943). M. F. K. Fisher wrote her description of the power of food in *With Bold Knife and Fork* (1969). The quotation can be found on page 101. James Carey's quotation can be found on page 180 of Robert Karl Manoff and Michael Schudson's *Reading the News* (1987).

As to Abraham Lincoln's weight, two friends from his young adulthood offered differing opinions to William Herndon. Nathanial Grigsby said Lincoln weighed 160 pounds; William Green claimed the weight was 214 pounds.

CHAPTER 1

I called upon a variety of modern and Lincoln-era resources to inform this chapter's discussion of childhood, culture, and corn. Lincoln's niece, Harriet Hanks Chapman, described his love for corn cakes to William Herndon (Wilson, Davis, and Wilson 1998). Her father, Dennis Hanks, similarly reported the crops the Lincolns grew in Indiana.

Louis A. Warren's extensive research into primary documents of the Kentucky and Indiana pioneering days resulted in two books. From these books I gained key insights into the culture of those places as well as the lives of Thomas, Nancy, Sarah, Sally, and Abraham Lincoln. I have used the Indiana information (Warren 1991) here and, as you will see, in the next three chapters.

In his *Two Years' Residence on the English Prairie of Illinois* (1968 reprint), John Woods wrote back home to London friends of his adventures and discoveries as he journeyed to Illinois in 1820, establishing his farm less than one hundred miles from Thomas Lincoln's Indiana homestead. His reporting of the American prairie agriculture and community culture provides immediate details of how crops were planted, how they grew, the yields per acre, and preparation for winter storage. His descriptions of the Americans he encountered and explanations of their way of life are almost like podcasts into the past. His descriptions in the second half of the book are particularly informative about both agriculture and native plants harvested for food by the settlers.

Two modern sources for corn growing, Douglas R. Hurt (1994) and Betty Fussell (1992), present a basis for understanding the historical importance of this grain. Lincoln-era sources, including the key farming periodical of the day the *Union Agriculturalist*, provide on-the-ground details of growing practices and harvest conditions.

Dennis Hanks's description of the way young Lincoln carried and ate corn dodgers is related on page 26 of Eleanore Stackhouse Atkinson's *The Boyhood of Lincoln* (1908).

My adventures in making hominy began with the *Union Agriculturalist* articles quoted in the text. I found more clues with the aid of early Lincoln Indiana friends Benjamin F. Irwin and Ira Emerson (Wilson, Davis, and Wilson 1998) and an 1840 edition of *The Family Magazine*, which I found online. Corn shellers were described by John McLean on page 88 in his 1919 book and by Richard Van Vleck in his article that I found on the American Artifacts website.

Three biographers provided descriptions and details of Mary Todd's childhood (Helm 1928; Baker 1987; Berry 2007). The names of the household slaves are detailed on pages 22–23 of Helm.

CHAPTER 2

On my search to re-create the only recipe Abraham Lincoln described, I found the details of his version reported by Walter B. Stevens (1998), page 105. Lincoln biographers David Herbert Donald (1995) and Walter B. Stevens (1998) evocatively took me to Ottawa, Illinois, and the site of Lafayette Square for his debate with Senator Douglas, while Louis A. Warren (1926 and 1991) portrayed the Kentucky and Indiana farms.

Although period cookbooks served as the primary sources for my exploration of the gingerbread man recipe, modern sources helped explain the differences in the amounts of ginger and the American agricultural history of sorghum (John J. Winberry, *Agricultural History*, 1980; Turner 2004; Smith 2007; Fiery Foods and Barbecue SuperSite article by DeWitt and Gerlach).

CHAPTER 3

The White House website provided concise information on the boyhood homes of the presidents.

I found key insights into the foods Lincoln enjoyed or, at least, could have eaten in the detailed recollections of his childhood friends and neighbors. Letters to William Herndon and interviews conducted by him (Wilson, Davis, and Wilson 1998) were almost as good as a shopping list: Dennis Hanks, pawpaws, honey; J. W. Wartmann, game, fish, wild fruits, and Lincoln's shooting skills; A. H. Chapman, Lincoln's hunting skills as well as the crops and livestock on the Lincoln farm; E. R. Burba, Lincoln hunting with his dog; Elizabeth Crawford, wild fruits, special foods for church gatherings, and Lincoln's claim that just potatoes for dinner were "poor blessings"; John Hanks described the Lincoln women as "good cooks."

Lincoln's stepmother, Sarah Bush Johnston Lincoln, recalled the wild and desolate conditions she encountered upon her arrival in Indiana to Herndon as well.

Louis A. Warren spent his life in the states of Lincoln's childhood. Born and educated in Kentucky, he was the editor of the *Larue County Herald* in Hopkinsville, near Lincoln's birthplace. Later he served as director of the Lincoln Library Museum in Fort Wayne, Indiana, for three decades. Warren brought his journalist's research skills and his familiarity with the lay of the land of both those states to his valuable and detailed exploration of the social and economic conditions of Abraham Lincoln and his parents. Warren's discoveries bring important insights into the childhoods of Thomas Lincoln and Nancy Hanks (Warren 1926). He also wrote extensive detail of the family's early Indiana neighborhood and farm experiences, including young Abraham's pulling fodder to pay for the ruined *Life of Washington* (Warren 1991). The description of the sound of Lincoln chopping wood as though it were three men can be found on page 143.

Lincoln's own description of his farming life appears in his 1860 campaign autobiography.

I found James Little's wonderful pawpaw memory at the Peterson Pawpaws website. Washington Irving's bee-hunting essay was printed in *The Crayon Miscellany* (1871).

John Woods's 1820 descriptions of foods and life (1968 reprint) were invaluable assets to understanding the pioneering Indiana culture. You can read his descriptions of pumpkins, vegetables, and seasonings on pages 155–61; rabbits running into logs on page 142; and frolics on page 154.

The staff of the Lincoln Boyhood National Memorial generously answered my questions both during my visit and in follow-up telephone conversations and e-mails.

CHAPTER 4

Once again I relied upon Louis A. Warren (1991) and David Herbert Donald (1995) for the known facts of the departure of the extended Lincoln family for Illinois and for Abraham Lincoln's first trip down the Mississippi. Ida Tarbell (1924) captured details of Lincoln's New Salem life.

I had the extraordinary benefit of reading firsthand descriptions of the river and New Orleans written by other young men near the time Lincoln made his journey. Reading their words as they encountered this vital city and dynamic river was almost as though I could see, smell, and taste the place as Lincoln would have experienced it. All of these resources are available through Google Books. Robert Baird's (1834) description of the cargoes at the levee can be found on page 280 and in H. Didimus (1845) on pages 6–7. Charles Sealsfield's (1828) description of the steamboat sound and smoke can be found on page 111. James Stuart's (1833) images of food for sale along the river on page 277 and George William Featherstonhaugh's (1844) tales of evening entertainment along the way on page 137 gave me additional details of a traveler's life on the river. Benjamin Moore Norman's (1845) positive descriptions of all the virtues, sights, and edifices of his hometown highlighted the marketplaces on pages 136–39, while John Purdy (1839) described the vendors' wares on page 185.

Lincoln's associates described the Mississippi adventure to William Herndon. John Hanks's key recollection that they "elected Abe cook" is somewhat contradicted by his remark that Lincoln "boarded at Carman's," the tavern in the town. However, I don't think the two are mutually exclusive. Lincoln could easily have prepared two of the three days' meals and gone up the bank and into the village for dinner.

Richard Campanella's (2010) analysis of the two Lincoln journeys provided helpful details including the possible construction of the flatboat. I found information about the speed and routes of steamboats at "The History of Steamboats," on the About.com inventors website. Robert Fulton is credited with inventing the practical steamboat when the *Clermont* made her round-trip from New York City to Albany in 1807. Fulton with partner Edward Livingston established steamboat routes between New Orleans and Natchez, Mississippi, beginning in 1814. These early boats traveled eight miles per hour with the downstream current and three miles per hour against the current upstream.

The slim volume by Thomas Reep, *Lincoln in New Salem* (1927), captures that village and its short history. Memories of Lincoln's life and impact in the village can be found indexed by the names of the residents I quoted.

I discovered the Lake Pontchartrain Railroad history on the New Orleans Past website and the barred owl gumbo in Alexander Wilson and Charles Lucian Bonaparte (1831) volume 4, page 284.

Robert Mazrim's (2007) wonderful descriptions of his archaeological explorations below New Salem's soil highlighted the sophistication of this frontier community with settlers bringing and wanting to buy china, glassware, and clothing in addition to rustic basics.

The barrels of oranges and lemons arriving in Springfield were advertised in the January 1, 1842, edition of the *Sangamo Journal*.

CHAPTER 5

George M. Harrison's culinary details dovetailed nicely with my perspective for this work. His lengthy letters to William Herndon form the basis for much of this chapter and our understanding of Lincoln's brief military career. Harrison's 1860 letter was quoted in Michael Burlingame (2006), pages 99–100.

William Souder (2004) quoted Audubon's respect for the hunting skills of the Native American on page 139.

Wayne Temple's (1981) explanation of Illinois militia equipment provided the information I needed to understand what the New Salem volunteers would have taken with them and how they were equipped.

I found details from the 1830 federal census online at Ancestry.com.

In the recipe section, I brushed up on my history of election cakes with Marian Burros's November 2, 1988, *New York Times* article, "Election Cake: A Noble Tradition."

CHAPTER 6

I first encountered the recipe for Mary Todd's almond cake in Poppy Cannon and Patricia Brooks (1968). However, the same recipe, or a close version, appears in countless other sources.

Paul M. Angle's (1935) work describing the increasingly sophisticated community of Springfield as it grew from a village into a city yielded many important details as I came to understand Springfield as the Lincoln family's home.

Ruth Painter Randall (1953), David Herbert Donald (1995), and Michael Burlingame (2008) all wrote of the events leading up to the James Shield's challenge of Lincoln and the duel. Each provided important facts and perspectives.

Judge Lockwood's skeptical assessment of his wife's new stove was related by Caroline Owsley Brown in her article "Springfield Society before the Civil War" in the *Journal of the Illinois State Historical Society* (April–June 1922) on page 477.

Springfield residents Mrs. William Black ("Took Tea at Mrs. Lincoln's," *Journal of the Illinois State Historical Society*, Spring 1955) and Caroline Owsley Brown wrote of parties and social activities in town and hosted by the Lincolns. These descriptions, no matter how brief, gave me important insights. I quote from them here and in the chapters that follow.

Eugenia Hunt Jones provided "My Personal Recollections of Abraham and Mary Lincoln," published in the *Abraham Lincoln Quarterly*, March 1945. She recounted Frances Todd Wallace's description of the wedding.

CHAPTER 7

Descriptions of Abraham Lincoln's speaking style and apparel were reported by the Herndon informants quoted, also by Harold Holzer (2004) on page 408. James O. Cunningham's recollection appears in Wilson (1943). Lincoln's genuine amusement in his stories was told by Helen Nicolay (1918), page 17.

Cunningham recalled the political picnic in "Lincoln on the Old Eighth Circuit" from Wilson (1943).

Wayne Temple (2004) quoted the Sunday school fire-pit barbecue description, while the Hanks-Lincoln wedding feast is recalled by Louis A. Warren (1926). News of the Jacksonville Fourth of July celebration appeared in the *Daily Illinois State Journal* of July 7, 1859. *The Cultivator* explained the economics of fattening a shoat into a hog in February 1860.

John Egerton (1993), page 276; Lillie S. Lusting (1939), page 6; and Daniel Beard (1920), page 136 all offer perspectives on burgoo; Samuel Corbley's first-person perspective appears in the *Indiana Magazine of History* (March 1906) on page 16.

CHAPTER 8

The National Park Service staff at the Lincoln Home National Historic Site in Illinois generously answered my questions and reviewed this and the three other Springfield-focused chapters that follow. Curator Susan Haake responded quickly and thoroughly to my e-mail requests and offered helpful perspectives as we visited on the telephone. I am especially thankful for her accurate measurements of Mary Lincoln's Royal Oak stove (discussed in Chapter 10). Haake and other staff members read and commented on the chapters in progress.

Along with information from Springfield residents cited in Chapter 6 notes, I found the home-life descriptions of Lincoln from Mary's perspective in Ruth Painter Randall (1953), where the overcooked chicken saga and "regularly irregular" comment are related on pages 88–89. Phillip Ayers's telling of his mother's experience with "The Lincolns and Their Neighbors" appears in Rufus Wilson (1943). Orville Hickman Browning (Pease and Randall 1925) made brief entries in his diary of parties he attended at the Lincoln home and of other Springfield social events during the legislative session.

The value of Harry Pratt's work (1943 book and article "The Lincolns Go Shopping" published in the Spring 1955 issue of the *Journal of the Illinois State Historical Society*) cannot be underestimated. His inclusion of the store-ledger entries gave me the data I used to put the family's grocery purchases into perspective. Additionally the *Springfield City Directory* for 1857–58 lists twenty-one restaurants. The 1859 listing shows thirty-two restaurants and saloons, and the 1860 directory lists twenty-eight restaurants and saloons.

I found the delightful description of Abraham Lincoln's carryout breakfast in Francis Fisher Browne (1995), page 206.

H. B. Masser's Patent Ice-Cream Freezer was advertised in the July 1855 edition of *Godey's Lady's Book*.

Dorothy Meserve Kunhardt wrote of the Lincoln boys' dog, Fido, and their neighborhood playmates in *Life Magazine* (February 1954).

The *Daily Illinois State Journal* offered a wide view of life in town. The circus was advertised in the July 2, 1856, edition. A porcelain steak maul was advertised in the January 4, 1858, paper. Ice availability was shouted on March 13, 1858.

Wayne Temple (2004) reported the corned beef and Ruth Painter Randall (1953) the chicken fricassee on page 339.

Charles Zane wrote of Lincoln and apples in the *Journal of the Illinois State Historical Society* in 1921.

Journalist Thurlow Weed colorfully described his meetings in Lincoln's home. His accounts can be found in volume 1 of his autobiography (1884) on pages 603–12.

I found the two additional food-related stories that Lincoln told in R. D. Wordsworth (1908), pages 14 and 41.

CHAPTER 9

Springfield newspapers and agricultural journals and magazines from across the nation brought forth a harvest of information on crops, seeds, and growing conditions. Fruit tree planting was mentioned by A. J. Downing in the December 1840 issue of *The Gardener's Magazine*, where he noted "Progress of Gardening in the United States." The pineapple controversy appeared in the September 1854 edition of *Valley Farmer*. The value of keeping a garden was highlighted in the 1854 *Report on the Commissioner of Patents*, page 323. That publication also fully described the qualities of beans on pages 323–38. The *Tennessee Farmer* sang the healthy praises of rhubarb in June 1837 on page 72.

In a 1982 landscape analysis and report for the National Park Service prepared by Robert R. Harvey & Associates, I discovered information about the Lincolns' apple trees as well as the copy of Simeon Francis's *Illinois Farmer* seed advertisement.

I found the date for the first canned tomatoes in Alan Davidson (2006). As to cooking the vegetables, in addition to suggestions from cookbook authors Miss Leslie, Mrs. Putnam, and Mrs. Bliss, agriculturalist Daniel Pereira Gardner (1854) suggested several simple preparations on pages 141, 494, and 803.

Emanuel Hertz (1938) reported William Herndon's observation of Lincoln, vegetables, and apples on page 166. The president's White House breakfast of baked beans was recounted by Wayne Temple (2004).

Temple also wrote extensively of Mariah Vance's relationship with the Lincoln family in two articles in *For the People*, the publication of the Abraham Lincoln Association (Winter 2004 and Spring 2005). I have called upon his work here and in Chapter 11.

CHAPTER 10

In addition to finding inspiration from the Red Bourbon turkey, much of this chapter relies on the kindness and inspirational work of the staff of the National Park Service. Timothy P. Townsend's essay "Almost Home" in *Abraham Lincoln: A Living Legacy*, published by the Eastern National Division of the Park Service, added depth and insights to my understanding of the family's life in their home at Eighth and Jackson. Floyd Mansberger's report of his archaeological findings not only of the Lincoln house yard, but of the neighbors' yards added depth to my analysis. Lincoln Home curator Susan Haake generously answered my questions and considered my theories. Once again, Caroline Owsley Brown in her article "Springfield Society before the Civil War," printed in the *Journal of the Illinois State Historical Society* (April–June 1922), and the Springfield newspapers provided key details. I took the closing image of the grief-stricken parents from David Herbert Donald (1995).

CHAPTER 11

Erica Holst told Springfield's telegraphic history in the *Quarterly Newsletter of the Papers of Abraham Lincoln*, the April–June 2009 issue.

David Herbert Donald (1995) set the stage for the Lincoln quotations that follow. The railroad quotation is from Lincoln's speech to the jury in the Rock Island Bridge case trial in Chicago in September 1857. The Rock Island Railroad hired Lincoln to defend them against the steamboat company who sued when their boat, the *Afton*, crashed against the pillars of what was the first railroad bridge across the Mississippi River and burned to the waterline. Lincoln argued that the rights of rail travel were the same as those of river travel. Nine of the twelve jurors agreed with him. The full text of Lincoln's argument can be found in volume 2, page 415, of his collected works (Basler 1953). Lincoln's expression of the value of his participation in the 1858 campaign is found on page 339 of volume 3, while his letter to Judd regarding expenses is also in volume 3 on page 337.

Paul Angle's comprehensive history of Springfield's early years (1935) provided details of that business community's growing and diverse population.

Two web sources yielded key information about William Johnson. Ronald Reitveld's article can be found on Abraham Lincoln Online and Michael Burlingame's article on *President Lincoln's Cottage Blog*, October 31, 2007.

As to oysters, Mark Kurlansky (2006) and Maria Eliza Ketelby Rundell (1823) expressed the same strategy for keeping oysters alive. Wayne Temple (1997) related the stories of Lincoln preferring his oysters cooked and serving fried oysters.

I found the details of Lincoln's New York experiences in Harold Holzer's reporting of *Lincoln at Cooper Union* (2004).

CHAPTER 12

Julia Taft Bayne's charming history of the time she and her brothers spent in the White House playing with Willie and Tad Lincoln gave me the descriptions I needed to develop a child's view of life in the White House.

For the inaugural journey, Victor Searcher (1960) detailed the trip and the only meals that were documented. Two *New York Times* articles offered views of the Astor Hotel: Christopher Gray's "Where Lincoln Tossed and Turned," September 24, 2009, and the anonymous "How We Dine," January 1, 1859. I read both articles online at the *Times* article archive.

Mary Lincoln's cousin Elizabeth Todd Grimsley relayed not only some of the events, but Mary's care and concern for her husband during her "Six Months in the White House" in the *Journal of the Illinois State Historical Society* (October 1926– January 1927).

British journalist Sir William Russell described a White House reception on page 64 of the first volume of his published diary.

Lydia Barker Tederick's "A Look at the White House Kitchens" from *White House History*, Collection 4, no. 20 (2010), offered valuable information on the below-stairs kitchens. The website Mr. Lincoln's White House detailed the employees. Mrs. Frances Seward's letter is quoted from Goodwin (2005) on page 405.

CHAPTER 13

I discovered *Bohn's Hand-Book of Washington* by Charles Lanman (1861) listed in an online auction of Lincoln and Civil War ephemera. When my not-so-high bid won, I was delighted to discover that this prewar tourist guide described not only the streets and sights, but also the cultural practices of the White House. It was just the thing I needed to guide me through Lincoln's Washington. I found the mounds of food description in David Herbert Donald (1995), page 336.

I could not have written about Lincoln's years in the White House without visiting the Lincoln Cottage and I am indebted to director Erin Carlson Mast for her generous support. She and her staff provided copies from their document collection, answered questions, and read the manuscript in progress. Matthew Pinsker (2003) and Elizabeth Smith Brownstein (2005) provided additional information about the Lincoln's time in this treasured retreat.

I relied on four writers' personal reminisces of Lincoln as they saw him in a relaxed setting: William Crook's descriptions were edited by Margarita Spalding Gerry in *Through Five Administrations* (1910); Mrs. Anna Byers-Jennings, in Victoria Radford's *Meeting Mr. Lincoln* (1998); Allan Thorndike Rice (1886), pages 418–19; and reporter Noah Brooks in P. J. Staudenraus's *Mr. Lincoln's Washington* (1967), pages 186–87. I found the description of the army bakery on pages 139–41 of Staudenraus.

CHAPTER 14

Dorothy Meserve Kunhardt and Phillip Kundhart, Jr., wrote of Abraham Lincoln's final journey home in *Twenty Days* (1965). The pictures and descriptions of the communities' actions helped me bring this work to its poignant ending. Mary Lincoln's final days are conveyed in Ruth Painter Randall (1953).

BIBLIOGRAPHY

PUBLISHED WORKS

Angle, Paul M. *Here I Have Lived: A History of Lincoln's Springfield, 1821–1865.* New Brunswick, NJ: Rutgers University Press, 1935.

Angle, Paul M., ed. *The Lincoln Reader.* New Brunswick, NJ: Rutgers University Press, 1947.

Atkinson, Eleanore Stackhouse. *The Boyhood of Lincoln.* New York: The McClure Company, 1908.

Baird, Robert. *View of the Valley of the Mississippi, or, the Emigrant's and Traveller's Guide to the West.* Philadelphia: H. S. Tanner, 1834.

Baker, Jean H. *Mary Todd Lincoln: A Biography.* New York: W. W. Norton, 1987.

Baldwin, Leland D. *The Keelboat Age on Western Waters.* Pittsburgh: University of Pittsburgh Press, 1969.

Bartelt, William. *"There I Grew Up": Remembering Abraham Lincoln's Indiana Youth.* Indianapolis: Indiana Historical Society Press, 2008.

Basler, Roy P., ed. *The Collected Works of Abraham Lincoln.* New Brunswick, NJ: Rutgers University Press, 1953.

Bayne, Julia Taft. *Tad Lincoln's Father.* Lincoln, NE: University of Nebraska Press, 2001.

Beard, Daniel. *American Boys' Handybook of Camp-lore and Woodcraft.* Philadelphia: J. B. Lippincott Co., 1920.

Beecher, Catharine, and Harriet Beecher Stowe. *The American Woman's Home, or, Principles of Domestic Science.* 1869. Reprint, Hartford, CT: The Stowe-Day Foundation, 1994.

Berry, Stephen. *House of Abraham: Lincoln and the Todds, a Family Divided by War.* New York: Houghton Mifflin, 2007.

Beveridge, Albert J. *Abraham Lincoln, 1809–1858.* Boston: Houghton Mifflin, 1928.

Boas, Norman F., MD. *Abraham Lincoln: Illustrated Biographical Dictionary: Family and Associates, 1809–1861*. Mystic, CT: Seaport Autographs Press, 2009.

Brooks, Noah. *Washington in Lincoln's Time*. New York: Century Company, 1895.

Browne, Francis Fisher. *The Every-day Life of Abraham Lincoln*. 1887. Reprint, Lincoln, NE: University of Nebraska Press 1995.

Brownstein, Elizabeth Smith. *Lincoln's Other White House*. Hoboken, NJ: John Wiley and Sons, 2005.

Buck, E. B., and E. P. Kriegh, comps. *City Directory for the Year 1859*. Springfield, IL: E. B. Buck and E. P. Kriegh, 1859.

Burlingame, Michael. *Abraham Lincoln: A Life*. Baltimore: Johns Hopkins University Press, 2008.

Burlingame, Michael, ed. *An Oral History of Abraham Lincoln: John G. Nicolay's Interviews and Essays*. Carbondale, IL: Southern Illinois Press, 2006.

Burlingame, Michael, and John R. Turner Ettlinger, eds. *Inside Lincoln's White House: The Complete Civil War Diary of John Hay*. Carbondale, IL: Southern Illinois University Press, 1997.

Burton, Orville Vernon. *The Age of Lincoln*. New York: Hill and Wang, 2007.

Campanella, Richard. *Lincoln in New Orleans: The 1828–1831 Flatboat Voyages and Their Place in History*. Lafayette, LA: University of Louisiana at Lafayette Press, 2010.

Carey, James W. "Why and How? The Dark Continent of American Journalism." In *Reading the News: A Pantheon Guide to Popular Culture*, edited by Robert Karl Manoff and Michael Schudson. New York: Pantheon, 1987.

Carr, Richard Wallace, and Marie Pinak Carr. *The Willard Hotel: An Illustrated History*. Washington, DC: Dicmar Publishing, 2005.

Carwardine, Richard. *Lincoln: A Life of Purpose and Power*. New York: Alfred A. Knopf, 2006.

Copway, George. *Indian Life and Indian History*. Boston: Albert Colby and Co., 1858.

Davidson, Alan. *The Oxford Companion to Food*. 2nd ed. Edited by Tom Jaine. Oxford: Oxford University Press, 2006.

Didimus, H. *New Orleans as I Found It*. New York: Harper and Brothers, 1845.

Digby, Kenelm. *The Closet of Sir Kenelm Digby Knight Opened*. Edited by Anne MacDonell. Released August 5, 2005. gutenberg.org/ebooks/16441.

Donald, David Herbert. *Lincoln*. New York: Simon and Schuster, 1995.

———. *Lincoln at Home: Two Glimpses of Abraham Lincoln's Family Life*. New York: Simon and Schuster, 1999.

Dunbar, Seymour. *A History of Travel in America*. Indianapolis: Bobbs-Merrill Co., 1915.

Dyba, Thomas J., and George L. Painter. *Seventeen Years at Eighth and Jackson: The Story of Life in the Lincoln Home.* Lisle, IL: IBC Publications, Illinois Benedictine College, 1985.

Eastern National Division National Park Service, comp. *Abraham Lincoln: A Living Legacy.* Virginia Beach, VA: Eastern National, 2006.

Egerton, John. *Southern Food: At Home, on the Road, in History.* Chapel Hill, NC: University of North Carolina Press, 1993.

Epstein, Daniel Mark. *The Lincolns: Portrait of a Marriage.* New York: Ballantine, 2008.

Eskew, Garnett Laidlaw. *Willard's of Washington: The Epic of Capital Caravansary.* New York: Coward-McCann, 1954.

Featherstonhaugh, George William. *Excursion through the Slave States, from Washington on the Potomac.* New York: Harper and Brothers, 1844.

Fessenden, Thomas. *The New American Gardener.* 15th ed. New York: Otis, Broaders and Co., 1842.

Fisher, M. F. K. *With Bold Knife and Fork.* New York: Putnam, 1969.

Flint, Timothy. *A Condensed Geography and History of the Western States, or the Mississippi Valley.* Cincinnati: E. H. Flint, 1928.

Fussell, Betty. *The Story of Corn.* New York: Knopf, 1992.

Gardner, Daniel Pereira. *The Farmer's Dictionary: A Vocabulary of the Technical Terms.* New York: Harper and Brothers, 1854.

Gerry, Margarita Spalding, ed. *Through Five Administrations: Reminiscences of Colonel William H. Crook, Body-Guard to President Lincoln.* New York: Harper and Brothers, 1910.

Goodwin, Doris Kearns. *Team of Rivals: The Political Genius of Abraham Lincoln.* New York: Simon and Schuster, 2005.

Harvey, Robert R., et al. "Lincoln Home Historic Site: Historic Grounds Report and Landscape Plan." Prepared for the National Park Service, 1982.

Helm, Katherine. *The True Story of Mary, Wife of Lincoln.* New York: Harper and Brothers, 1928.

Herndon, William H., and Jesse W. Weik. *Herndon's Lincoln: The True Story of a Great Life.* Springfield, IL: Herndon's Lincoln Publishing Co., circa 1920.

Hertz, Emanuel. *Abraham Lincoln: A New Portrait.* New York: Horace Liveright, 1931.

Hertz, Emanuel, ed. *The Hidden Lincoln: From the Letters and Papers of William H. Herndon.* New York: Viking Press, 1938.

History of Sangamon County, Illinois. Chicago: Inter-State Publishing Company, 1881.

Holzer, Harold. *Lincoln at Cooper Union: The Speech That Made Abraham Lincoln President.* New York: Simon and Schuster, 2004.

Hurt, R. Douglas. *American Agriculture: A Brief History*. Ames, IA: Iowa State University Press, 1994.

Irving, Washington. *The Crayon Miscellany*. Philadelphia: J. B. Lippincott and Co., 1871.

Kappler, Charles J. *Indian Affairs: Laws and Treaties*. Vol. 2. Washington, DC: Government Printing Office, 1904.

Keckley, Elizabeth. *Behind the Scenes, or, Thirty Years a Slave and Four Years in the White House*. New York: G. W. Carleton and Co., 1868.

———. *Behind the Scenes, or Thirty Years a Slave, and Four Years in the White House*. Edited by Frances Smith Foster. Champaign, IL: University of Illinois Press, 2001.

Kunhardt, Dorothy Meserve, and Phillip B. Kunhardt, Jr. *Twenty Days: A Narrative in Text and Pictures of the Assassination of Abraham Lincoln and the Twenty Days and Nights That Followed*. New York: Harper and Row, 1965.

Kurlansky, Mark. *The Big Oyster: History on the Half Shell*. New York: Ballantine Books, 2006.

Lanman, Charles. *Bohn's Hand-Book of Washington*. Washington, DC: Casimir Bohn, 1861.

Mansberger, Floyd R. *Archeological Investigations at the Lincoln Home National Historic Site, Springfield, Illinois*. DeKalb, IL: Northern Illinois University Press, 1987.

Mazrim, Robert. *The Sangamo Frontier: History and Archeology in the Shadow of Lincoln*. Chicago: University of Chicago Press, 2007.

McClure, Col. Alexander K. *"Abe" Lincoln's Yarns and Stories*. New York: Western W. Wilson, 1901.

McClure, J. B., ed. *Anecdotes of Abraham Lincoln and Lincoln's Stories*. Chicago: Rhodes and McClure Publishing, 1891.

McLean, John. *One Hundred Years in Illinois: 1818–1918*. Chicago: Peterson Linotype Co., 1919.

Miers, Earl Schenck, and C. Percy Powell, eds. *Lincoln Day by Day: A Chronology, 1809–1865*. 1960. Reprint, Dayton, OH: Morningside, 1991.

Miller, Marion, ed. *Life and Works of Abraham Lincoln*. Centenary ed., Vol 5. New York: Current Literature Publishing Co., 1907.

Nicolay, Helen. *Personal Traits of Abraham Lincoln*. New York: Century Co., 1918.

Nicolay, John G., and John Hay. *Abraham Lincoln: A History*. Vol. 1. New York: Century Co., 1890.

Norman, Benjamin Moore. *Norman's New Orleans and Environs*. New Orleans: B. M. Norman, 1845.

Ostendorf, Lloyd. *Abraham Lincoln: The Boy, the Man*. Springfield, IL: Phillip H. Wagner, 1962.

Packard, Jerrold M. *The Lincolns in the White House: Four Years That Shattered a Family*. New York: St. Martin's Press, 2005.

Pease, Theodore Calvin, and James G. Randall, eds. *Diary of Orville Hickman Browning*. Vol. 1, 1850–1864. Springfield, IL: Illinois State Historical Library, 1925.

Peck, J. M. *A New Guide for Emigrants to the West*. Boston: Gould, Kendall and Lincoln, 1837.

Petersen, William J. *Steamboating on the Upper Mississippi*. Iowa City: State Historical Society of Iowa, 1968.

Pinsker, Matthew. *Lincoln's Sanctuary: Abraham Lincoln and the Soldiers' Home*. New York: Oxford University Press, 2003.

Pratt, Harry E. *The Personal Finances of Abraham Lincoln*. Springfield, IL: Abraham Lincoln Association, 1943.

Purdy, John. *The Columbian Navigator*. London: R. H. Laurie, 1839.

Radford, Victoria, ed. *Meeting Mr. Lincoln: Firsthand Recollections of Abraham Lincoln by People, Great and Small, Who Met the President*. Chicago: Ivan R. Dee, 1998.

Randall, J. G. *Mr. Lincoln*. Edited by Richard Current. New York: Dodd, Mead and Co., 1957.

Randall, Ruth Painter. *Mary Lincoln: Biography of a Marriage*. Boston: Little, Brown and Co., 1953.

Reep, Thomas P. *Lincoln at New Salem*. Petersburg, IL: Old Salem Lincoln League, 1927.

Report on the Commissioner of Patents for the Year 1854—Agriculture. Washington, DC: U.S. Government Printing Office, 1855.

Rice, Allen Thorndike. *Reminiscences of Abraham Lincoln, by Distinguished Men of His Time*. New York: North American Publishing Co., 1886.

Root, Waverly, and Richard de Rochemont. *Eating in America: A History*. Hopewell, NJ: Ecco Press, 1995.

Russell, Sir William Howard. *My Diary North and South*. Boston: T. O. H. P. Burnham, 1863.

Schurz, Carl. *The Reminiscences of Carl Schurz*. Vol. 2. New York: Elibron Classics, 2005.

Seale, William. *The President's House: A History*. Washington, DC: White House Historical Association with the cooperation of the National Geographic Society, 1986.

Sealsfield, Charles. *The Americans as They Are; Described in a Tour through the Valley of the Mississippi*. London: Hurst, Chance and Co., 1828.

Searcher, Victor. *Lincoln's Journey to Greatness: A Factual Account of the Twelve-Day Inaugural Trip.* Philadelphia: John C. Winston Co., 1960.

Smith, Andrew F., ed. *The Oxford Companion to American Food and Drink.* Oxford: Oxford University Press, 2007.

Souder, William. *Under a Wild Sky: John James Audubon and the Making of the Birds of America.* New York: North Point Press, 2004.

Staudenraus, P. J., ed. *Mr. Lincoln's Washington: Selections from the Writings of Noah Brooks, Civil War Correspondent.* South Brunswick, NJ: Thomas Yoseloff, 1967.

Stevens, Walter B. *A Reporter's Lincoln.* Edited by Michael Burlingame. Lincoln, NE: University of Nebraska Press, 1998.

Stewart, Amy. *Wicked Plants: The Weed That Killed Lincoln's Mother and Other Botanical Atrocities.* Chapel Hill, NC: Algonquin Books of Chapel Hill, 2009.

Stuart, James. *Three Years in North America.* Edinburgh: Robert Cadell, 1833.

Tarbell, Ida. *In the Footsteps of the Lincolns.* New York: Harper and Brothers, 1924.

———. *The Life of Abraham Lincoln.* Vol. 1. New York: Macmillan Co., 1928.

Tebbel, John, and Keith Jennison. *The American Indian Wars.* Edison, NJ: Castle Books, 2003.

Temple, Wayne C. *Alexander Williamson: Friend of the Lincolns.* Racine, WI: Lincoln Fellowship of Wisconsin, 1997.

———. *Lincoln's Arms, Dress and Military Duty during and after the Black Hawk War.* Springfield, IL: State of Illinois Military and Naval Department Public Affairs and Retention-Recruiting Sections, 1981.

———. "Mariah (Bartlett) Vance Daytime Servant to the Lincolns." *For the People.* Abraham Lincoln Association. 6, no. 4 (Winter 2004); 7, no. 1 (Spring 2005).

———. *By Square & Compass: Saga of the Lincoln Home.* Rev. ed. Mahomet, IL: Mayhaven Publishing, 2002.

———. *"The Taste Is In My Mouth a Little …": Lincoln's Victuals and Potables.* Mahomet, IL: Mayhaven Publishing, 2004.

Thomas, Benjamin Platt. *Lincoln's New Salem.* Springfield, IL: Abraham Lincoln Association, 1934. quod.lib.umich.edu/l/lincoln2/0566928.0001.001?rgn=main;view=fulltext.

Townsend, William H. *Lincoln and the Bluegrass: Slavery and Civil War in Kentucky.* Lexington: University of Kentucky Press, 1955.

Turner, Jack. *Spice: The History of a Temptation.* New York: Alfred A. Knopf, 2004.

Turner, Justin G., and Linda Levitt Turner. *Mary Todd Lincoln: Her Life and Letters.* New York: Alfred A. Knopf, 1972.

Warren, Louis A. *Lincoln's Parentage and Childhood: A History of the Kentucky Lincolns Supported by Documentary Evidence.* New York: Century Co., 1926.

———. *Lincoln's Youth: Indiana Years, Seven to Twenty-one, 1816–1830.* Indianapolis: Indiana Historical Society, 1991.

Weed, Thurlow. *The Life of Thurlow Weed.* Edited by Harriet A. Weed. Boston: Houghton, Mifflin and Co., 1884.

Weik, Jesse William. *The Real Lincoln: A Portrait.* Boston: Houghton Mifflin, 1922.

Whipple, Wayne. *The Story-Life of Lincoln: A Biography Composed of Five Hundred True Stories Told by Abraham Lincoln and His Friends.* Philadelphia: John C. Winston Co., 1901.

Whitney, Henry Clay. *Life on the Circuit with Lincoln.* Boston: Estes and Lauriat, 1892.

Williams, C. S. *Williams' Springfield Directory City Guide & Business Mirror, for 1860–61.* Springfield, IL: Johnson and Bradford, Booksellers and Stationers, 1860.

Williams, Susan. *Food in the United States, 1820s–1890.* Westport, CT: Greenwood Press, 2006.

Wilson, Alexander, and Charles Lucian Bonaparte. *American Ornithology, or, The Natural History of the Birds of the United States.* Vol. 4. Edinburgh: Constable and Co., 1831.

Wilson, Douglas L., Rodney O. Davis, and Terri Wilson, eds. *Herndon's Informants: Letters, Interviews, and Statements about Abraham Lincoln.* Urbana, IL: University of Illinois Press, 1998.

Wilson, Rufus Rockwell. *Lincoln among His Friends: A Sheaf of Intimate Memories.* Caldwell, ID: Caxton Printers, 1943.

Winters, B., comp. *Springfield City Directory for 1857–58.* Springfield, IL: S. H. Jameson and Co., 1857.

Woods, John. *Two Years' Residence on the English Prairie of Illinois.* Chicago: Lakeside Press, 1968.

Wordsworth, R. D., comp. *"Abe" Lincoln Anecdotes and Stories.* Boston: Mutual Book Company, 1908.

COOKBOOKS

Acton, Eliza. *Modern Cookery in All Its Branches, Revised for American Housekeepers by Mrs. S. J. Hale.* Philadelphia: Lea and Blanchard, 1845.

An American Lady. *The American Home Cook Book.* New York: Dick and Fitzgerald, 1854.

Andrews, Julia C. *Breakfast, Dinner, and Tea: Viewed Classically, Poetically, and Practically.* New York: D. Appleton, 1860.

Bliss, Mrs., of Boston. *The Practical Cook Book: Containing Upwards of One Thousand Receipts.* Philadelphia: Lippincott, Grambo and Co., 1850.

Bryan, Mrs. Lettice. *The Kentucky Housewife*. Facsimile of 1839 ed. Bedford, MA: Applewood Books, n.d.

Cannon, Poppy, and Patricia Brooks. *The Presidents' Cookbook: Practical Recipes from George Washington to the Present*. New York: Funk and Wagnalls, 1968.

Child, Lydia Marie. *The American Frugal Housewife*. Boston: American Stationers' Co., 1836.

Corson, Juliet. *Miss Corson's American Practical Cookery and Household Management*. New York: Dodd, Mead and Co., 1885.

Crowen, Mrs. T. J. *Every Lady's Cook Book*. New York: Kiggins and Kellogg, 1854.

Economic Cookery: Designed to Assist the Housekeeper in Retrenching her Expenses, by the Exclusion of Spirituous Liquors from her Cookery. Newark, NJ: Benjamin Olds, 1840.

Francatelli, Charles Elmé. *The Cook's Guide, and Housekeeper's & Butler's Assistant*. London: Richard Bentley, 1857.

Hale, Sarah J. *Mrs. Hale's New Cook Book*. Philadelphia: T. B. Peterson and Brothers, 1857.

Irving, Lucretia. *Irving's 1000 Receipts, or, Modern and Domestic Cookery*. New York: Cornish, Lamport and Co., 1852.

Lee, Mrs. N. K. M. *The Cook's Own Book, and Housekeeper's Register*. Boston: Monroe and Francis, 1842.

Leslie, Miss Eliza. *Directions for Cookery in Its Various Branches*. Philadelphia: Carey and Hart, 1840.

———. *Directions for Cookery in Its Various Branches*. 20th ed. Philadelphia: Carey and Hart, 1845.

———. *Miss Leslie's New Receipts for Cooking*. Philadelphia: T. B. Peterson, 1852.

———. *Seventy-Five Receipts for Pastry, Cakes, and Sweetmeats*. Facsimile of 1828 ed. Bedford, MA: Applewood Books, n.d.

Lustig, Lillie S. *Southern Cook Book: 322 Old Dixie Recipes*. Edited by S. Claire Sondheim and Sarah Rensel. Reading, PA: Culinary Arts Press, 1939.

Nicholson, Elizabeth. *What I Know, or, Hints on the Daily Duties of a Housekeeper*. Philadelphia: Willis P. Hazard, 1855.

Putnam, Mrs. E. H. *Mrs. Putnam's Receipt Book and Young Housekeeper's Assistant*. New York: Phinney, Blakeman and Mason, 1860.

Randolph, Mary. *The Virginia House-Wife Or, Methodical Cook*. Washington, DC: Davis and Force, 1824.

Rundell, Maria Eliza Ketelby. *American Domestic Cookery, Formed on the Principles of Economy, for the Use of Private Families by an Experienced Housekeeper*. New York: Evert Duyckinck, 1823.

———. *A New System of Domestic Cookery: Formed upon Principles of Economy, and Adapted to the Use of Private Families, with the Addition of Many New Receipts, by a Lady*. London: Thomas Allman, 1840.

Simmons, Amelia. *American Cookery*. Facsimile of 1789 2nd ed., 1796. Bedford, MA: Applewood Books, n.d.

Tyree, Marion Cabell. *Housekeeping in Old Virginia*. 1879. Reprint, Louisville, KY: Favorite Recipe Press, 1965.

Vollmer, William. *The United States Cook Book: A Complete Manual for Ladies, Housekeepers, and Cooks*. Translated by J. C. Oehlschlager. Philadelphia: John Weik and Co., 1859.

WEBSITES

About.com Inventors: http://inventors.about.com
"The History of Steamboats." About.com.Inventors.
http://inventors.about.com/library/inventors/blsteamship.htm.

Abraham Lincoln Online: http://showcase.netins.net
"Abraham Lincoln at the Willard Hotel." Abraham Lincoln Online.
http://showcase.netins.net/web/creative/lincoln/sites/willards.htm.

Reitveld, Ronald. "Lincoln Memories: Visiting the William Johnson Gravesite." Abraham Lincoln Online. http://showcase.netins.net/web/creative/lincoln/news/rietveldmem.htm.

American Artifacts: www.americanartifacts.com
Van Vleck, Richard. "Hand-Held Corn Shellers." *Scientific Medical & Mechanical Antiques*. no. 15. www.americanartifacts.com/smma/sheller/sheller.htm.

American Livestock Breeds Conservancy: http://albc-usa.org
"Bourbon Red Turkey." American Livestock Breeds Conservancy.
http://albc-usa.org/cpl/bourbon.html.

Ancestry.com: www.ancestry.com

The Closet of Sir Kenelm Digby Knight Opened. Edited by Anne MacDonell. Released August 5, 2005. www.gutenberg.org/files/16441/16441-8.txt.

Fiery Foods and Barbecue SuperSite: www.fiery-foods.com
DeWitt, Dave, and Nancy Gerlach. "Ginger: The Gentle Heat." Fiery Foods and Barbecue Supersite. www.fiery-foods.com/article-archives/91-other-spicy-ingredients/1798-ginger-the-gentle-heat.

Kentucky State University: www.kysu.edu
"KSU Pawpaw Program." Kentucky State University.www.pawpaw.kysu.edu.

Lincoln Boyhood National Memorial: www.nps.gov/libo/index.htm

Mr. Lincoln's White House: www.mrlincolnswhitehouse.org

National Archives: www.archives.gov
"Featured Documents," National Archives & Records Administration.
   www.archives.gov/exhibits/featured_documents/dc_emancipation_act/.

National First Ladies' Library: www.firstladies.org
"Mary Lincoln Biography." National First Ladies' Library.
   www.firstladies.org/biographies/firstladies.aspx?biography=17.

National Park Service's American Battlefield Protection Program:
   www.nps.gov/history/hps/abpp

New Orleans Past: http://neworleanspast.com
"Around Lake Pontchartrain: 1830 Pontchartrain Railroad." New Orleans Past.
   http://neworleanspast.com/aroundlakepontchartrain/id53.html.

Peterson Pawpaws: www.petersonpawpaws.com

President Lincoln's Cottage Blog: http://lincolncottage.wordpress.com
Burlingame, Michael. "A Little-Known Story of Lincoln and William Johnson."
   October 31, 2007. http://lincolncottage.wordpress.com/2007/10/31/a-little-
   known-story-of-lincoln-and-william-johnson/.

Steamboat Times: http://steamboattimes.com
"A Pictorial History of the Mississippi Steamboat Era." Steamboat Times.
   http://steamboattimes.com/flatboats.html.

U.S. Army Quartermaster Foundation: http://qmfound.com
"Early Army Rations." U.S. Army Quartermaster Foundation.
   http://qmfound.com/army_rations_historical_background.htm.

U.S. Department of Agriculture: www.usda.gov
"Sugars." USDA Snap-Ed Connection. snap.nal.usda.gov/nal_display/index.php?info.

White House: www.whitehouse.gov
"The Presidents." White House. www.whitehouse.gov/about/presidents.

NINETEENTH-CENTURY AGRICULTURAL NEWSPAPERS

American Agriculturist

American Farmer

The Cultivator (New York State Agricultural Society)

The Gardener's Magazine

Illinois Farmer

The New Genesee Farmer and Gardener's Journal

Prairie Farmer

Tennessee Farmer

Union Agriculturist and Western Prairie Farmer

Valley Farmer

NEWSPAPERS, MAGAZINES, AND JOURNALS

Agricultural History

American Cookery (The Boston Cooking School Magazine)

Daily Illinois State Journal

The Family Magazine, or Monthly Abstract of General Knowledge

Godey's Lady's Book

Harper's New Monthly Magazine

Indiana Magazine of History

Journal of the Illinois State Historical Society

Life Magazine

Lincoln Editor: The Quarterly Newsletter of the Papers of Abraham Lincoln

New York Times

Sangamo Journal

White House History

DOCUMENT COLLECTIONS

Cutter Papers. Collection of the Lincoln Cottage. National Trust for Historic Preservation, Washington, DC.

Menu collection. Minnesota Historical Society, St. Paul, MN.

INDEX

Page numbers in *italics* denote recipes.